Still Cruising

Bagheera

Even the most conventional families are sometimes apt to dream a little. Adventures on the Discovery Channel may ignite a quiet flame . . . but a Caribbean holiday is generally as far as they will get. Understandably, few families have the guts or the wonderful spirit of the Copelands. On their circumnavigation they dropped anchor in unheard of places where a yacht was as strange as the space shuttle. As a result the children have memories that will help them cruise through life with a following wind and sunlight on their shoulders.

—*Jol Byerley, Yacht Captain, broker, racer, author, radio personality and raconteur. Nelson's Dockyard, Antigua*

Colin, Liza, Duncan, Andy and Jamie

Still Cruising

Australia to Asia, Africa and America

by
Liza Copeland

1995
Romany Enterprises

Canadian Cataloguing in Publication Data

Copeland, Liza, 1946-
Still Cruising

Sequel to: Just Cruising

ISBN 0-9697690-1-6

1. Copeland, Liza, 1946- — Journeys. 2. Bagheera (Yacht). 3. Voyages around the world 4. Yachting. 5. Children— Travel. 1. Title
G440.C664A3 1995   910.4'1   C95-910731-2

Romany Enterprises
3943 W. Broadway
Vancouver, B.C.
Canada V6R 2C2
Tel: (604)228-8712
Fax: (604)228-8779

Typeset by Vancouver Desktop Publishing Centre, Vancouver, BC
Printed in Canada by Hignell Printing Ltd., Winnipeg, Manitoba

To
Andy, Duncan, Colin and Jamie
my family and wonderful cruising companions

Contents

Author's Note

Metric measurements have been used throughout this book with the following exceptions:

Yacht lengths are in feet as this is common practice.
3.28 feet = 1 metre

Distances at sea are measured in nautical miles.
1 nautical mile = 1.85 kilometres = (1.15 statute miles)

This unit has been used traditionally for ease of navigation, because:
1 minute of latitude = 1 nautical mile,
1 degree of latitude = 60 nautical miles.

A knot = one nautical mile per hour.

Weights of fish are generally discussed in pounds (and it certainly sounds more impressive!)
2.2 pounds = 1 kilogram

It might be useful for you to know also that:
4.55 litres = 1 imperial gallon
3.78 litres = 1 us gallon

All **prices** are quoted in us dollars

Acknowledgements

Again my gratitude goes to our friends both at home and around the world who have been so enthusiastic and supportive.

Special thanks go to Nancy Garrett, Brenda de Roos and Diana Gatrill who have been unfailing in their encouragement, help and recommendations with the manuscript, despite a gruelling timetable. Thanks also go to my proof readers Caroline Baker, Richard Beattie, Jimmy and Shirley Faure, Peter Grove, Graham Kedgley and Dave Seller for picking up the small errors that are so easy to miss; also June Mauthe for her organisational consistency and many hours on the computer.

I much appreciate the kind words from Gary Hoyt, Tom Service, Ken and Keith Beken, Kerry McPhedran and Jol Byerley.

Alison Kinsey, my step daughter, has my gratitude not only for managing all our affairs whilst we cruised, but also for her editing and level-headed help in choosing the photographs. I am grateful also to my nephew Andrew Hodson for his photos of the family, Pat Tandurella, Annette and Tanil Tuncel from *Kelebek*, and the Services from *Jean Marie*.

My Canadian distributor Nancy Wise never ceases to amaze me with her enlightening suggestions. Giselle Lemay, my graphic artist, and Joanne Langley, for her work on promotional sheets, have my appreciation for their patience and attention to detail.

Finally I would like to thank my children not only for being such wonderful cruising companions but also for their support and suggestions whilst writing. Heartfelt thanks go to my husband Andy, who, due to the success of *Just Cruising*, was stimulated to even greater diligence editing this book, particularly with the cruising tips in Appendix A. I also thank him for being encouraging and accepting of my new demanding career as a writer and speaker.

Prologue

For years we had dreamt of harnessing the wind and travelling to exotic lands. At best we hoped to spend two years sailing our yacht *Bagheera*. Our plan was to explore the Mediterranean with its diversity of cultures and cuisines, while keeping passages short for our young family; then to cross the Atlantic for a Caribbean visit, before selling our vessel in the United States.

My earlier book *Just Cruising* tells how those plans unfolded—also how, instead of taking the boat to Florida, we were enticed to Australia to become Canada's 'Tall Ship' during the Australian Bicentenary celebrations. A perk of being a participant was a one-year working visa and we took this opportunity to replenish the cruising kitty and give our children a normal school year. We particularly wanted to see how they did socially as well as academically, because now that we were almost two thirds of the way around the world we were very tempted to keep on going!

Still Cruising recounts how we completed our circumnavigation—cruising through South East Asia, the Andaman Islands, Sri Lanka, India, the Maldives, Chagos, the Seychelles, down the East African coast to Madagascar, around the Cape of Good Hope (or the Cape of Storms), then to the United States via South America, the Caribbean, Cuba and the Bahamas.

Often sailing to remote and little known destinations this part of the trip was very different to much of our earlier travels. Some places were known for pirates or bandits, whilst in others there were no inhabitants and we had to be totally self-sufficient, as there were also few other yachts for camaraderie and support.

We visited islands where the last overseas visitors were the Japanese during World War II, where they were amazed by our children's freckles, and where customs and lifestyle were very different to ours, with people still wearing their traditional dress, cooking their national foods and entertaining themselves with their old story telling, dances and plays. These were also areas of stunning scenery, fascinating wildlife and unbelievable serenity.

In *Still Cruising* you will read about some of our richest, most exotic cruising and travelling adventures, including our greatest challenges at sea.

Bagheera ready to leave Australia

Australia and
South East Asia

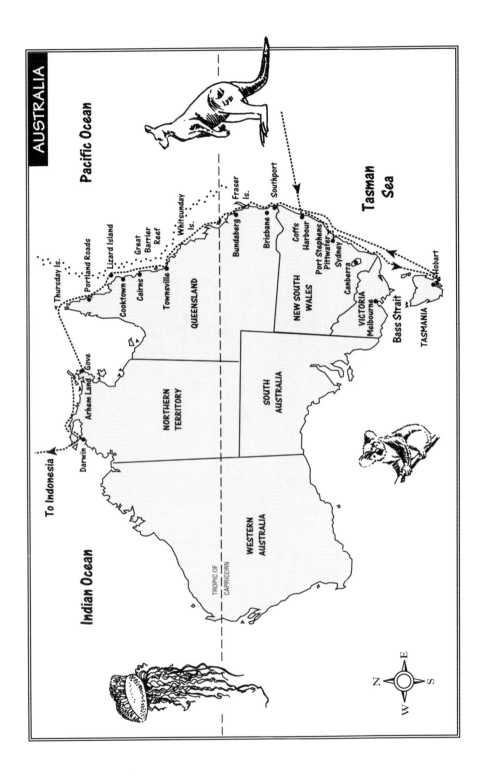

AUSTRALIA

Pacific Ocean

Tasman Sea

Indian Ocean

To Indonesia

Thursday Is.
Portland Roads
Lizard Island
Cooktown
Cairns
Townsville
Great Barrier Reef
Whitsunday Is.
Fraser Is.
Bundaberg
Southport
Brisbane
Coffs Harbour
Port Stephens
Pittwater
Sydney
Canberra

Darwin
Arhem Land
Gove

NORTHERN TERRITORY

QUEENSLAND

WESTERN AUSTRALIA

SOUTH AUSTRALIA

NEW SOUTH WALES

VICTORIA
Melbourne

Bass Strait

TASMANIA
Hobart

TROPIC OF CAPRICORN

N
E
S
W

1. The Australia Coast –Sydney to Darwin

In all we spent twenty months in Australia, representing Canada in the Bicentennial celebrations Tall Ships events in Tasmania and Sydney in our Beneteau First 38, *Bagheera*, then living in Pittwater twenty miles north of Sydney for over a year. The boys went to regular school and played community sports. Andy worked as the 'Winch Doctor', helped out on Beneteau yachts at Boat Shows and painted houses, while I was employed as a psychologist for the Department of Health. We made several trips inland in a friend's camper van, including visits to Expo in Brisbane, south to Melbourne and to the capital, Canberra.

With every trip our admiration for the country increased, with its exotic bird and animal life, brilliant flowers and sunsets, and dramatic, varied scenery. The boys were especially impressed that Australia hosts many of the world's most dangerous 'nasties', such as salt water crocodiles, sharks, box jelly fish and funnel-web spiders of which we saw several!

We felt completely at home 'down under' and it was a wrench saying farewell to so many friends at our dockside party on Easter Saturday in 'The Puddle,' at the southern end of Pittwater. There were classmates of the boys and their families, work acquaintances, new cruising friends, my cousins, and several of Andy's contemporaries from the Fleet Air Arm of the Royal Navy. In particular Neville and Shirley Lockett had been wonderfully hospitable, as well as providing our mailing address.

Finally the lines were cast off and we were on our way. But we were not alone, there were stowaways on board, our friends the Tandurellas had sneaked below!

Like our experiences when leaving England it took a while to re-acclimatize to the lifestyle. While Andy couldn't wait for the challenge of the ocean, Duncan, Colin and Jamie, now 12, 10 and 6 respectively, and I felt a real vacuum. It was hard leaving this now familiar area, with a settled life of school and work, in which we had all been independent. The boys had grown, (at first Duncan kept bumping his head!), and the boat seemed much smaller. There had never been three for school before, two went either side of the main cabin table but there was no comfortable place for the third, except the cockpit table, but initially it frequently poured with rain. When I suggested the chart table Andy complained, "but that's my workshop and office!"

So we eased into the lifestyle gently, harbour-hopping up the New South Wales coast with short trips and frequent stops to visit friends and new sights.

For the first time we had to consider our 7'2" draft, due to the many bars at inlet entrances, but the tricky piloting was always worth it. In

Our stowaways – the Tandurella family

pretty Iluka, across from Yamba, we enjoyed walking in one of the few surviving littoral rain forests and were fascinated by the strangling figs, long vines that strangle the parent tree. Later the fishermen gave us a huge bag of the shrimp and tiny octopus that they were unloading.

From Ballina Andy's cousins drove us through lush, rolling farmland to Byron Bay where their beautiful home had panoramic views of the ocean full of surfers, long sand beaches, and mauve sunsets over the inland hills. After a visit to the 1901 lighthouse that marks the most easterly point of Australia we stopped at Gary's pharmacy to restock our medical supplies. They were labelled carefully so we would have no problems with future authorities, legal requirements for possessing medications varying widely around the world.

Southport is sheltered from the ocean by a long sand-spit running up from Surfer's Paradise. We had barely dropped the anchor when a dugong, or sea cow, ambled past. It was about three metres long, and we decided, a cross between a pig and an elephant.

Duncan rushed below to our reference books. "Dugongs are actually distant cousins of elephants," he told us excitedly. "They were almost hunted to extinction because it was believed that their oil cured lung and rheumatic illnesses. And guess what? They shed tears if they are wounded."

I phoned some friends who lived down the coast at Broadbeach. "I'm so glad you've arrived," said Diana. "I rang up the local newspaper to tell them you were coming and the reporter wants to see you tomorrow."

We had been given the odd mention by the press during the Tall Ships Events but this was unexpected! Diana also arranged a doctor's appointment for me, as I had been experiencing considerable pain in my arm.

"Typical tennis elbow," the doctor announced, "probably from carrying all those groceries and jerry cans of fuel, from what you've told me. The only real answer is complete rest for a month." Some hope on a boat!

Over a delicious dinner of local Moreton Bay Bugs, tender crustacea which look like a long-armed crab or short-tailed lobster, we discussed the weather with Diana and Reg. With the offshoot of yet another cyclone and gusts of 50 knots expected, we were beginning to despair.

"Why don't you go inside, up the Broadwater?" Reg suggested.

"But what about the depths, you know we draw over seven feet," replied Andy.

"You'll have to go easy," said Reg thoughtfully "but it should be all right. The channels do silt up but the bottom is soft and one can usually find a way through."

We poured over the chart that night and decided to risk it. We agreed on an early start. We finally headed up the Broadwater at 8:00 A.M. in torrential rain and stopped for the night at the Never Fail Islands. "Never fails to do what?" we wondered, as the wind howled all night long. With more rain the next day and poor visibility we carefully felt our way down the narrow, winding channels. We passed two yachts aground, but could not get close enough to help them.

Rounding a bend we found a rented house boat anchored in the middle of the narrow channel. With 40 knots of wind from behind it was hard to slow down quickly, we could only head for the shallows.

Ironically the charters didn't understand what they were doing wrong, and one called out, "It's a beaut spot for fishing!"

I will not repeat my husband's expletives as we slithered past them, bumping bottom yet again.

We heard *XXXX*, Alan Bond's 200' three-masted schooner, on the radio and the voice sounded very familiar. John Bardon was an old friend from our Caribbean charter days in the '60s so we asked Brisbane radio to connect us.

"You're lucky you're inside," John told us. "Bumping bottom is minor compared to being out here. It's foul, with a constant 45 knots and very unpleasant seas. We can't go in because it's too rough to go through the bar at Southport," he continued. He sounded as cheery as ever. A seasoned captain of over twenty years, it would take more than that to faze him.

Not being out in the huge ocean swells more than compensated for a few sandy groundings in the narrow passages, we agreed. At times it was scary, however, often being blown under bare poles down the narrow channels at eight knots, despite the engine being in full reverse! We pulled into the dock in Manly thankfully.

The next morning there was a brilliant blue sky and barely a whisper. I did a much needed laundry and we helped American yachts, *Sunshine* and *Unicorn* tie up, the boats we had seen aground the day before. After the trauma of the last few days we all felt we deserved dinner out that night!

Sailing up to Bundaberg, also in sunshine, we passed the huge (598 square km.) all-sand Fraser Island. There were many 4-wheel drive vehicles being ferried across, outback driving being a rapidly booming craze. Almost in the tropics, we were charmed by Bundaberg, a sugar, rum and market-gardening town. Suited climatically and topographically to grow almost any fruit or vegetable it is enhanced by a winding river and undulating foothills. It was in this lush pastureland that we saw a few acres for sale.

"Perfect," cried Duncan, "for livestock, horses, fruit, vegetables and an aviary. Let's buy it?"

It even had river frontage and a billabong water hole. I think Duncan, our budding farmer as well as aspiring vet, was only finally pacified when later we met a New Zealand couple who coincidentally had bought the land next door. They invited him to visit them anytime.

Bundaberg is only fifty miles south of the first part of the Great Barrier Reef, an atoll called Lady Musgrave. Eight kilometres around, the white sandy island with its sparkling turquoise lagoon and raised surrounding reef could not have been more picture perfect. Although visited by many day-tourists it was immaculate, falling within the effective fully protected area of the well documented Barrier Reef zone.

Jamie, with a new mask, was ecstatic. He kept squeezing my hand and pointing to another wonder underwater—he would look up, gasp for breath and say, "Mummy, it is SO beautiful."

It brought back memories of running charter boats in the Caribbean. Guests new to snorkelling all had the same reaction.

At low tide we explored the windward reef. The boys found mollusks (shells), nudibranchs (sea slugs), echinoderms (sea stars, sea cucumbers, sea urchins) galore, and Jamie was thrilled to find one giant clam shell that he could actually sit inside and another that spat at him!

The Great Barrier Reef is the world's largest living organism. Stretching from just south of the Tropic of Capricorn it ends in the Torres Strait, just south of Papua New Guinea. Like a huge serpent it winds its way up the Queensland coast, at some points just a few miles off the shore while at others it is as much as 320 kilometres away. It ranges in width from 16 to 240 kilometres and encompasses 2,600 coral reefs and about 320 coral islands.

The coral is formed by a marine polyp that is closely related to the sea anemones and jellyfish of the family *Coelenterata*. The significant difference is that the coral polyps form a hard exterior surface by excreting lime. This hard skeleton remains when the polyps die and over millions of years a reef gradually builds up.

Basically reefs are either fringing or barrier; the fringing reefs growing up around the islands while the barrier reefs are generally further out to sea and enclose a lagoon of deep water. Coral cannot survive in temperatures below $17.5°c$. and the water also must be salty. The coral gradually grows to the surface with live coral surviving at a maximum depth of 10 metres as the water must also be well-lit. This is because the coral needs the tiny single-celled plant Zooxanthellae, which needs light, to produce limestone. When the reef breaks the surface a coral cay may form. Birds which inadvertently drop seeds help stabilize these islands. When rainwater solidifies the limestone into beach rock and dense vegetation takes root the cay develops into a coral reef island.

In 1975 the Australian government passed the Great Barrier Reef Marine Park Act, which allows enjoyment and particular uses of the reef while preserving its natural beauty. Now over 98% of the reef is protected marine park. One of the reasons for these regulations was the crown-of-thorns starfish scare in the 1970s when this starfish, which eats coral, had an unexplained explosive increase in numbers.

The bay in Middle Percy is a lovely spot, with a long sandy beach lined with rustling palms. Once ashore Duncan knocked down a coconut and we enjoyed its refreshing juice while exploring a hut that was filled with 'yachty's' mementos.

"Daddy, we will have to leave something too, like the picture you did on the wall in Madeira," said Colin.

On the wall in Funchal, Andy had drawn the cat logo on our spinnaker that is symbolic of *Bagheera*, the black panther in Rudyard Kipling's Jungle Book. Later he made another fine reproduction back on board adding all our names and the date. We walked up to the homestead the next morning, a pretty three kilometre trail with dramatic changes in vegetation from the pandanus of the sands below to the forest of the rich red soil above. We arrived at 'Andy's' just before the rain started, a perfect excuse to stay for lunch, but first he showed us around. A homesteader for several years he kept chickens, geese, and ducks at the back, with cattle, horses, sheep, wild goats, emus, kangaroos and dogs elsewhere on the property. Also the most wonderful passion fruit we have ever tasted.

"Any chance of buying some?" I asked 'Andy'.

"Of course, pick yourself a bag," he replied. The fruit disappeared in no-time; the flavour remains one of our favourites.

The Whitsunday Islands are the most developed of the Barrier Reef islands. They were named by Captain Cook who recorded that he had sailed through on July 3rd, 1770, Whitsunday. In fact, he was a day out as he hadn't calculated for crossing the International Date Line! The seventy odd islands are scattered on both sides of the Whitsunday Passage and are easily accessible. Having heard so many positive attributes of the islands we were looking forward to getting to this tropical paradise. I have to admit we were disappointed as they didn't seem tropical at all. We had visualized typical remote Caribbean or South Pacific islands but the Whitsundays are continental islands, mountain peaks from two drowned coastal mountain ranges. Their geologic make-up, vegetation and wildlife is similar to that on the mainland. Without question some were spectacular but the miserable weather inhibited extensive exploration.

After stocking up in Mackay we called in at Brampton Island, Palm Bay on Long Island, Cid Harbour, Hamilton Island, Whitehaven Bay and Nara Inlet. Ironically the highlight of our visit to the Whitsundays was a touristy day on Hamilton Island where we rented a motorized buggy. The boys were delighted, all taking a turn at 'driving'. We toured the motor bike museum and Andy was amazed to find a model similar to the 1929 Raleigh he had owned as a teenager. We all played squash, and Jamie had a thrill later when he swam across a pool with Buttons, the resort's tame dolphin. We were also pleased to find other boats heading north, British *Tournel of Mawes*, and Australian *Yaraandoo 11* with Canadian *L'Ami Pierre*, a 37' Beneteau, who had children aboard.

Finally in Cairns the weather cleared. Although it continued to be windy there was sunshine everyday and we breathed it in like nectar. Every yacht billowed with drying bedding and clothing, the bleach bottle having been used liberally on all the mould that spreads virulently on board with damp conditions.

Although we had experienced some pleasant diversions, and the odd nice day, having the wettest April on record and being threatened by five potential cyclones had made the trip up the coast a long haul. Contrary to many people's expectations one is seldom 'battened down' on a boat. As we had sailed mostly in the tropics we were generally on deck, in the water or ashore. However on the few occasions, such as at this time, when we were confined below decks I had to admit life on board can take on a whole new dimension. We even considered buying a television!

However, with the sun enveloping us in attractive Cairns with its broad palm-lined streets, we were all in good form when our Australian-Canadian friend Mary Light came for a visit.

"We have to go to the Tablelands, before we leave Cairns. You'll love them," she informed us with her usual infectious enthusiasm. "Traditionally people take the train," she continued. "It's a spectacular steep ascent with fifteen tunnels. It was built in 1888 and even goes through the Barron Falls Gorge, but it will be quite expensive for the whole family and limits us doing any more exploring. Let's rent a car instead."

It was indeed a dramatic climb up to the top of the Macalister Range, through the hillsides of broken granite and lush forest. At times we glimpsed the railway high up on its sleepers, and when we reached Kuranda we went to see the old railway station, attractively decked in tropical flowers and ferns. Once past Atherton we entered the lovely rolling farmlands of the plateau. This is one of the richest growing areas of Australia, due to the fertile volcanic soil and ample rainfall, and the dozen national parks protect the remains of what was once a massive tropical rain forest.

We stopped frequently, once to visit a furniture factory. Here Mary bought us a chopping board made from local woods, a beautifully turned wooden egg for Colin, and spinning tops for Duncan and Jamie. Mary, with characteristic directness and charm, had the delighted carpenter machine them especially for us!

Mary charmed everyone, including Aussie Bou our budgerigar!

Finally we came back to the coast, down a long winding road, which, Mary informed us, had only been a one-way dirt track in her youth. Fringed by the long golden-red grass glowing in the sunset we gradually descended to the deep blue Pacific Ocean. Huge platters of seafood at lively Barnacle Bill's restaurant made a perfect ending to the day.

It was a beautiful sail up the shore, the high hills, with vegetation in many varied tones of green, dropping dramatically to the ocean. In

Cairns we had replenished our fishing tackle box and soon after leaving we caught a fish.

"Great timing for dinner!" I said prematurely.

It was a fine but energetic tuna and it escaped from the gaff before we could anoint it with alcohol, our method for getting fish on board. Fortunately we soon caught another and I quickly put a few drops of gin on its gills and down its gullet. It instantly went limp and Andy easily lifted it into the bucket—a so much kinder and cleaner death compared to bashing the poor creature over the head with a winch handle with blood and scales flying everywhere! We found the method infallible, sometimes the larger fish become 'alive' again, but a few more drops of alcohol (now kept in a squeezy bottle for the purpose!) and it's 'game over'.

Low Islets is distinct with its one hundred year old lighthouse on the sandy cay. Exploring the reef we were fascinated by the soft corals, and how the baby giant clams, with their bright green, blue and purple mantles, excavated holes in the hard coral in which to protect themselves.

Lizard Island, 160 nautical miles north of Cairns, is the most northerly of the Barrier Reef resort islands and with its turquoise seas, many white sand beaches, great diving and long walks, is justly named a jewel.

While anchoring in Watson's Bay, the boys noticed the ruins of a house ashore.

"Let's go and have a look at it," suggested Colin.

The stone ruins had been the home of the Watsons and we learnt of their tragic story. In 1881 Mrs. Watson, a settler's wife whose husband was away in their only boat starting a new fishing depot, was attacked by aboriginals. Apparently the house had been built on aboriginal ceremonial ground. One servant was killed but Mrs. Watson with her son and a Chinese servant managed to escape to sea in a beche de mer (sea cucumber) cooking barrel. Unable to find fresh water, they died on another island. Mary Watson was found with her baby in her arms but she left behind a detailed diary. Her story is told at the Cooktown museum and a dry fountain has been built to her honour.

Lizard Island was named after the monitor lizards found here when Captain Cook spent a day trying to find a way out to the open sea. Apparently, although Cook recognized that something to the east was making the waters calm, it wasn't until he went aground, on what became Endeavour Reef, near Cooktown that he realized the extent of the Barrier Reef. Cook climbed the steep hill at the north end of Lizard Island. Being able to see the darker blue of the passes with the elevation, he located several routes to the distant Pacific.

We also climbed up to what is now called Cook's Look. It was a hot, steep, rugged ascent, although easier for us with the well-marked path than it had been for Captain Cook. To the west were the yachts at anchor, silhouetted in the brilliant turquoise water, to the east was a panoramic view of the outer reef.

"Being here really makes one appreciate Cook's truly remarkable seamanship and navigating skills," Andy remarked.

We spent ten delightful days in Watson's Bay. There is an attractive barbecue area ashore and it was here that we became acquainted with many other yachtsmen, as everyone at this point was a long distance cruiser. There were also other children for the boys, prompting Duncan to suggest,"Let's have a treasure hunt for my birthday."

It was a great success. We made 'lizards' the theme of this, his thirteenth birthday, and Andy decorated a fine lizard-shaped birthday cake. With all the practice gained at cake decorating on the trip, he was becoming a real professional.

The traffic, sediment and brackish water had made the diving by the channel on the inside of the reef disappointing, and we were itching to dive on the outer reef. However it wasn't that easy, as much of the reef is uncharted. Divers in Cairns had told us of 'Cods' Hole', located close to Lizard Island, and we were determined to see the 1.5 metre potato cod, members of the grouper family, which were common there. We had been waiting for a calm day, but it continuously blew 20-25 knots. Now Andy was agitating to get moving north.

"Why don't I check it out with the resort?" I suggested.

"It's a great day to go to the Hole," assured Bill, who ran the water sports. "Don't worry about the wind, it always blows harder in Watson's Bay, as it funnels between the hills. Low tide today is at 1:00 P.M. so you will be sheltered from the Pacific swells out at the reef."

We decided to try, so collected some friends from other boats, also a lady who had been camping on the shore, relaxing after finishing her term as mayor, and headed out into wind. It was a bumpy ride but the sea conditions were good at Cormorant Pass.

I was on the helm, Andy on the bow, as we approached one of the mooring buoys, laid to stop the reef from being damaged by boats anchoring.

Suddenly Andy called back urgently, "Stop! Go in reverse."

I backed off. "What's the problem?"

"It's very shallow."

"The depth sounder says 75 feet."

The water was so clear it seemed like ten.

It was a wonderful dive in perfectly calm water, only a few yards from the raging Pacific Ocean. It was all we had hoped for from the Barrier Reef with huge schools of brilliantly coloured fish, massive coral, and the enormous potato cod that liked their noses stroked and to feed from people's hands.

We had caught one of the remoras, or suckerfish, which regularly attached themselves to the hull of *Bagheera*, and Andy dove down with the cut up pieces in the bucket. He held out a morsel to the nearest giant. As the cod approached it opened its huge mouth and Andy's outstretched arm disappeared inside!

"A little eerie," Andy admitted later as he described the sensation of his arm being sucked into the huge, toothy maw that was easily a third of the length of the cod's whole body. Andy had emptied the rest of the fish from the bucket!

There were also several sharks around. Although sharks always bear watching, particularly in the passes and on the outer reef, and one has to be extremely careful when shooting fish if there is blood in the water, they are generally not aggressive in clear, sunlit tropical waters. The reef's most unpleasant creatures are actually less dramatic, such as the stonefish, with their highly venomous spines that lie hidden on the bottom, looking just like stones. We always wear plastic reef shoes when exploring the reef and intertidal zone. Other concerns are the box jelly fish, whose sting can be fatal, but they are found only in coastal water and in certain seasons. When shell collecting, we also had to be careful of the cone shells which can thrust a barb of highly toxic venom into their prey. We always use tongs to pick them up for an examination.

It was time for Mary to leave. She had been a wonderful guest with endless stories and games for the boys, and technical talk with Andy, as she still sailed her own boat in Vancouver. As always I had found her positive, stimulating and refreshingly down to earth. It had also been good to talk to someone from home who could fill me in on 'the news' and put life in perspective. Still with whirlwind energy, Mary now 75, had experienced a couple of setbacks with cancer. The skin cancer on the top of her head had necessitated some hair removal; undaunted she brought a headscarf to match every outfit. She was thrilled to be flying out. To the last minute true to form she charmed the resort manager into giving us six loaves of bread on her way to the airport.

We continued around the 'top' of Australia with mostly strong south-easterly winds, but still sheltered from the great Pacific swells by the reef. Navigation through the inner passage is busy rather than difficult, although distances at times were hard to judge. It was most reassuring to check on our new radar that a black patch of reef, which seemed only a stone's throw away at dusk, was actually two miles off.

Although the coast was mostly deserted, we generally anchored for the night, sometimes getting fish or shrimp from the commercial fishermen. We also saw the local sights, such as the pearl oyster farms and aboriginal paintings, and the arrival of the replica of the longboat *Elizabeth Bligh* (re-inacting Bligh's voyage after the mutiny on the *Bounty*), as we headed north to Portland Roads, the Flinders Group, Escape River, and Mount Adolphus Island.

Sailing close to Cape York, we photographed this most northerly point of Australia then headed into the Torres Strait. The Melanesian people on Thursday Island were lively, and we found the atmosphere surprisingly West Indian. The tides here were amazing. Due to the meeting of the two great water masses of the Pacific and Indian Oceans

Exploring the intertidal zone

locations only a short distance apart could have tides with times and heights completely different.

The Gulf of Carpentaria seemed an extraordinarily loppy sea, although maybe it was just our getting used to the ocean again. We made our landfall in the attractive bauxite town of Gove after two days, having been accompanied by a brown boobie bird for much of the trip. We had arrived in time for an Aboriginal open day with vendors and dancing. We were also introduced to an Aboriginal delicacy—giant sized maggots called witchery grubs. Of course the purists eat them alive!

The Yacht Club in Gove is most hospitable and we all gathered there most evenings. On the notice board was a significant tip.

Check your dinghy carefully before climbing in, crocs find them very comfortable!

Saltwater crocodiles, a protected species, are now becoming a menace to man, (who is a favourite delicacy), particularly in this northern area of Aboriginal owned Arnhem Land. This area is not accessible without a permit but for the most part we found it uninteresting, and with gory tales of crocodile attacks we weren't desperate to go ashore on the mainland. We were able to have several pleasant 'barbies' on the islands, however. Now travelling with a delightful group, about eight to ten boats, we cooked ashore and shared our catches of the day. Duncan, having taught himself the guitar coming up the coast, added harmony to our campfire songs. Every night we were treated to a backcloth of brilliant fiery-red skies.

Periodically we had visits from the Coast Watch, who patrolled by plane, making contact with us by radio. We had been calling in our position every day, as instructed by an old naval friend of Andy's, who was now head of Sea Safety Canberra. On one occasion the coastguard took our photo and it was presented to us in Darwin.

We were fascinated by the charts in this area which was not frequented by large ships. Soundings often dated back to Flinder's time, a British navigator who charted this area in the early 1800s. Interestingly it was Flinder's consistent use of the term Australia that led to the acceptance of the name. Rocks were noted that had been sighted over the years, none quite in the same position but presumably the same one! We gave all the sightings a wide berth.

The water up here is often murky. One morning we rose early to leave with the group only to find our anchor wouldn't come up. We presumed it was on a coral head, but whatever direction we tried it wouldn't come free. It wasn't an appealing prospect to go into the water, with possible crocodiles or box jellyfish around, but it had to be done. Andy finally dove down and freed the chain, but he came up looking pale. Barely able to see a foot in front of him, he had found it spooky and frightening groping around in the gloom.

There was very little wind as we approached Darwin. Used to sailing 150 nautical miles a day, we hadn't anticipated the recent light airs and the motoring that would be required.

"We're pretty low on fuel," Andy told our Alaskan friends on *Uhuru*, whilst chatting on the radio.

"Don't worry, we have plenty," they replied. "Come alongside and we'll give you a jerry can."

We arrived in Darwin at 9:00 P.M. There seemed to be a huge number of boats.

"It looks as though there's a good turnout for the Darwin Ambon Race," I commented.

We anchored well out, having heard of the massive rise and fall of the tide here, up to 7.8 metres.

The next morning the Dutch family from *Helena Christina* came by in their dinghy.

"Hi *Bagheera*, we've all been wondering when you'd arrive. There are THREE BOXES of mail for you in the race office!"

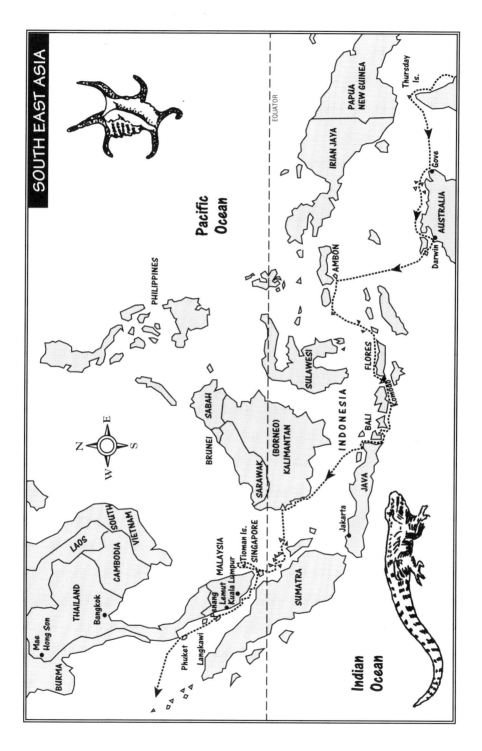

SOUTH EAST ASIA

EQUATOR

Pacific Ocean

Indian Ocean

BURMA
Mae
Hong Son
THAILAND
Bangkok
LAOS
CAMBODIA
VIETNAM
SOUTH

Phuket
Langkawi
Penang
Lemut
Kuala Lumpur
MALAYSIA
Tioman Is.
SINGAPORE
SUMATRA

BRUNEI
SABAH
SARAWAK
(BORNEO)
KALIMANTAN

PHILIPPINES

SULAWESI

INDONESIA

Jakarta
JAVA
BALI
FLORES
KOMODO

AMBON

IRIAN JAYA

PAPUA
NEW GUINEA

Darwin
Gove
AUSTRALIA

Thursday Is.

N
E
S
W

17

2 The Darwin Ambon Race

The Darwin Ambon Race attracted us as we had all enjoyed the camaraderie of the Atlantic Race for Cruisers in 1986. The boys, in particular, hoped to find other boats with children on board.

The race also facilitated our way into Indonesia as the entrance fee included a cruising permit, and officials were organized to greet boats on arrival. In the past, all vessels wishing to cruise Indonesia had been treated like large ships, having to submit a non-refundable $500 application, with permission often not granted! By 1989, recognizing the revenue brought into remote parts of the country, Indonesia was encouraging yachtsmen, and cruising permits were down to $200. Nevertheless, permission took six to eight weeks and frequently an arduous search was required on arrival to find the various officials. One of our friends, for example, took five days to clear into Timor.

All was action-stations at the Darwin Sailing Club. The committee were most welcoming in the race office, and glad to unload the three large boxes of mail.

"You must be popular people," the chairman said, smiling at the boys.

"Actually", replied Colin, who had already been thumbing through the envelopes, "I think most of it is school books!"

"How many entries do you have for the race?" I enquired.

"Over forty, so far, and we're pleased that about half are international yachts. There are several different nationalities but I think you are the only Canadians. By the way, we've arranged for a local doctor to give all the immunizations you'll need if you're interested. The details are on the notice board, with a lot of other information. Feel free to come along at any time if you have any questions."

"The next ten days are going to be really busy," commented Andy as we went to join friends in the club. "I've several things to do on the boat, including installing the water tank Beneteau has just sent."

"And I will have to do a massive laundry and a huge shop, besides trying to get ahead with school before the trip," I added. "Boys, you had better make lists of all your favourite foods and anything else you need so I can stock up on them in case we can't get them in Indonesia. I gather the shopping here is great."

There was also a major decision to make. Amongst our mail was a letter from our good Vancouver friend, Peter Grove. I had written to Peter earlier about our concern for Duncan's schooling. When Duncan had returned to Correspondence he had started Grade 8, the beginning of High School. This was much more demanding than the Elementary Programme and took far more time. Duncan was often labouring more than five hours a day, working by himself, which was tough for anyone let alone a teenager who had just experienced a very dynamic and successful regular school year. He really missed the life at Pittwater High School with his mates, the hum and competition of the classroom, his independence from us, and both school and community sports. So I had asked Peter to enquire about the possibility of Duncan being offered a place at St. George's School in Vancouver which takes boarders. I wasn't really thinking of his going immediately, but wanted to have the information for a possible future decision. Peter's letter, informing us that Duncan had been offered a place for September, in two months time, put us in a quandary.

Andy and I mulled it over at length. We certainly didn't want Duncan to leave us, and felt he was getting a very enriched life. However, our trip had initially been planned for only two years. When extending the time to six years, we recognized the importance of analyzing this decision from the point of view of every family member. The last thing we wanted was to compromise Duncan's future, particularly by turning him off schoolwork. High School is also an important part of the Canadian lifestyle, and we didn't want him later to feel he had been deprived of the experience. Our final conclusion was that it was only fair to let Duncan himself make the decision. As the deadline date was already due he could only have two days.

Duncan's initial reaction was that he wanted to stay on board, but after a few hours he came back with the questions—where was the school exactly, what was it like, what sports did they play, would he know anyone there, which countries would he miss, would he be joining us for all the holidays . . ? I told him that the school was just nineteen blocks from our house; that I knew of at least four boys from his Vancouver Elementary School, who now went to St. George's; that Peter Grove, his godfather, lived only four blocks away and that he had already invited Duncan to spend the weekends with his family; and that his four sisters, Andy's daughters, couldn't wait to see him! Then we poured over the school atlas.

"You'll miss much of the Indian Ocean," I concluded, "but you should be able to join us in Thailand for this Christmas and South Africa next year. And in the summer you will be able to come to Kenya, and join us for a safari. The Easter holidays are too short for a visit but maybe you could go skiing."

Boarding school wasn't a new concept to Duncan. His cousins, who had grown up in Malaysia, Africa and Saudi Arabia, had always gone to England to school and loved it. We encouraged him to talk with our cruising friends, who he now knew well. Predictably there were some extreme reactions but most were objective in helping him to balance the pros and cons.

Finally he gave us his decision.

"I think I'll go back," he told us. "It's not that I want to leave you and the boat, although high school is much more fun than correspondence. The biggest thing is that if I don't go back I won't play sports until I'm in Grade 10, and then it's too late to get on to any teams. I'll be way behind everyone else."

It was a sad choice for us but we felt that it was the right one for Duncan. Thank goodness my father had left me money to pay for it!

Time was running out for our chores and some sightseeing. It was a quick bus ride into town, and easy to find our way around. Although there had been various attempts to start communities in this area, mostly due to British fears that the French or Dutch would get a foothold on Australia, it wasn't until 1869 that Darwin was founded on its present site. Initially growth was accelerated by the discovery of gold in Pine Creek in 1871 but when gold fever died down the town developed erratically due to the harsh climate. It was during World War II, when Darwin became an important base for the Allies against the Japanese, that the town became firmly established.

On Christmas Day, 1974, Cyclone Tracy all but flattened the town. In true outback style it bounced back. Darwin is now a thriving, modern city, a centre for the mining activities in the Northern Territory and a stepping stone for tourists. We found the new town attractive, with good facilities for stocking up, an extensive library for research for school-work, and an excellent museum of Arts and Sciences.

It was in the museum that we learnt about the aboriginal rock paintings that we had been seeing up the coast. The figures and images were grouped in two major styles: Mini and X-ray. Mini is the older (in Arnhem Land dates between about 7000 to 20,000 years ago) and generally depicts spirit creatures in the shape of humans. These are often in composed scenes acting out rituals of love, hunting or battles. X-ray art is a more generic art collection from up to 9,000 years ago to the present. As the name suggests, this art depicts the internal features of the subjects.

We also enjoyed the stuffed birds and underwater collections in the museum, eyeing with awe the huge blue box jelly fish, or sea wasp. With a body the size of a large salad bowl, and twenty tentacles which are three metres long and covered with millions of stinging capsules, it is claimed that only a well-aimed bullet kills humans faster.

"And look what it says here," said Andy. "They prefer murky water! It still makes me shudder when I think of that dive to free the anchor chain."

But it was 'Sweetheart' that caught the boys' attention.

"You have to come and look," said Jamie pulling my arm. "You won't believe how big this crocodile is."

Now stuffed for posterity 'Sweetheart' was a huge salt-water crocodile and a local personality, notorious for attacking small boats. Apparently he ate propellers and a fuel tank before coming to his end!

High on our priority list was organizing a trip to Kakadu National Park. Since starting our voyage, we had made a point of trying to see the local sights and travelling inland to get the flavour of the culture. I investigated using local buses, renting a car and taking organized tours. For Kakadu the organized tour was by far the best deal with a luxury air-conditioned bus, meals, tours of the various art sites and a river cruise. The company even decided that being six, Jamie could go free!

It was a wonderful day. As we left at 5:30 AM, we were illuminated by a brilliant full moon on our right while a huge orange sun rose to our left. The tour stopped for morning tea at a place where the boys could enjoy tame kangaroos, emus and donkeys, then continued into the park itself, in total a two hour drive. In 1981 UNESCO called Kakadu one of the world's last great natural reserves and it was declared a World Heritage Site. It is now leased to the government by its aboriginal owners. Situated between the South and East Alligator Rivers, the park consists of two distinct regions—the high, rocky Arnhem Land escarpment, with its incredible gorges and waterfalls, and the low floodplain, lagoons and billabongs drained by the rivers.

Our driver was informative and happy to stop at a moment's notice. There were Jabiru birds, dingoes and water buffalo, and huge, eight metre high termite mounds, which take ten years to grow just a third of a metre.

After a stop at the Four Seasons Hotel, which is shaped like a crocodile, we explored the impressive Nourlangie Rock to see the aboriginal rock art. This is reputedly the most vivid display of X-ray art in Australia. Here the artists used a wide range of colours to illustrate the local wildlife. In particular, fish are featured, as this style paralleled the emergence of fresh water in the area. Giant perch dominate several of the friezes with their anatomy revealed in great detail. There are also striking male and female figures in the company of ancestral heroes, which represent the birth of a tribe. The white figure is that of Namarrkon, the lightning man, who was feared for his power and violence.

Until recently the aboriginals repainted the art which has helped it withstand the effects of rain, wind and time, and encouraged the people to renew their ancestral ties to the 'Dreamtime'—the creation of the world. The red soil from the area obviously influenced the colours of the paintings. I had already discovered the permanence of the dye from the soil in the boys' clothing!

"But when are we going to see the crocodiles?" the boys asked, as we climbed back in the bus.

Without doubt the highlight of their day was the Yellow Waters cruise. We were visiting at a good time as it was the dry season (April-November) when many of the water holes have dried up. This forces the wildlife into a few narrow waterways which is excellent for viewing. There are two types of crocodiles, the dangerous saltwater variety and the smaller freshwater, or Johnston's, that are generally considered harmless to man.

Almost immediately we saw saltwater crocodiles. They were close by and impressive, particularly when they snapped at a bird in flight and we glimpsed their teeth in action! Saltwater crocodiles live primarily in coastal rivers and swamps, although they are also found in fresh water and in the open sea. Their main sources of food are crustaceans, birds, small reptiles, fishes and mammals. They can grow to be six metres long and hide from their prey by floating submerged in the water with only their nostrils, eyes and small strip of body showing. Although seemingly half asleep resting in the water-lilies, their eyes, mere slits, watched every action and reaction in the water; they are ever alert for an opportunity—especially to consume humans!

Whilst the boys and I watched in awe, Andy was looking through the binoculars and exclaiming, "This is fantastic, I can't believe the varieties of birds here."

Our guide was knowledgeable and delighted to have passengers who were so interested. He pointed out the different herons and egrets, having to talk loudly above the noisy magpie geese. There were large flocks of green pygmy geese, plumed whistling ducks, wedge-tailed eagles and many more. Some claim that Kakadu is Australia's premier bird sanctuary and that sighting over seventy species a day is not uncommon.

The boys talked about the visit the entire way back on the bus, with Duncan thumbing through our bird guide and coming up with more tidbits of information.

As I put Jamie to bed, and we had finished yet another discussion about the 'man-eater' or 'devil's lizard' crocs, he asked me if we would also be going to bed soon.

"No, it's tonight that Judy, my schoolfriend, and her husband Chris, who we met in Melbourne, are arriving," I reminded him. "And they don't get here until two in the morning!"

Planning to go offshore cruising themselves, Judy and Chris had welcomed our invitation to get some offshore experience and finish the practical requirements for their navigation course. We looked forward to their company and help in watchkeeping as (heaven forbid!) autopilots and windvanes were not allowed on the race.

The anchorage off the Darwin Sailing Club is up to a mile offshore due to the extremely shallow bay. It had not proved as awkward as expected, although we were thankful for the dinghy trollies provided that night. Judy and Chris's arrival coincided with one of the lowest spring tides of the year, with the water an unbelievably long muddy walk from the club.

More annoying than the tide had been the standard offshore wind in the morning and onshore wind at night. This guaranteed a soaking both ways in the dinghy which was uncomfortable and could be embarrassing, such as my leaving a 'pool' in the doctor's office when we went for our immunizations!

The immunizations suggested for South East Asia included gamma globulin (hepatitis A), typhoid, paratyphoid A&B and tetanus (TABT), cholera, polio, mencevax (meningitis), and malaria pills. A once-weekly dose of chloroquine was advised as a prophylactic for malaria. We carried fansidar as a treatment and were warned there were some chloroquine resistent areas (such as Thailand and East Africa) where we should take paludrine in addition, or preferably the expensive mefloquine.

Knowing that several yachtsmen were going to be in the doctor's office at the same time we opted to arrive later than the appointed time, which resulted in us being at the end of the line. For three hours our cruising friends came out of the surgery clutching their arms, looking pale, and telling us how awful the experience had been. Finally it was our turn.

"Who's next?" asked the doctor after Andy and I had tried to suffer in silence.

"I'll go," volunteered Jamie, who had recently survived shots at school.

We had opted for the oral typhoid as there is often a severe reaction to TABT, but the boys still needed the tetanus. As the needle went into Jamie's arm he let out a loud scream and that was the final straw for Colin. If Jamie and so many of the adults had found it so traumatic, it was not for him. It was hard to tell who was the more upset, Colin because of the prospect of the injection or Andy about Colin's refusal!

We returned to the sailing club where Colin used the hand-held radio to call his friends on *Helena Cristina* to explain that he couldn't stay the night as planned because he had refused to have his shots.

"You mean you wouldn't have your shots?" repeated twelve year old Agnita incredulously, in her delightful singsong Dutch accent. "Oh, no!"

Within minutes the whole fleet knew the story, and were sympathizing with Colin!

"But what are you going to do?" our friends asked later.

"Colin has agreed to have them another day," I replied.

The office staff and even the doctor's wife came in early for Colin's appointment.

"It's fine," said Colin matter-of-factly. "I've come to terms with it now."

Two minutes later he came out smiling, totally flooring us all.

As always, we were 'on the double' the final days before the trip. *Bagheera* had to be taken around to the wharf for us to fill up with water and take on fuel from a truck. A huge shop was accomplished to cater for seven on board and to stock up on western foods like cereals, snacks, and long life milk, and fresh foods such as potatoes, onions, carrots, cabbage and apples. We loaded up on paper products, not forgetting Andy's phobia about running out of 2-ply toilet paper! A sack of 'strong' bread flour was collected from the baker, meat was vacuum packed and frozen solid by the butcher and I finally managed to get all the items on the boys' lists.

In the evenings we relaxed, participating in the race dinner, and enjoying a variety of foods from the stalls at the Mindil Beach market. Meanwhile, the Dutch girls helped Colin buy some gemstones and Jamie choose a 'didgeridoo', the aboriginal wind instrument with a deep resonant sound, that is made from a long hollow tube.

"A real bargain," Jamie informed us proudly, holding up his miniature instrument. It was unbelievably tuneless, as we were to be frequently reminded!

The final night was spent dining with our recent cruising mates, with the grand finale of Andy anaesthetizing us with his infamous flaming hot rum or 'poor man's' liqueur. In the morning boats would be heading in many directions, either taking part in the race, following different routes to either the Mediterranean or South Africa, or continuing along the Australian coast.

We have a great memento of the evening in our visitor's book from Peter and Shirley Billing on *Clypeus*.

Bubble, bubble toil and trouble,
Fire burn and cauldron bubble,
Measure large of sunsoaked rum
In the cauldron mix and turn
Skin of orange, juice of lime,
Heat it up and bubble fine;
Stir in sugar, mix it up,
Set afire and light the cup.
For a charm or powerful trouble,
Like a hell broth boil and bubble.
Bagheera's brew makes friends worldwide
But sailors, beware of the falling tide.'

—*Macbeth Act IV* with apologies

Back on board I had made a point of removing as much packaging as possible, while I was stowing the goods away. We had become increasingly aware of the problem of non-biodegradable products, particularly plastic, which are abandoned and an eyesore all around the world. Garbage amasses fast on a boat so we leave as much ashore as possible, where it will be disposed of appropriately. At sea we sort for different disposal methods; biodegradables (cut up small) go in the ocean, while other items are kept for burning or to be buried. When possible we keep plastics on board until we reach port, where we check out the municipal facilities. This is important in developing countries where disposal methods are often poor, if they exist at all.

The race started on July 22nd. After enjoying a champagne breakfast and clearing customs we headed out to the start. The winds were light and while we concentrated on hoisting our spinnaker we were drenched from behind. Several friends had piled onto *Yaraandoo* with the intent of sending us off in style.

Out came the buckets and we drenched them back!

Gradually our spinnaker filled. *Yaraandoo* escorted us across the bay, then we called our final goodbyes. It was goodbye to friends and goodbye to Australia, our home for almost two years.

"I still think you should have got residency status with your job, Mummy, then we could have stayed," sighed Duncan. "I really like Oz."

I sympathized. Then, my watch over, I went straight to bed and was instantly asleep. Whatever time of day we leave I always do the same, a combined result of physical and emotional exhaustion, and coping with the motion of the sea again.

It was a pleasant 600 nautical mile trip with the odd squall adding some excitement, particularly when we blew out our 'cat' spinnaker. We called in our position daily on the race radio schedule and had frequent conversations with other yachts, several of whom could be seen most of the way. After three days, the finish line was in sight but we were becalmed. Gradually the wind filled in from behind bringing boats with it, and a group of us finished within seconds. Although fifth boat over the line, we couldn't sail to our race rating, laden as we were with cruising gear.

"Over the side with those schoolbooks!" declared Andy. The boys, of course, thought that was an excellent idea!

We anchored, with a stern line ashore, off the attractive village of Amahusu about six nautical miles west of the city of Ambon. The people were charming, with huge dark eyes and big smiles, and most welcoming.

As promised, the entry procedures were streamlined although we had to think carefully when completing our cruising itinerary so as not to close any options. The only problem was getting copies made. Having heard the Indonesians required multiple copies of boat documents and crew lists we had run off many in Darwin—only to find on arrival that the officials all wanted to stamp one sheet, then have copies made of that. There was only one photocopier in the village and forty-two yachts!

By the next day all the boats had finished, and the atmosphere was festive for the welcoming celebrations. The locals were immaculately and vibrantly dressed and the children, who had been given the day off school, glowed with enthusiasm.

We were entertained royally with singing, dancing and music. The culmination was a magnificent banquet that introduced us to a variety of Indonesian fare. Meat, fish and rice dishes, and the sweet deserts, were distinctly flavoured with the renowned spices of this area of the Moluccas (Maluku)—the famous Spice Islands of the East Indies.

New friends for Jamie and Andrew, from Wildfire, in Ambon

Meanwhile, on the beach, dug-out canoes with brilliantly coloured sails had been arriving for the beach sports. There were races on the sands, canoe races and tug o' war. We thought all the women petite until the opponents for the women's tug o' war showed up, but they good-naturedly roared with laughter when Chris, decked in a skirt and floppy sunhat, filled in for me in the finals.

For the yacht captains there was an ancient ritual. Several of them grasped the underside of a huge log of bamboo and were invited to breathe in the fumes of a potent plant that was burning in a pot held by one of the local men. The excitement was great as the captains were 'driven by the spirits' and stampeded around the beach with the inevitability, it appeared, of the 'spirits' luring their victims to a sodden finale!

The celebrations continued with a formal prizegiving in Ambon city, dances in the evening, and becak (bicycle cab) races. Even the ubiquitous bemos buses were barred from the street for this last event. The locals excelled in peddling these three-wheeled taxis, used for urban transpor-

Yacht captains 'driven by the spirits'

tation. The yachtsmen, however, found the co-ordination of speed and steerage somewhat hazardous, with the streetside drainage ditches looming ahead all too frequently!

The village of Amahusu is as attractive as its people, with houses and gardens not only beautifully maintained but cultivated with artistic pride. Knowing well the tropical vegetation of the Caribbean, we were amazed by the many varieties of trees and flowers, several of which we had never seen before.

It was particularly lush because, unlike the rest of Indonesia, this was Ambon's wet season. We had experienced some torrential showers, although these were, of course, before the hosing to our water tank burst, and we lost all our carefully caught supply into the bilge!

"Thank goodness we had all those immunizations in Darwin", Andy commented, as we lugged water of questionable quality from the shore. We chlorinated it heavily, which worked well for everything except a good cup of tea.

There had been little tourist development in Ambon. The city, however, is large and could provide all necessary supplies. All we really needed was produce. The markets were cheap with a large selection of fruit and vegetables, but I had already been warned, "Take Andy with you. There are some persistent 'leeches' who insist on helping you, and you will end up paying a fortune."

So Andy and I went together and ended up with a bargain! Glancing in the window of a jewellery store on the way, I saw some attractive pendants. We chose a fish that was intricately segmented in 22 carat gold. After some negotiation it cost just $5.00 more than its gold value.

It was the first of many handcrafted treasures that we were to collect in our travels through exotic, diverse Indonesia.

3. Indonesia

Ambon to Komodo

Stretching 5,200 kilometres from the Asian mainland to the Pacific Ocean, the Indonesian archipelago embraces 13,677 islands, of which 6,000 are named and under 1,000 permanently settled. Most of the islands are mountainous, and the area, known as the Ring of Fire is the home of over 400 volcanoes. Some of these have erupted with devastating effects, such as Krakatoa in 1883 when 30,000 people were killed. However, the volcanoes also bring life, as the ash, rich in chemicals, is very fertile. With its soil and high humidity, Indonesia has some of the most productive land in the world.

Tanah Air Kita, the Indonesians' name for their homeland, means 'Our Land and Water'. With a total area of five million square kilometres, little more than a third of the country is land. Barely larger than Australia's state of Queensland, it supports a fast growing population of over 185,000,000, making Indonesia the fifth most populous country in the world at the time. With the break-up of the USSR she has now moved up to fourth.

The original people are thought to have come from India or Burma while later migrants, the Malays, came from Indo and southern China. From the 7th century there have been well-developed societies in the archipelago. The people today are a fascinating mix of these and subsequent migration waves—Chinese, Indian, Melanesian, Portuguese,

Polynesian, Arabian, English, Dutch and American. Reputedly there are over 300 ethnic groups. Because of the size of the archipelago, and isolation due to the islands, jungles, swamps and highlands, ethnic pockets have remained, so that besides the diversity of cultures, there can also be a time lag of hundreds of years.

From Ambon we headed west, determined to see as much of this complex country as possible.

"Let's go somewhere remote," suggested Andy.

Amongst other islands we decided to stop at Wangi Wangi, which on the chart looked well removed from any of the well-populated areas.

It was pleasant sailing except for the line squalls, but these were useful for catching water. Andy rigged a cloth water trap and tube to the gooseneck, where the boom and mast join. We filled two 25 litre cans with water that ran down the mainsail in ten minutes! It was the beginning of a system that became far more sophisticated and even more productive as time went by. In the remote areas we were able to rely on this system for our entire freshwater supply.

"It appears to be a raised atoll, like Niue in the South Pacific," I commented on arrival, seeing the weathered coral cliffs.

We sailed down the west coast of Wangi Wangi, attractive with its sandy beaches and huge palms. There were several trading schooners at anchor by large boat sheds, but like many of the islands of Indonesia there was a continuous shallow fringing reef with a very deep drop-off. This made anchoring a problem for us. We couldn't go over the reef with our draft, and neither Andy's back nor our electric anchor windless could cope with hauling up our anchor and chain from much more than 90 feet. Unsuccessful in finding a passage into one of the secluded bays, we had to use the staked channel into the harbour by the large town.

Even before the anchor was down *Bagheera* was surrounded by scores of dug-out canoes loaded with noisy, excited people, who all wanted to come on board. Not only was it overwhelming but it was devastating to our newly painted topsides.

"Put all the fenders out, quickly," Andy called frantically as another canoe crunched into our hull. "Liza, get the mat fenders as well. Duncan, you push them off with the dinghy oars."

At the same time we gestured and used physical restraint to indicate that no-one was to come aboard. We held them off but more canoes kept on coming.

"Look at the dock," cried Colin suddenly.

Busily occupied on board, we hadn't realized that crowds had also now filled the long jetty. It was packed with people who, as we looked up, called out and beckoned us to go ashore. We couldn't understand this extreme reaction. Indonesians had been curious previously but none before had acted in this frenetic way.

Finally, to our relief, a man arrived who could speak some English.

"I'm a government officer," he told us, "sent from Java to counsel the people of this island in family planning. I'm used to foreigners but the local people were amazed when you arrived. You are the first overseas visitors to the island since the Japanese left at the end of World War II, and they have never seen a boat like this before."

"No wonder they're reacting this way," exclaimed Andy. "What do you think we should do?"

"The 'Head Official' would like to show you around. He is waiting on the jetty. I'll come back with you. By the way this is a Muslim town so you should dress conservatively, especially the ladies."

"Why don't some of us stay on board," I suggested, thinking how vulnerable *Bagheera* would be if left unattended.

Duncan, Colin and Jane, a friend who was travelling with us to Singapore, agreed to stay behind.

The headman greeted Andy, Jamie and me with ceremony and took us on the tour accompanied by, or so it seemed, most of the island's 3,000 inhabitants. It was a pleasant town, the homes attractive with tiled roofs, and there were some new two-storey buildings with glass windows, unusual for much of the tropics. What started as a royal tour however became increasingly like a mob scene. Everyone wanted to shake our hands and feel our white skins, especially Jamie's. Finally 'guards' had to form a barrier around us to hold off the crowds.

What a relief it was to return to the jetty and climb into the dinghy!

Back on board, Duncan, Colin and Jane had managed to hold the fort, although they had discovered there had been petty theft. Anything loose on the deck, such as thongs and clothing, had been taken, and also, to our dismay, a $100.00 spinnaker snatch block. The shackle from the other block had also been removed but fortunately they had not figured out how to open the block itself, so it was still on the spinnaker sheet, the line attached to the sail.

Others claimed similar experiences with theft when we talked on the radio that evening.

"Unbelievable," reported Skip on *Endymion*. "As we were giving out gifts on the port side we were being stolen blind off the starboard."

We left the next day, not wanting to stand guard yet another night, and sailed towards the southern Lesser Sundas, or Nusa Tenggara Group, which stretches from Timor to Bali. The anchorages were serene and the diving spectacular at the remote islands on the way. We caught up on school, found some new shells for our collection and read up on the history, fauna, flora and religions of the Isles. We dined mostly from the sea, with Andy and Duncan, our spear fishermen, finding fish and lobster in abundance. The olive green and salmon coloured shells of the painted lobster were so beautiful I was reluctant to kill them but, with a delicate garlic butter, they made a sumptuous supper!

An overnight trip took us to a small bay at the west end of Flores, close to Labuhanbajo. It was dry here in the rain shadow, with sparse vegetation, but the angular hills and thatched huts provided an attractive setting. We had learnt by this time the advantages of anchoring away from the towns, both in order to avoid the tedious official paperwork and being over-whelmed by curious people. Meanwhile, we could still get to town by dinghy to see the sights, meet locals in their own setting, and visit the markets.

Once anchored, Andy and the boys rushed to the long sandy beach for a soccer game. Jane joined them but I declined. It was time to clean up and I wanted peace, quiet and space. About once a month I'd try to get the boat to myself. Then I could complete a massive spring clean, tidy-up and reorganize the food in two to three hours. What a difference it made having no bodies to manoeuvre around, and no-one questioning what I was doing!

Normally back before I am finished, on this occasion the family was gone a long time. Ashore two backpackers had come up to them enquiring about the Canadian yacht. Not only were they from our home town, Vancouver, but they had just graduated as boarders from St George's School. It was an unbelievable co-incidence and what a fortuitous one. Both boys were so positive about the school, so encouraging about Duncan's return and full of pertinent information that was invaluable to a new boy! We thoroughly enjoyed the lads and invited them to cruise with us to Komodo, to see the dragons, setting sail the next morning.

Sandwiched between Flores and Sumbawa, with many other small islands, Komodo is a mere 36 kilometres long, and 16 kilometres at its widest point. The waters around the island have the reputation of being the most tempestuous in Indonesia. As we sailed up the straits the waves tossed us high, spray drenched us, and the rip tides and whirlpools buffeted *Bagheera* from side to side. The island itself was desolate, its east coast an eroded cliff that plunged steeply to the sea, with deep black ravines gouged into the solidified volcanic ash.

"This is great dragon country!" remarked Duncan with a grin.

It was Saturday. Friends had told us we should be at the Sunday feeding of the Komodo dragons.

"They are truly formidable," they'd said. "The children will love them."

Although seeing the dragons had been our reason for coming to Komodo, our friends had also suggested we spend a few days on the island.

"The village is great, really traditional, one of our best stops," they'd enthused.

We had been hoping for the opportunity to meet some Indonesians who lived a more traditional lifestyle, after our memorable visits with the local people in the South Pacific. Amazingly, although Wangi Wangi hadn't had recent visitors, much of their lifestyle was quite western, so this was an unexpected bonus.

We anchored off the government camp at Loh Liang. Komodo is a protected national park, but visitors' permits only cost us 50 cents each. Our allotted guide spoke some English and suggested we go for a close look at the dragons that afternoon.

"How close?" I asked anxiously.

"Just a few feet away but don't worry, I will be taking this."

He reached for a long stick with a pronged fork on the end. It didn't look sturdy enough to fight off the ferocious attacks we had heard of. Over thirty humans reputedly had been torn apart over the years, including one two days before in nearby Rinca—the boys couldn't wait to get going!

It was the best time of year for dragon hunting. Dragons are sun worshippers and during the dry season, May-September, there are more of them out looking for food (about 2000 on Komodo) than in the wet season, December-February. Our guide stressed that we must never wear red, as it could be mistaken for blood, and we must never go looking for these monster lizards without him. Although the dragons prefer goat, deer, or wild pig, if particularly hungry or threatened the largest and most aggressive will attack humans, generally creeping up on them from behind. Just their bite can kill. Although they are not poisonous, they can pass on an infection from the carrion they eat, for which there is no known cure.

The Komodo dragons, locally called ora, are confined to the small islands of Komodo, Padar, Rinca, Uwada Sami, Gili Motong and Western Flores, an area of under 1000 square kilometres. They are the largest of the monitor lizards that are found throughout Asia, Africa and Australia, growing up to 3.5 metres long with a weight of over 150 kilos, which can increase to 200 kilos after a good meal. Although mentioned by early fishermen and pearl divers, and their skins taken (but too scarred to be prized) by Chinese traders since the twelfth century, the area's isolation and strong ocean currents ensured the monitors' survival. In 1912, a Dutch scientist, P.A. Ouwens, 'identified' the dragons, and they were protected in 1915, although at times still hunted until 1937.

During the hot, dusty, half-hour walk, we were entertained by shrieking sulphur-crested cockatoos and equally noisy friar birds. The dragon-watching site at Banunggulung, a fenced area at the top of a ravine, was built to enable tourists to watch the dragons safely, and regular feedings have enticed a group of the creatures to take up residence. There were several docile dragons lounging in the dried-out river bed below. The guide went down ahead, assuring us they were not hungry; we followed, some more enthusiastically than others!

Covered in tough, dappled, grey-brown, scaly skin, with thick powerful legs and razor sharp claws, the ponderous lizards moved slowly, if at all. But their pink/yellow forked tongues, the sensor for both smell and taste, constantly flicked in and out, just like ribbons of fire.

"Wow," whispered Jamie as he clutched my arm tightly, "they really are true dragons!"

We were all held spellbound. Then two young ora, with pale yellow speckles, approached Duncan inquisitively—more than a little nerve-racking for his mother—but they were easily guided away by the pronged stick, and Duncan was thrilled when he was given the stick to use himself.

Meanwhile the guide searched for babies. Hatching after an eight month incubation period, they live in the trees for their first year, as adults will eat any young who are under a metre long. No luck, but he did find a strong plastic-like web that stretched for about four metres, built by a 14 cm ugly, poisonous, but not deadly, Nephilia spider.

We ate back at the camp, our lively fellow visitors making up for the sparse fare of rice or noodles with tea. They were staying in the guest house, called a losmen, which had spacious cabins, but there were more people than beds.

"Maybe we could sleep on the beach?" began one backpacker.

"Maybe you didn't see the dragon at the garbage dump right by the beach," replied another.

"Any room on your deck?" someone asked.

"Sorry," we replied, "we've already picked up two extras in Flores."

Duncan using our guide's pronged fork on a young Komodo dragon

The losmen floor rapidly won the vote when a photo album appeared with gory pictures of a child ripped apart by a dragon some years before.

On Sunday morning we returned to Banunggulung in time to hear the piercing squeals of the sacrificial goat as it was being slaughtered for a dozen now-frenzied Komodo dragons. What a transformation. From our 'theatre', or 'cage' overlooking the river bed we watched these massive animals. Blood-crazed due to their highly developed sense of smell, they clambered over each other, their twenty claws scraping on the others' scales. Visible were shark-like layers of backwards-slanting dagger teeth that could saw through the toughest of meat. One was hissing loudly, its tail arched, ready to strike.

Komodo dragons consume prey faster than any other wild animals, including lions and crocodiles, and large pieces of goat just disappeared, no chewing, no gulping, just gliding down. Our guide told us he had seen a 45 kilo dragon consume a 35 kilo pig in under twenty minutes and that, if really driven by hunger, they would swallow horns, hooves, bones—everything. Only the stomach and intestines are generally shunned.

Some of the twenty or so guests started to wander away to watch the dragons lumber slowly, but curiously gracefully, down the track on the other side of the fence, maybe heading for a snooze in their burrows. Suddenly there was a scream.

Unwittingly, a couple had wandered out of our protective 'cage' and a dragon was ambling right between them! Quickly their guide steered the dragon away and they nipped back through the turnstile. Our guide told us that as these dragons were fed so regularly and were not the oldest, largest or most cantankerous, it was unlikely they would attack people here, which is why he had been able to take us into the ravine. However, you can never be too careful with a dragon!

Kampung Komodo, the village, is about a half-hour walk from the south of the camp. We went by boat and anchored off. Dry, sparse hills, with only the fan-leafed palms breaking the horizon, rose steeply behind the line of buildings along the shore, the dome of the mosque standing high at the far end.

Children swarmed around our dinghy as we reached the sands, the population density being evident wherever we went. Although here there were only five hundred people, it seemed crowded for such a small village. Many small brown arms helped us carry the dinghy up the sandy beach.

After paying our respects to the Kepala Kampung, the headman, we wandered through the tightly packed rows of houses. These all stood on stilts, about two metres high, with pointed thatched or corrugated roofs, woven palm walls, and steep retractable ladders.

We were escorted by a throng of children. They were fascinated by the boys' freckles.

"Freckles" we told them. They chanted back delighted "Feckles, feckles," doubling over with laughter.

Later, a lady couldn't resist a shy touch of Colin's face. She gestured her surprise that his face was smooth, not bumpy at all from the freckles!

We were beckoned into one of the homes and offered a most welcome Bintang beer, brewing having been introduced by the Dutch. The room was furnished functionally for every aspect of family daily life, with other touches of Dutch heritage evident in the heavy wood furniture and lace tablecloths.

The store held little but a few rusty cans and the sweet goods that all Indonesians favour. Our hosts told us that Komodo is one of the driest regions of Indonesia and very little grows, certainly not rice, the usual Indonesian staple. However, some of the villages did have gardens at the government camp where there is year-round water, so they can grow a few subsistence root and green vegetables. The main staple is fish and squid, along with the numerous chickens and goats that roam the village. Goats, sold for feeding the dragons, also provide good business from the tourists.

They explained that the people were descendants of convicts who had been exiled to the islands from Flores in the sixteenth century. Others had come later from Sumbawa and elsewhere and now they were known as the Bangsa Komodo. Their ancestors had all built their bamboo houses high off the ground and as close to the water as possible as they were terrified by the 'monsters' they had found.

"How do you find living with the 'monsters' now?" we wanted to know.

Although the villagers still lived in awe of these lizards, the largest on earth, familiarity with the dragons' habits and the use of the forked stick had given them some control. Usually the people stayed close to the village and in the past the dragons had stayed away. However, with the increase in tourism, the dragons had become more used to people and to a diet of goat. On occasion, they were now boldly entering the village at night to poach.

Indonesians are governed from Java. As this village seemed so remote from Jakarta, the capital, we asked about community decisions.

"Adat," one lady answered.

Adat is the ancient unwritten law or custom which regulates the actions and behavior of each inhabitant and each event of every village in Indonesia; it covers a total way of life, be it land ownership, ceremonies of birth, marriage and death, courtship, building houses, or praying for rain. Although it is rooted in religion, particularly animism, it is not one in itself. Like most of Indonesia this village practised Islam, but all religions (the most common being Islam, Christianity, Hinduism and Buddhism) are modified to fit Adat. The Indonesians say 'Religion comes in from the sea, but customs come down from the mountains.' Adat is a product of centuries of habit and is rigorously performed without question. We found it a fascinating contrast to our western technological age, with its values constantly challenged and changed.

Along the shore was a myriad of different types of boats, or *prahus*. With a history of inter-island and distant trading—the Chinese for sandalwood and beeswax over a thousand years ago, sixteenth century Europeans for the spices of the Moluccas, and the Dutch for the valuable commercial cargoes of sugar, tobacco and teak—Indonesian vessels range from large trading ships up to 100 feet long to small local fishing boats. Designs are varied, and include monohulls, catamarans, trimarans, and single and double outriggers. Built of wood, little metal is used, most being fastened with trunnels (originally treenails), and few have engines. Although abundant by day we saw few travelling at night and, if they were, they generally had no lights. As wood reflects poorly they also didn't show up well on radar which meant watches were busy.

In the past the Bugis pirates from Sulawesi, known as 'bogeymen', roamed the seas in their tall, seven sailed ketch-rigged *pinisi*. They were justly feared by local sailors. But neither we, nor any of our friends, experienced any signs of aggression and there had apparently been no attacks by pirates for years.

A wizened old boat builder worked with the ease of a master craftsman on a squid fishboat hull. His only tools were a saw, brace and bit, and adze. We watched, mesmerized by his rhythmic strokes, the finish, silky smooth. The boat was built from local wood, steamed and bent to shape with the planks edge-fastened.

"Amazing," commented Andy, "it's being constructed back to front!"

Unlike western builders, who make a frame on which to secure the planks, here they put in the frame and stringers after all the planking was complete.

We found the boys playing with the local children at the water's edge. Jamie was deep in conversation regarding our inflatable dinghy. The fact that he was speaking English and his new friends were speaking Bahasa Komodo, one of the three hundred or more Indonesian dialects that is similar to Biman, the language of Eastern Sumbawa, mattered not at all. They communicated perfectly and were totally at ease. Jamie said his goodbyes using a few words of Bahasa Indonesia, which is similar to Malay, and is now the official language taught in Indonesian schools. Apparently, the need for a national language was identified in the early twentieth century when the Indonesian nationalists found themselves addressing their revolutionary meetings in Dutch!

The following evening we left the village and went out to the island of Pulau Lasa for a refreshing dive. It was our last evening with the Canadian boys who had joined us in Flores as we were sailing for Bali the next morning. We lit a fire on the sandy spit. A local lad joined us, offering a selection of pearls. Everyone sang, accompanied by Duncan on the guitar, watching the final rays of the sun. We were thoroughly content.

Like Marco Polo, Kublai Khan, adventurers from Portugal, Spain, Holland and Britain during the Age of Discovery, the Dutch who created an empire, and the Yankee traders, we had gained much wealth from this land. The wealth from our visit, however, was without material gain. It was the rich experience of beholding an ancient wonder of nature, an awesome lizard that is strikingly similar to fossils that date back 130 million years to the age of the dinosaurs. It was also the unexpected pleasure of meeting the people who have lived with the dragons, the Bangsa Komodo. In this country, which is one of the earliest places man has lived, we had enjoyed a group of people whose way of life has changed little from village life centuries ago.

4. Indonesia to Singapore

Bali and Borneo

W e've had a very fast passage," Andy informed me, as he handed over the watch at 10:30 PM. "We'll arrive in Bali in the middle of the night at this rate, so I suggest we take a dog leg south and arrive at dawn."

It sounded a logical idea but what a mistake. When we turned back to the north-east we just stayed in one spot! It was hard to believe. With 30 knot winds we were hurtling along. The log recorded speeds of seven then eight, even nine knots as *Bagheera* surfed down the waves, but the SATNAV, our electronic satellite navigator, does not lie.

I plotted our position on the chart, then another half an hour later, and a third within the hour. Our position was almost the same and at one point we were going backwards! There was a huge current against us and no-one had warned us.

"It's unbelievable," exclaimed Andy on the radio the next morning. "We've just logged 57 miles but covered only 21 over the ground. Didn't anyone else have a similar experience?" he asked incredulously.

"No," they all answered.

To frustrate us further it was Independence Day, a civil holiday, so customs was closing at mid-day! As we got close to the shore, we picked up some speed, and after going through the reef into Benoa harbour, *Bagheera* positively 'flew' along. It was 10:30 AM when we anchored and there was more than enough time to clear in with the officials—and learn about the current.

"At this time of year the south equatorial current and north-east monsoon combine to build a head of water between the converging north and south island chains," they explained. "This pressure is only relieved by the water gushing out through the narrow passes between the islands and it's especially strong on the falling tide. You probably had the current at its worst!"

There were several other yachts at anchor. Some had sailed straight from Darwin whilst others had been on the race.

"What a pleasant surprise," I called out to Richard and Gabrielle on *Catriona-M*, good friends from the race. "I thought it was a final good-bye in Ambon."

"We have decided to go to Singapore for the shopping," they called back, "and stopped here on the way. We're so glad we did, it's wonderful."

Everyone loved Bali, and without doubt, it stands out in our memories as one of the most beautiful islands in the world. Although some of it has been exploited by tourism, the rest of the island is magical. Not only is it picture perfect with its towering volcanoes, emerald green sculptured rice paddies, exotic birds, ornate temples and carvings, colourful festivals and brilliant flora, but its happy people have a fascinating culture.

Catching the bemo bus from the harbour, we crossed the causeway and made a quick trip that afternoon to the popular holiday destination of Kuta. We knew it would be touristy but it was also great fun. The town was alive with vendors; brightly-coloured clothing, kites and parasols were strung up on display, along with stalls of local carvings, silver, leather, batik, puppets and art brimming full with goods. Fakes were in abundance too with Gucci handbags, designer clothing and Rolex watches.

The long sandy beach was filled with tourists. They were being massaged, manicured, and pedicured, all the while bargaining furiously! A charming lady talked us into buying a pineapple. It was sweet and juicy and she peeled it beautifully, a geometric work of art, with none of the fruit wasted but not a glimpse of skin or spores left.

"That's amazing," declared Colin, fascinated by the design.

"Delicious, let's have another," was Duncan's typically more concrete response! With an impish smile the lady deftly carved the next one.

A kite display caught Jamie's attention. Kite flying is a popular local sport and we had seen the amazingly graceful kites swooping and fluttering along the way. The kites were all birds, feathers and claws painted onto the brightly-coloured material wings, their papier maché heads sporting beady eyes and ferocious beaks. Jamie decided on a purple one. We couldn't believe it was only $1.50.

Friends came over when we were back on board *Bagheera*.

"How about joining us for an island tour?" they suggested. "It includes a local dance, visits to local craftsmen, such as stone carvers, weavers, the painters at Ubud, and gold and silver jewellers, the presidential palace and up to a volcano. We also get lunch."

"Sound's a great idea," I replied.

"Yes, we'll get an idea of places we would like to go back to when we rent a car," agreed Andy.

Barely out of the capital, Denpasar, the stone carvers of Batubulan were working at the roadside. Artisans chipped away furiously, creating the massive 'monster' statues. These, it seems, can liberate heroes, gods, demons, or whatever you fancy! They become the guardians of the temples, bridges, even restaurants, and now, of course, are sold as tourist souvenirs. The rock is soft and surprisingly light.

"But too big for the boat," said Andy, guiding me away!

Next stop was at a theatre, to see a Barong dance. Music, dance and drama are at the centre of Balinese life and the tinkling sound of the xylophones can be heard at all hours of the day and night. With two thousand dance troupes on the island, there are dances for every occasion, whether honouring a temple god, celebrating a wedding, a tooth-filing ceremony, or exorcising evil. Cremations are some of the most lively celebrations of all. The Barong-Rangda, or Kris dance, is one of the most violent of the Balinese dances and often used as an exorcism.

The outdoor theatre was a colourful one with bright banners and umbrellas. The backcloth was an ornate temple gate and at the side stood a typical tiered-roofed temple. In a decorative setting of its own sat the gamelan orchestra. The men were dressed in pink, their headdresses gold. Their percussion instruments were traditional gongs, drums and xylophones, made out of bronze, wood and bamboo. Likened to the beating of an insect wing or a river trickling over rocks at night, the gamelian performance was a show in itself. Contrasts were dramatic both in tempo and volume, from the slow to the frenetic and from the haunting to the deafening. Their facial expressions followed the mood, one minute alive the next in a trance.

The Barong dance is about the forces of magic, the clashes of good with evil. Good is portrayed by the lion-like, fun-loving Barong, decked in a huge, ornate headdress, two men playing his body. Bad is Rangha, the queen of the witches, who has entrails around her neck and fangs protruding from her mouth! All facial features and limbs speak in this classic dance and the movements of the dancers are incredible, many being exaggerated forms of traditional work, such as men using prehensile toes to climb coconut trees. With the sudden changes of characters— varying between the comic to the grotesque, movements going from motionless to jerky, the stage filled to overflowing, to one person moving a single finger in a trance-like state—there was never a dull moment.

At the height of the performance the Barong's supporters rush to kill the witch, boldly flourishing their kris knives. Rangda puts them in a trance and the knives turn to stab their owners. The Barong then casts his spell to stop the kris from harming the men. As the men rush around crazily, dramatically trying to stab themselves, the gamelan gets louder and louder, until it is almost unbearably deafening. Only when Rangda left defeated, as good must always triumph over evil, did it become quiet. The men, however, are still in a trance and a priest always has to be present to sprinkle them with holy water to bring them back to the real world. A chicken is then sacrificed to propitiate the evil spirits.

"What's for lunch?" the boys asked as we left. It had been an early start as well as an exhausting performance, and they were ravenous.

"Chicken, of course!" said Andy.

"How about snakes, anteaters, porcupines and centipedes!" suggested our guide with a twinkle in his eye.

"Oh yuk!," they predictably replied. In fact, these are Balinese delicacies!

As usual there were several rice dishes, with side dishes to go with them. The food was spicy, liberally flavoured with chili, garlic, tumeric, ginger and aromatic leaves. Fruits included the exotic zirzak, starfruit, mangosteens, durian (if you can bear the rotting meat smell), mangoes, passion fruit and, to our surprise, strawberries. They told us that on the high hills of Bali temperate fruit and vegetables grow well, and that strawberries are a national favourite.

We continued on our way up the 'tourist corridor', stopping next at Celuk, the centre for silver and gold. The jewellery was intricate and artistically displayed, but the prices were shocking.

"I really like those earrings," Jane told me, "but they want $125! What a rip off for silver!"

"I'll give you $20," she said boldly at the counter. They settled on $25!

I loved the textiles, batik and ikat, with their vibrant colours and unique designs, and bought some lengths at $4.00 a piece, hoping I'd be able to have some made up. Friends had found seamstresses did excellent work very inexpensively. I would also be going to the stores to look at ready made goods as Kuta and Sanur are designer clothes capitals of Asia.

'Mas' means gold, but the town of Mas is the centre for wood carving. The Balinese sculpt in wood, bone, horn and gnarled roots, the last being one of our favourites. The works are intricate, but sadly the number of similar items gave an assembly line impression. The boys particularly liked the theatre masks and the brightly painted ducks, frogs and tropical fruit. The ones Andy and I liked were very expensive but fascinating as they were so different from our western design—although I'm not sure I would want them in my home!

"Come over here," Colin called in one centre. "You have to see this one." The figure was grotesque, exuding fear, and really quite scary!

Everywhere, vendors hovered at the roadside, at times overbearing with their sales patter. We were charmed, however, by two young boys. They came up shyly and had some boxes that had been beautifully carved, and in an original design.

Ubud, situated in the hills behind Denpasar, is the cultural centre of Bali. Referred to as calm and peaceful in the guide book we were disappointed to find the tourist development which had occurred. Ubud is renowned for its art although it is only recently that artists have painted to sell. Most paintings used to be for the temples and were generally narratives with mythological themes that were taken from Hindu epics. A series of panels illustrated a story. In the 1930s, under the influence of European painters, single scenes came into vogue, although in many ways the style remained the same. Balinese paintings are busy, with canvasses packed full. A forest will have hundreds of branches, leaves and animals and sometimes dozens of stories appear to be happening at once.

We continued to the Elephant Cave, Gua Gadjah, a former Buddhist monastery which dates from the 11th century. The carvings here also portrayed many stories, with forests, waves, animals, and people running in panic. I had a moment of panic when I saw the enormous demon peering down on us from above the entrance, his hands splitting the rock apart!

It was hard to imagine that the small village of Bedula had been the former capital, but the guide had a story about the last king who ruled from here, that really appealed to the boys. Apparently King Bedaula had magical powers which allowed his head to be chopped off and then replaced again. One night he had his trick done for some guests, but the servant managed to drop the king's head in the stream and it floated away! Frantically trying to find something to replace it, the servant found a pig and quickly popped its head on the kings shoulders instead!

The scenery along the route to Tampaksiring is spectacular, with a lush green valley and immaculately terraced rice fields climbing up the hillsides. Looking down we caught a glimpse of Gunung Kawi, the two rows of blackened memorials built for the Balinese royal family in the 11th century. They stand in dramatic seven metre high niches cut into the sheer rock faces. Together with Gua Gadjah they are the earliest monuments of Balinese art.

In contrast is the former president Sukarno's retreat, a grandiose twin palace built in 1954. It overlooks the sacred cleansing stream at Tampaksiring that is known as the 'Fountain of Youth'. For over a 1000 years, on the same day each year, villages have worshipped a stone here because it is 'adat', the customary law we were told about in Komodo.

The 1717 metre high Gunung Batur volcano bellows and glows red when it erupts, throwing out rocks and debris. As the cloud descended it was easy to imagine the crater as the home of the spirits.

"Anyone for a swim in the hotsprings?" said our guide, as we passed the springs bubbling up in the lake. Later swimmers told us the water was freezing!

Back in the harbour several yachts with children had arrived. Among them was *Cool Change* with the Runge's on board. We celebrated Shannon's thirteenth birthday the next day. We had last seen the family in Bora Bora in the South Pacific, having arrived the day before Shannon turned eleven. I also gave a party for Colin, as I would be away for his birthday in September. Ten kids arrived. After the usual party games I suggested each tell us about a memorable event in their travels. How amazingly cosmopolitan this group of children was, so naturally chatting about sights and cultures around the globe. One story stimulated another, and another and another . . .

When friends toured the island we looked after their boats, running their engines for an hour a day to keep their freezers cold. Then it was our turn to go away. Renting a car for three days we headed straight for the hills, and so much enjoyed the cool airs, the contrasting scenery and the friendly people. We stayed in small guest houses and the owners taught Duncan to play the bamboo xylophone. Our meals were cooked from their own fresh foods and we were introduced to salaks, a palm fruit in a snakelike skin. Not only are salaks delicious but, unusual for the tropics, they are also crunchy and we found them quite addictive!

Whether the land, the buildings, the gardens, the people, or the food, everything in Bali is made to look beautiful. Even the humblest of dwellings is transformed by carved wooden doors, and frames around the windows, with flowers and religious offerings giving a continuously festive air.

It was a mixture of religion and historical events that caused this unique, artistic culture todevelop. One reason was the productive sawah wet-ricefield growing system, already in existence in the 9th century, which provided abundant food and gave people time for the arts. Due to the fertile volcanic soil and high rainfall this system of terracing is ideal for Bali, giving very high yields and many crops a year. Technically complex and delicate to manage, however, because of the water that is required, it developed the strong spirit of the community, or kampung, and a discipline of tradition. The people practised animism, the belief that every object has a hidden power and a soul, and the worship of the spirits was an everyday practice.

The Hindu religion came to Bali from Java during the 11th century. Meanwhile, in Java itself, Islam was on the rise and during the 15th century many of the scholars, artists, dancers, musicians and intelligentsia from the declining Hindu Majapahit Kingdom moved to Bali. It is from this time, with the combination of tradition, Hinduism and a highly intelligent, artistic people, that Bali's vital culture began.

Most of the 2.5 million Balinese today are Hindu and life from birth to death centres around religion. Balinese Hinduism has developed quite differently to Hinduism in India as it is combined with the practices of animism. Although the people worship the same gods as the Hindus in India, such as the trinity of Brahma, Shiva and Vishnu, the animistic spirits are more closely related to their day-to-day lives.

Temples are in abundance, 20,000 of them! Driving around the island they were everywhere: in houses, markets, courtyards, cemeteries, beaches, rice paddies, on mountain tops, and at most intersections incense is burnt to prevent any mishaps. Villages have at least three communal temples, with a temple of origin, a temple for the dead and a temple for the spirits. The Balinese believe that there are spirits everywhere and much of their lives are taken up with making artistic offerings to appease them. Every morning offerings are laid out, on high shelves for the good ones, and on the ground to placate the bad.

The good spirits, those that bring prosperity and good health, are thought to come from the mountains, while the giants and demons come from the ocean. The Balinese thus have one of the few island cultures that don't turn their eyes towards the sea. Their sacred mountains are considered 'north', the sea 'south'. As these are considered their cardinal points they align their villages from north to south. The Balinese religion divides most concepts into polarities; the sun and moon, day and night, heaven and earth, and good and bad. Even the evil witch Rangda plays the useful good role of guarding the temples. The Balinese believe that the interaction of these opposites provides harmony to their world and determines their fate.

The grandest of the temples, although somewhat touristy now, is the 'mother temple' at Besakih. Built up high, on the majestic mountain of Gunung Arung, thirty separate temples are stages on the seven terraces. Known as the 'Navel of the World' this is where all the gods and goddesses are said to live. It is Bali's equivalent of Delphi, which we had visited while in Greece.

Temple festivals are a frequent occurrence and we came across a parade for an odalans, or temple birthday. The men came first, playing their gamelan instruments, their lively music setting the festive tone. The women followed, all dressed in bright yellow, their fruit offerings piled a metre high above their heads. They chattered non-stop and there was frequent laughter. The procession was a long one, with over a hundred ladies taking part.

The temple was beautifully decorated inside with streamers, brightly-coloured sunshades and flowers. As they entered, the ladies piled up the offerings, decorations in themselves.

"What a wonderful occasion," I commented afterwards, "but what a pity to waste all that delicious food."

I was pleased to learn that the gods are happy to fill themselves on the spirit and the food is taken back home later for a feast!

Returning through Ubud we saw what is considered to be one of the most exciting and visually spectacular dances, the Kechak, or Monkey Dance. It tells a tale from the Ramayana, the Hindu epic that is comparable to 'The Odyssey or The Iliad'. Instead of the gamelan, accompaniment is provided by the all-male choir who, in perfect unison, chant the chak-a-chak sound of the monkey army. It was quite eerie with this strange chanting, in the dark, shadow-filled room lit only by flaming torches, especially when the men, naked to the waist, threw out their arms to the centre and shook their hands wildly.

Back on board I again started my daily vigil of visiting the travel agents and airline offices in Sanur and Denpasar. Making the decision for Duncan to return to school had been difficult, but getting a flight back to Vancouver was proving impossible, and nothing happened unless one went to the office in person. Finally, Thai Airlines had two cancellations but they were in the executive class. I checked, day after day, but none came up in the economy section. By the time I picked up the ticket I knew the staff quite well.

"Don't worry too much about the extra cost," said the sympathetic manager, "I've thrown in the flight to Jakarta, and the executive fare includes the hotel you'll need for your overnight stay in Bangkok."

Little was he to know that we were also going to be moved up to first class from Tokyo to Seattle. Duncan was in seventh heaven—leg-room and food all the way!

Family and friends greeted us at the Vancouver airport, a wonderful reinforcement for Duncan that he was indeed returning home. It was then back to reality with a vengeance for me, buying his uniform and sewing on the nametapes!

Duncan settled into St. George's School well. I spoke to all his teachers and was happy with the programme. My final words were with the sports director. Rugby was mandatory and I commented that Duncan might not take to such a physical contact sport. How wrong a mother can be! I stayed a few days after the term started, talking to Duncan regularly on the phone.

"Guess what?" he told me gleefully one night. "We're doing the Galapagos Islands in science."

"Well, you should have a head start on that topic," I replied.

"Actually, we had a quiz this morning. After I correctly answered every question the teacher said he might have to give me a different assignment!"

I continued on to England, primarily to see my sister and family, then to Singapore to rejoin *Bagheera*. It had been wonderful catching up with so many of our family and friends and I had thoroughly enjoyed the luxury of baths, washing machines, dishwashers, cars and SPACE!

Meanwhile Andy was having an interesting trip. The Bali officials had warned of pirates off Borneo, so he went there in company with *Time* and *Uhuru*. Jane had stayed on board and an Australian, Neil, joined for the trip to Singapore.

The three hundred nautical mile sail from Java to Kalimantan, the Indonesian part of Borneo, was a busy one. There were many oil rigs along the route, but these were easy to see as they were lit up like cities. Oil is a major source of revenue for Indonesia. In contrast to our earlier night passages in Indonesia there were hundreds of fishing boats. These small dugouts were unlit, and up to 100 nautical miles offshore. They were impossible to see; time after time Andy heard a faint shout, or saw a fisherman in the glow of the navigation lights frantically paddling away. One wonders how the fish are preserved so far from land, and how many men are lost in the frequent tropical squalls.

Contrary to the warnings, the coastal people of Kalimantan were very friendly, and welcomed us into their villages.

Their lifestyle was primitive, but they insisted on sharing their basic diet of coconuts and fish. Andy invited them back for coffee, and, as always, the local people loved coming on board, being fascinated by our boat.

One day *Bagheera* was pursued, then boarded, by a naval patrol. The officers were astonished that our permit showed we had permission to cruise the coast, but were quite happy when invited to have a beer and have their photos taken! They said no yachts had been there before. Our careful planning in Ambon had paid off.

Kalimantan is criss-crossed by giant, navigable rivers, and the three yachts decided to go up the Padang Tikar. After manoeuvreing past the many fishing platforms they finally anchored twenty miles upstream

Village in Kalimantan

where the river was still half a mile wide with the steaming jungle dense along its banks. The villagers were curious but friendly, although communication was difficult as they spoke no Bahasa Indonesia. Previously our phrase book had been very useful and our attempts at pronunciation the cause of much spontaneous laughter and consequent camaraderie.

Sadly *Bagheera's* time here was then cut short. A spider bite Andy had suffered in Bali had become very swollen and painful, and anti-biotics and painkillers we had on board were to no avail. They sailed quickly for Singapore, but did manage a visit with King Neptune as they crossed the equator. It was Jane and Neil's first crossing in a yacht and they had to endure the traditional initiation rites. As usual the captain ran out of shaving cream!

There was one untoward incident during the trip, a near collision at sea. It was with a huge Indonesian wooden vessel, visible by its two faint steaming lights. As they were on a collision course, Andy changed his heading to go astern. It made no difference, so he changed course again. Finally only a 'crash' jibe saved the day. He was close enough to see the other vessel's planks. It reminded us that you can never take navigation lights for granted, or trust that everyone will follow the international

Bagheera is visited by the Indonesian military

King Neptune's visit

rules. The vessel had mounted its lights backwards, with the forward one higher than the aft.

After a brief stop at Tanjung Penang for the formalities required to clear out of Indonesia, *Bagheera* anchored off Changi Sailing Club at the northeast end of Singapore Island. The outpatient's clinic at Changi hospital was extremely efficient and, after the wound had been drained and intensive anti-biotic treatment administered, Andy was completely recovered by the time of my arrival.

An excited family met me at the airport. It was the longest time we'd been apart.

"What's Singapore like?" I asked

"Great for shopping," replied Andy, "particularly for the boat!"

"And I LOVE 'Lucky Plaza'!" said Colin.

5. Singapore and Malaysia

Tioman Island

B*agheera* was one of a throng of local and international yachts on moorings and at anchor off the Changi Sailing Club, a thriving racing and cruising club situated near the notorious wartime prison camp. Temporary membership is offered to overseas yachts, and there are showers, a bar and restaurant. We gathered with friends in the bar that evening, eager to find out about their purchases of the day. Singapore was proving a shopper's paradise for all. (Although recently friends told us that due to the strength of the Singapore dollar prices are no longer as favourable.)

Dinghies were high on many people's lists. With chafe from the docks and deterioration from the sun, many tenders were on their last legs, their owners fed up with patching and pumping.

"What make of dinghy did you decide on?" we asked John and Ines on *Quahlee*.

"A Japanese Achilles," John replied. "We're thinking of buying an outboard too. They're also unbelievably cheap," added Ines.

"I know," said Martin from *Kinta III*, "Judy and I were looking at a Mariner 9.9. It was built in the States and retails here for half the price."

The conversation turned to cameras, videos, TVs, electronics, and other equipment . . . prices all too good to be true.

Richard from *Catriona-M* came to join us, having just been to the office. "It's all right for some," he said, looking pointedly at us.

"Oh really, have we won a million?" replied Andy with a grin.

"No but there's a fax saying you're getting a new dinghy under warranty." The sailing club always put incoming faxes on the counter so they were open reading for one and all!

"How did you manage it?" everyone chorused.

"I've been writing, faxing and phoning the manufacturers continuously since we arrived," explained Andy. "Let me tell you after all those split seams and the transom falling off we deserve it."

Our new dinghy also needed a new outboard we decided, but we didn't expect to end up with two! It happened as we sold our old Yamaha 8 hp to *Wildfire* for some cash and a Mercury 3.2. This small Mercury became our commuter engine, taking us efficiently to and from the dock. With its internal fuel tank it gives us more room in the dinghy itself, and is less likely to be stolen as it is too small to attract the local fisherman. Then we splurged on one of the Mariner 9.9s. With this we could do 15 knots on the plane with the whole family aboard. It was wonderful later for exploring outer reefs, and here in Singapore it saved us the hot, humid walk to the food stalls in Changi village.

Singapore is renowned as the food centre of Asia and the food stalls with their many vendors proved it for us. Wonderful spicy aromas—Indian, Thai, Chinese, Malaysian and Indonesian—drifted down as we tied up the dinghy and our mouths were watering by the time we entered the market itself. We could get satay from one stall, szechuan chicken in another, rotis across the way, lemon grass soup around the corner. There were hot, spicy foods for Andy and me, and a variety of milder dishes for the boys. A pint tumbler of Singapore's famous fresh lime squash was the perfect refreshing accompaniment. On an extravagant day we spent three dollars per head, usually it was two. There was always a crowd of yachtsmen and the communal tables worked well.

"Why don't they do this back home?" I commented. "It is such a good idea." By the time we returned to Vancouver this model had been adopted by all the shopping centres.

Singapore consists of the main island of Singapore, which is separated from the Malaysian Peninsula by the narrow Johor Strait, and many adjacent islets. The main island is predominantly flat, much of it being reclaimed land. With a population of three million the original jungle and swamps have mostly been consumed for residential and industrial use.

Strategically located on the shipping route between the Indian Ocean and the South China Sea, Singapore is a major world port, its principal trading partners being the U.S., Japan, Malaysia, China, Taiwan, Germany, U.K. and Hong Kong. Although always a trading centre, it wasn't until Sir Thomas Stamford Raffles arrived from England in 1819 that the modern city was founded. Under the British it became a great port and one of their principal overseas naval bases. In 1942, during World War II, it was captured by Japan, but only held for three years. After a brief two year link with Malaysia, in 1965 it became an independent sovereign state, remaining in the commonwealth and becoming a member of the United Nations.

Economically Singapore has grown from strength to strength, primarily due to the skills of its Prime Minister Lee Kuan Yew. Governing Singapore from 1968 to 1990, as head of the People's Action Party, he was able to realize a remarkable vision and the changes in the last few decades have been vast. Singapore is now a modern, thriving centre. Whoever we spoke to, whether Indian, Chinese, Malay or British expatriate, they expressed their pride in the new buildings, cleanliness and landscaping, the high standard of living and their positive feelings about a totally honest and very efficient, albeit somewhat dictatorial government.

One taxi driver told me, "We're never worried about how our tax money is being used. If there's a hole in the road today, it will be fixed by tomorrow."

How many places in the world could you hear that?

Singapore's main shopping area is over an hour from Changi by bus. After catching up on school assignments, completing many loads of laundry, and several visits from the refrigeration man, (with the entire boat torn apart), we indulged ourselves in a day off to explore. The plazas on Orchard Road were fascinating and, as everyone had told us, the prices were amazing but it was an exhausting experience. We all looked at clothing, then Andy at boating goods, Jamie in toy stores, Colin in gem shops while I tried to co-ordinate them all!

We also wanted a video camera, our original one having long since given up the ghost. A waterproof one seemed the answer to the salt and humidity that is inevitable on a boat but we found these were expensive and limited in function. There seemed to be no end to the options in size, make and model, and aggressive salesmen who all but dragged us into their shops or booths to show their wares. First we had to decide on the system we wanted. In Canada we are on the American NTSC, but the PAL system is used by the rest of the English speaking world and is a much superior method. We finally chose NTSC for easy use at home, re-enforced when American friends offered us their small NTSC TV for immediate playback. They had been out buying themselves a large multi-system TV for viewing worldwide.

Our old video had been one with a separate heavy pack. As it was a chore to carry around, it had often been left on board. The newer models seemed light until we heard of the SONY handycam, the smallest unit yet. It was to be on the Singapore market in two weeks time. Overwhelmed by a full day of shopping it was easy to decide it would be best to wait for it.

Caught up on school, chores and suburbia, but knowing a friend was visiting Singapore in a week's time, we headed up the East coast of Malaysia with *Asteroid* for a few days of cruising. While I had been away the boys had frequently been invited over to the seventy foot American *Asteroid* by ten year old Katherine. They loved their visits, particularly because there were several hundred videos on board!

It was an easy trip in glassy seas. We relaxed in the cockpit, the light breeze refreshingly cool after the heat and humidity of Changi. The water gurgled by and Clayderman played softly from our cockpit speakers. It was delightfully soporific, except I was supposed to be on watch and alert!

We stopped at the picturesque island of Bibu for the night, and went snorkelling in the turquoise seas. It was unbelievably warm and lovely to be submerged in the sea again. Our swim was cut short though by some small stinging plankton. They left no mark but their sting was acute, especially when we came out of the water, and we quickly doused ourselves with vinegar.

A pretty island with jagged hills and white sand beaches, Tioman was reputedly used as a setting for the film 'South Pacific'. Stuart, the skipper of *Asteroid*, came over as soon as we had anchored.

"Try to clear-in right away," he urged, as we were now in Malaysia. "Yerge has chartered a bum-boat tomorrow to go down to the waterfalls and it would be great if you could join us."

The bum-boat was basic with a very noisy engine but the outing was fun with Yerge and Marguerite, the owners of *Asteroid*, their children Katherine and two year old Rule, and their crew. We bounced down the rapids and swam in the pools, then had a wonderful back massage under the sparkling falls. Following a delicious picnic lunch prepared by *Asteroid's* cook, and a snooze, we swam amongst the coloured corals. Hot spicy crab at a beachside stall made the perfect ending to the day. We joined Carl from *Omni*, while the boys dined in style at the Tioman Island Resort!

After school the next morning we took *Bagheera* to one of the small off-lying islands. The beach was so white the glare was painful, but the diving was incredible in the crystal clear water.

As we swam to the rocks Andy suddenly stopped. "Look," he said pointing, "there are some HUGE parrot fish over there."

They were a deep blue-green and much higher and wider than the Caribbean and South Pacific varieties we'd seen.

"Let's try to get closer. We'll creep up. No splashing," he warned the boys.

Undisturbed by the intrusion the fish let us swim amongst them. It was an amazing sight. At four to five feet long they absolutely dwarfed six year old Jamie. We followed them to the coral where they merged with the hundreds of colourful smaller fish. The strong current then whisked us back to *Bagheera*.

That evening while watching the frigate birds come home to roost we could see a storm was brewing. Soon we were surrounded by flashes of lightning and in contrast to our day of paradise it was a terrible night. *Bagheera* tossed around violently in the heavy squalls, jerking abruptly on the anchor, while the rain teemed down ceaselessly. Andy was up and down our hatch like a Jack-in-a-box checking our position to make sure *Bagheera* was holding fast and that we were in no danger from other boats, their anchor lights at times being completely obliterated. There was a tense moment as a boat drifted past us. He was completely disoriented it seemed as he shouted to us to check our anchor as we must be dragging!

It was unbelievably hot and humid below, and we were all exhausted in the morning. There was still a bad swell, and as I'd already had to take a seasick pill, I decided to take the boys to the resort to do some school work. They did a fine morning of work although it cost a fortune in drinks!

It was beautiful ashore, the rain having added a freshness and the golf course sparkled even greener than usual. It would be hard to find a more picturesque setting, and a course that was more immaculately tended. We went for a walk up the coast, to the airstrip and next village. A mere six kilometres, but we were dragging our feet on the return. The sea was peaceful, the sky promised a quiet night. The boys went over to *Asteroid* and Andy and I settled down in the cockpit with a sundowner and our books, relishing the peace. I'd barely read a page when we were swarmed by flies, hundreds of them! Leaping below we battened down the hatches, but, attracted by the lights, the flies had got there first. They were everywhere and I spent the evening sweeping the battle field as they died!

We returned to Singapore the day before Peter Leech's visit. A former business partner of Andy's in yacht brokerage we thought he would enjoy meeting some of our yachting community, so invited him to join us on board. There's nothing like a visit, particularly by someone from home, to get one motivated into the cleaning mode and *Bagheera* was sparkling for his arrival. There had been just one crisis that morning—the head had got blocked. Definitely Andy's least favourite job, and he was not in good humour by the time he had it reassembled and working.

"This is not to be blocked again," he ordered. "If it is, the person who does it will fix it themselves."

Ten minutes before we were due to go ashore to pick Peter up at the Changi Sailing Club dock I found water splashed around the basin so took a sheet—one sheet!—of toilet paper to clean it. I started flushing it down the head but to my horror it wouldn't pump away. I almost called out, then stopped myself. Which was worse, I pondered, having no working head with thirty people visiting or telling Andy that the head was blocked again. There was no contest. Dealing with thirty people's bathroom needs was far easier than facing fireworks from Andy at that moment!

It was a great afternoon, the scene people imagine of yachties—one continuous party after another and no worries in the world! Peter was fascinated by the stories and as I listened, I too was impressed by the exciting lives we were all leading, and the wonderful camaraderie between us. After all, I rationalized, every lifestyle has its problems. As the beer supply in the fridge got lower a few people went quietly up to the foredeck whilst others used the facilities back on board their own boats. Andy and Peter were none the wiser, amazingly their bladders had held out!

The party continued from lunch to dinner, a gaggle of dinghies constantly round the boat. We had known most of the people since Australia but three new yachties also showed up. They were in fancy dress, their dinghy decorated in streamers and balloons.

"I know you don't know us," the lads called out with engaging smiles, "but it looks a great party and we're Canadians too."

"Come on board," I called back. "You've certainly taken a lot of trouble to get invited."

Peter generously took us out to dinner that evening. We stopped at the Sim Lim Plaza on the way, and while Peter was buying some gifts he saw some 'pull-back' toy cars.

"I'll have to get you one of those, Jamie," he said. "It will really go well on the floor in my hotel."

The Marco Polo dining room served a delicious meal—it is lovely to use elegant china, silver and linen once in a while and remind our children it exists! Then we went up to Peter's room. I don't think that I've ever seen a corridor quite as long, a fine track for a car, particularly one with so much speed. Whilst we used Peter's phone, Colin and Jamie kept themselves and several hotel guests happily entertained.

While waiting for our replacement dinghy to arrive from France we were taken to several of the sights of Singapore—the zoo, the bird park, Sentosa Island and the Science Centre—and each time were struck by the efficiency, planning and cleanliness of the island. The buses always ran on time, the MRT train stopped precisely at the line in every station. There was no litter anywhere, and there was even a $200 fine for not flushing a public toilet! We were also impressed by the way people worked and the speed with which things could be done. We had first hand experience with a car repair.

Hamid, an Indian friend of my brother-in-law, had kindly invited us for a tour of the island, only to have the airconditioning on his Mercedes fail. He and Andy diagnosed the problem as a damaged belt pulley, so we drove to a garage for a replacement. We were on our way to the Jurong Bird Park twenty-five minutes later!

Both the bird park and the zoo in Singapore have been beautifully designed and landscaped, with as many natural barriers used as possible. We particularly enjoyed the walk-in aviary which is spread over two hectares. It holds over three thousand birds, with a stunning variety of species.

"They have a parrot show like Las Palmas," called Colin.

"And look at the scarlet ibis over there," said Andy. "Do you remember the flocks of scarlet ibis in Venezuela that made a luminous red blaze across the sky as they returned every night?"

At the zoo more memories were jogged by the giant tortoises, Australian marsupials and Komodo dragons. We were also introduced to the orangutans. We'd been attracted to them right away, but in the show they were priceless characters, trying to do a trick on the trainer before he could do it on them, then howling with laughter at the fun of it all.

Hamid took us to Little India for lunch; the meal was an Indian curry, thick with coriander and turmeric. The boys were fascinated that Hamid ate with his fingers as is the tradition. Indians make up about 6% of the population of Singapore. Tamil is one of the official languages, along with English, Malay, and Mandarin as 77% of the population is Chinese.

After my sister had lived in Singapore almost thirty years previously she had returned home with a dinner service. Six years her junior it made a lasting impression on me. I didn't consciously set out to buy china but quite by chance, whilst I was looking for a dustpan and brush in a tiny jumbled store, some pieces caught my eye. They were 'Royal Porcelain' made in Thailand; not only was the pattern attractive the price was right too, and within no time I had ordered a service for twelve! The owner of the shop couldn't believe his luck and on top of the existing 25% discount offered to give me an additional 30% off. Three days later I went to pick it up. As the store was so small he carried the boxes outside. Squatting on the pavement I counted the pieces, not only were there twelve place settings but I had ordered extra serving platters and bowls, cups and saucers, coffee and tea pots besides. All looked perfect and the total bill was $149.00 us. I couldn't believe my bargain although I have to admit Andy wasn't quite so elated when I brought it all on board!

One day several of us went in our dinghies to an outer island. In contrast to Singapore Island there was no modern development here. The people all lived in the traditional way, many of them in houses on stilts along the river. We went up the winding river for lunch, listening to the birds in the thick verdant jungle that crowded its bank. On our return we checked on the Cal 40′ *Uhuru*. Bert and Mary Lou had gone trekking in Nepal for a few weeks and had left their boat on a mooring. When we saw it we gasped in horror. The swallows which roosted nightly on all our boats had found uninhabited *Uhuru* particularly attractive. The decks were inches deep in swallow pool—what a welcome home!

It was almost the end of October so the boys were planning their Halloween costumes. Although mostly a North American celebration we found that kids everywhere love to join in. Anchored at Changi we had met few children ashore but fortunately there were several aboard other boats, and many North American adults who knew just what Halloween was all about. Most of the fleet took part, the adults re-living their youth, carving melons for pumpkins and having as much fun dressing up as the kids. For the party afterwards, Andy excelled himself with a cake decorated as a gruesome skull. The kids went off by dinghy to trick-or-treat around the yachts, Katherine and Colin as ghostly vampires, Jamie a canine devil, and we also had a magician, a rabbit, a diver, a Mexican, . . . and an Arab snake tamer with convincing cobras that writhed around his neck!

Boats were now starting to leave, heading north for Malaysia and Thailand. Richard and Gabrielle on *Catriona-M* invited us to race with them in the King's Cup Regatta in Phuket. The *Kinta's* would also be part of the crew. It sounded fun and we enthusiastically accepted, providing we had received the new dinghy. At the time, although the paperwork showed that the dinghy should have arrived in Singapore, Lufthansa had been unable to locate the package.

Dusty Trembly came to dinner the evening before his departure. Since meeting him in Cairns, we had become very fond of this single-hander, a mere 75 years young, since meeting him in Cairns. He frequently came over to *Bagheera* for a coffee or to be the 'neighbour' or 'relative' who was required for several of the school assignments. A veteran seaman who had crossed the Pacific sixteen times, Dusty was now completing a circumnavigation in his Peterson 44 *Magnum*, although he still returned to Denver every winter to do ski patrol—"Just to keep fit," he told us. A retired doctor, psychologist, U.S. Airforce test pilot and Boeing 747 jumbo jet captain, he had our full admiration.

He left the next morning in *Magnum* with John and Ines in *Quahlee* and Warwick in *Valentine*. The boats left in a trio but within a few minutes we heard John on the v.h.f. Radio.

"*Magnum* and *Valentine* this is *Quahlee*. Sorry we have engine problems so we are returning to the anchorage."

Andy roared off in the dinghy to see if he could help. Not long afterwards John came on the radio again.

"*Magnum* and *Valentine* this is *Quahlee*. We seem to have fixed the problem so we're heading out again."

Barely two minutes later we heard Andy.

"Mayday, Mayday, Mayday. This is the Yacht *Quahlee* I think John is having a heart attack, any medical people please come over. Repeat *Quahlee* calling Mayday, Mayday, Mayday. John has collapsed and we require immediate medical assistance at the Changi anchorage."

I rushed up on deck. *Quahlee* was quite close but Andy had the dinghy.

I could see a couple already rushing over. Then Andy appeared on deck, jumping into our dinghy to get Doctor Dusty who was still anchoring. After dropping Dusty on *Quahlee* he came to get me. Meanwhile, Carl on *Omni* had called the military base and arrived with a paramedical squad complete with oxygen and stretcher in his dinghy.

A medical doctor, a cardiac nurse, a paramedic and oxygen within minutes were at John's side but it was to no avail. The team all went on working although in their hearts they knew there was no hope. It was hard to give up on a friend, especially one who was just beginning to live his life-long dream. It was Ines who finally said in a broken voice, "It's been too long, much too long."

I went with her to the hospital. There were endless papers to be signed and permission for the autopsy to be given, then the awful wrench of leaving John behind.

Ines felt strongly that she wanted the body returned to Australia for a family funeral. We went to the Australian consulate for advice and they recommended a local undertaker. The procedure is complicated as Australia requires a lead-lined coffin, when coming from overseas. We finally had one arranged at huge cost but when it arrived in Australia we found they had ripped us off, having used a regular coffin with no lining at all. Thank goodness the Australian officials were most understanding.

As the yacht club phone was too public, I took Ines to the apartment of our friends Dorothy and Sam Shaw, whom we had met while cruising up the Australian coast. Dorothy is a nurse and immediately took Ines under her wing. Meanwhile John's brother arrived from Australia and many of the difficult decisions were made. Ines hoped she could continue cruising but she needed time to organize her life. Andy arranged for *Quahlee* to be hauled out for storage while Ines and I sorted through the boat, packing John's things away and putting aside all the perishable goods.

The evening before the haul-out we went to dinner with the Faures, longtime friends of my sister. Even before we were up the next morning friends came by *Bagheera*.

"Did the police get hold of you?" they enquired. "They went around *Bagheera* several times last night, illuminating the boat and calling on the loud hailer. We all wondered what you'd been up to!"

Our second visitors had the answer. "Dusty's had a problem," they told us. "He told the coastguard you could help him out."

Dusty had left the previous day, still emotionally and physically debilitated by John's death, but anxious to get going north. During the afternoon the wind died so he started the motor. He was on the south side of the island off the Raffles Light when the plug of his gear box fell out, the gears seized and he lost the use of his engine. This stranded him right in the very busy shipping lane, with strong currents and a rocky shore downstream. All he could do was anchor for the night. He was in ninety feet and the holding was poor. In this position *Magnum* became the turning mark for all the big ships leaving the Malacca Strait and heading east.

At Changi we were out of range on the v.h.f. radio. We hadn't planned a single side-band radio contact until the next day, so Dusty called the coastguard to contact us. They phoned the yacht club who said we weren't members and they couldn't get hold of us. Ironically, as they were speaking we were a few feet from the office having a drink on the club's deck with Jimmy Faure, who had just finished his term as commodore. It was after we had left to have dinner that the marine police came to our boat.

Fortunately we had met some members of the Republic of Singapore Yacht Club, which was close to Dusty's present position on the south side of the island. Due to the reclaimed land around the coast the club house is now up the river but they arranged permission for Dusty to use the club's mooring buoys, which were between two islets nearly a mile offshore. We couldn't leave immediately, however, as Andy had promised to supervise the hauling of *Quahlee*, but we found another boat that was heading in that direction and they readily agreed to tow Dusty in.

As *Quahlee* came out of the water we could see the cause of her engine problems. The water intake was thickly covered in barnacles which had thrived in the rich, soupy water off Changi, and now we knew the cause of the constant blocking of our head! After ensuring that the boat was safely in a cradle ashore we left in *Bagheera* and, by taking the inner route, arrived at the mooring just ahead of the *Magnum*.

As we helped Dusty tie up we could see the toll it had taken. He had been up all night, traumatized by the huge freighters that were heading straight for him. We gave him a good meal and several tots of whiskey hoping that, secure on the mooring buoy, he would recover with a good night's sleep .

The club bum-boat took us in early the next morning and we made our daily call to the dealer about our new dinghy. Finally they had located it and said it would be delivered that afternoon. The boys were very excited when we unpacked the large carton. It was a complete unit, with new floorboards and all the trimmings including, to Jamie's delight, a flag that flew from the bow!

"I wonder if they are giving us any warranty," I commented to Andy. This was after all our fourth new dinghy, and the third one supplied under our original warranty! As he glanced through the documents, his face lit up with a smile.

"It seems they are!" he replied.

Dorothy and Sam Shaw came over to see us, kindly picking up extra copies of my annual Christmas newsletter on their way. I'd sent out over a hundred two weeks before, our annual link with all our friends. They took us to the food stalls for dinner. Dusty was still too tired to join us but he had been able to arrange a mechanic to fix the gear box.

It was now urgent we leave for Thailand to be there when Duncan arrived for his Christmas holiday. It was hard to believe his first term had almost gone by, most of it while we had been in Singapore. We checked out with the authorities the next morning, only to find later that Dusty had a streaming cold and was really under the weather. He was plainly not fit enough to leave, and when he came to dinner that night we persuaded him to stay in Singapore until he had fully recovered.

We phoned our goodbyes to Jimmy and Shirley Faure, and Dorothy and Sam Shaw, who had been so hospitable during our stay, also the Kearns family. We had enjoyed Des and Susie Kearns and their three daughters, and had been able to help their eldest get the job as nanny board *Asteroid*. Previously they had lived in Vancouver but we had barely met. We also had another link. Des had originally sailed from New Zealand with Bob Bailey, our good Pacific cruising pal on *Belair*. We were to learn later that after we left Singapore the Kearns took Dusty to their home and nursed him back to health.

We headed north to Malaysia on Andy's birthday, November 30th. It was pelting with rain, which made the navigation even more demanding as we passed through the shipping lane. The ships seemed to come up in no time at all, towering over us as they passed. We could fully appreciate Dusty's traumatic night. The sun conveniently came out for lunch. I had decided to have some western delicacies for a change and served smoked salmon, duck and orange paté, and Cambozola cheese. We even had capers, courtesy Ines.

The Malacca (Melaka) Strait is renowned for pirates. The Singapore officials advised sailing in company and stopping at anchor by the Malaysian shore every night. There had been no recent attacks by pirates, however, and none of the seventy odd yachts ahead of us had reported any problems.

"What do you think?" Andy asked. "It would be nice just to deadhead for Port Kelang."

"Let's go for it," I agreed.

The next morning Skip on *Endymion* graphically reported on the radio how they had warded off 'a pirate attack' that night!

6. Malaysia and Thailand

Port Kelang, Kuala Lumpur, Lumut, Penang, Langkawi, Phuket, Bangkok, Mae Hong Son

Skip's story of a vessel aggressively approaching their boat had put us on the alert but we arrived in Port Kelang some thirty hours later without incident. It was much muddier than we had expected; in fact we learnt that the meaning of Kuala Lumpur, which is further up river, is 'muddy estuary'. With memories of thick mud on our deck when anchoring in estuaries in England, we were pleased to find an available mooring buoy. Perched up on stilts, the Royal Selangor Yacht Club was most welcoming. After luxurious hot showers we enjoyed the company of Warwick, an Australian single-hander in his 60s from *Valentine*, for dinner. Meanwhile the boys had found a swimming pool and a TV room where they could sprawl out on huge comfortable cushions.

Early the next morning we joined Warwick for the train ride to Kuala Lumpur, Malaysia's capital. It was a delightful trip back in time, through rice paddies, bananas groves and lively villages, the homes so close to the track that we felt part of the local life. Originally founded by eighty-seven adventurous Chinese miners looking for tin, Kuala Lumpur now has a population of over a million. Although a thriving city full of modern concrete buildings, it still has impressive relics from Colonial days. The Keretapi Tanah Melayu Malayan Railway Station and administrative office are particularly remarkable; their towers, arches, pillars and domes in flamboyant Moorish style being far more like a mosque than the ultra modern Masjid Negara National Mosque opposite.

The Central Market with its many stalls was a hive of activity. A selection of Chinese 'chops', or name stamps, caught our attention. Colin had started a collection of turtles in different stones and we decided to have a chop made with his name and its meaning on the bottom and a turtle fashioned on the top. It took just an hour to carve.

We returned with Warwick by taxi, as the fare was very reasonable and found the modern highway such a contrast to the earlier trip by train. Colin had decided to stay on board for the day and when we returned to *Bagheera* we found him most distraught.

"Aussie Bou flew away," he told us. "I could see him struggling in the water for a long time but then he drifted out of sight."

It had taken him over half an hour to attract the attention of the club ferry boat and although they had combed the river they had found no sign. Our little budgerigar was a great character and we were desolate. We had been hoping to leave that afternoon so took *Bagheera* to the club dock to fill with water and fuel, planning also to enquire about pet stores. A few minutes later a man walked down the ramp towards us. He moved slowly, his hands cupped together.

"I believe you have lost a bird?" he said, carefully showing us a small area of green and yellow feathers.

Unbelievably, Aussie had flapped his way downstream for half a mile, staying afloat for over an hour. The man had been alerted by the sea gulls who were diving at Aussie, and had been able to reach him from the dock. Our little bird looked surprisingly perky after his ordeal but had to suffer a severe wing trim that evening so he couldn't fly out of the cabin again.

We decided to maximize our sightseeing time in Malaysia by continuing to travel at night. The trip up to Lumut was extremely busy. For many miles off the coast the sea was 'saturated' with fishing nets all laid at right angles to the shore and thus to our course. Although a few had lights, most were not visible. All we saw were white buoys at the bow and then a faint impression of buoys disappearing into the distance. Fortunately, the nets were quite deep and we didn't get entangled.

After a swim at Pangkor Island, we arrived at Lumut in the afternoon and found it a delightful town. That evening in the picturesque Perak Yacht Club we met several new people and learnt about the forlorn looking boat, *DX*, with a broken mast which was anchored off. Tragically, the owner of the boat had died of botulism from a can of mushrooms, when half way across the Indian Ocean. The crew had been rescued by helicopter from Diego Garcia, south of the Maldives, abandoning the yacht. Amazingly, in the middle of the ocean, the Canadian yacht *Lorelai* had sighted *DX* some weeks later. They knew all about the situation as they had helped monitor the ham frequencies during the crew's rescue. They decided to claim it for salvage and towed the 40' boat 2000 miles east back to Lumut. It reminded us to check all cans for bulging or fizzing on opening, which could possibly be caused by this bacterium. Apparently the owner had boasted about what a good deal he'd had on cans before leaving Australia.

While the boys and I were completing school the next morning, Andy went to clear customs which was nine kilometres away. Chan, who ran the yacht club with his family, kindly offered to take him to the bus station and while talking we learnt that Chan frequently took visitors on inland tours. It sounded ideal so we arranged to leave at 8:00 the next morning. A group of us went to the Monday evening market in the town that night, enjoying the food and the extroverted vendors. One lady in particular had us in fits of laughter and when she had successfully talked her latest customer into buying a basket full of produce she turned to us.

Holding out a mangosteen she beckoned to the boys. "Here, here, take, take, delicious no? Queen Victoria's favourite!"

Apparently Queen Victoria offered a handsome reward to anyone who could get a mangosteen back to her that was edible. The segmented sweet, juicy pulp is indeed delicious and our saleslady soon had a bagful in our hands.

It was a magical trip inland with Chan and we were particularly impressed with the good use of the land and the remarkable variety of the crops. According to Chan, it was the Japanese who taught the Malaysians how to grow paddy rice and several other crops. Previously, the British had cleared the land for rubber. As we arrived at one rubber plantation, new grooves in the bark were being made and the white sap oozed out, dribbling into the collecting cups below. The boys felt the pellets of congealed latex that were tossed in heaps on the ground when the cups were full. They would be collected in bulk at a later date. They didn't look like rubber but the texture was the same. To our surprise modern hybrid rubber trees are thin but have the same yield as the old massive ones, although a slightly shorter productive life.

Rubber was first grown in Malaysia at Kuala Kangsar, the royal town of the state of Perak. Here Chan took us to see the impressive palace of the Sultan. The Sultan was at that time serving as King; the Sultans of the thirteen States serve as royalty on a rotation basis. Chan explained there are three main ethnic groups in Malaysia—the Malays, Chinese and Indians. The Malays control the government, while the Chinese dominate the economy.

Here also is the Ubadiah Mosque, its onion shaped golden cupolas and thin minarets spectacular against the bright blue sky. In dramatic contrast were the limestone cave temples outside Ipoh. Perak Tong was impressive with its huge stalactite caves full of altars and resounding loud gongs, and a huge buddha sixty-seven metres tall; but it was the turtle pond at Sam Po Tong that most interested the boys!

Ipoh is renowned for its fine cuisine and the superb fish Chan ordered for lunch which was delicately spiced with ginger and peppers, was unsurpassed by any of our other Malaysian meals.

The trip from Lumut to Penang was the last overnight passage we had to make that was off the Malaysian coast; we set off at 6:30 that evening. The fishermen were more numerous than ever and our log is filled with comments such as 'hundreds of fishing boats, every combination of lights and no-lights possible, fishing floats everywhere'.

I came on watch at 10:30 P.M. and for the most part managed to zig-zag my way through the fleet, although at times huge detours were necessary to get around the end of a string of floats. Motoring, as the wind was light, Andy had also furled the sails to increase visibility. The night was pitch black with an occasional glimmer from the moon, just fleeting enough for me to see at midnight that we were about to run over a buoy. I quickly put the engine into neutral so we wouldn't snag a line with the propeller. It was at that moment that I heard an engine astern. The noise rapidly increased, an unlit boat was approaching fast, obviously heading for us.

Rushing below to wake up Andy, I grabbed a long t-shirt thrown down earlier as it was a hot night. If pirates were coming at least I should have some clothes on! In a flash Andy was on deck beside me with our search light. We could see the boat clearly now. It was about 20' long with two men on board. Andy shone the searchlight directly at them. Immediately blinded, they veered away, dropping back towards the buoy I had just run over, then disappearing into the darkness.

I handed over the watch at 1:30 A.M. having had no further incidents. However, as two more 'attacks' happened during Andy's watch, he remained on deck until it was light.

Was it angry fishermen, potential pirates or just bullies? Later we were to hear that the fishermen are often aggressive on this stretch, protective of their self-defined fishing territory. This was the location of

Skip's 'pirate' experience but we had heard of no actual boarding of small yachts in this area for years and, judging from recent cruisers' reports, there has been none since. Those most at risk seem to be the large freighters who have only a small crew and have much more of value on board than a small yacht.

"Did you have a gun?" is a question we are frequently asked.

"No we didn't," we reply.

"But why not?"

Just carrying a gun on a boat presents problems, let alone using it. On entering foreign countries one is usually asked to declare all firearms. They are then deposited ashore with the authorities until the owner leaves the country. This means that at the times you would need the weapon the most, such as sitting at anchor or cruising the coastal waters, you don't have it on board. On departure you must retrieve your weapons from your Port of Arrival which means sailing back upwind (well over two thousand miles in Indonesia) or expensive travel overland.

So what if you don't declare your gun and hide it away on the boat? Unfortunately officials do regular searches, particularly if the vessel is American, as a high percentage of Americans start out armed. If firearms are found the boat is usually impounded. If the owner is lucky it might be just a large fine, if unlucky he may end up in prison, a horrific proposition.

If you carry a gun you have to be prepared to use it, be accurate, be lethal, and know the consequences of your action. If you shoot someone you have to be able to prove it was in self-defence—to your person, not to your property. Furthermore we felt using a gun against several armed boarders would be difficult, with retaliation almost certainly terminal.

However, we weren't entirely unprepared. The searchlight was effective and, once blinded, our would-be aggressors were unable to tell whether we had guns or how many people were on board. We had an antique knife in a wooden cover by the chart table and, like every other yacht, amongst our safety equipment we had a flare gun, or Very's pistol, which is lethal at close range.

Vulnerable items such as the dinghy and outboard were made easily identifiable, thus less attractive to steal, by painting them with florescent stripes and the boat's names. They were also locked up or disguised so that it required considerable time and effort to steal them. As no-one likes to face a guard dog we taped a dog's ferocious barking. We never had to use it but are convinced it would be effective!

Without doubt, the question of whether to carry firearms on board will be an ongoing debate amongst yachtsmen, and we were fascinated by a subsequent discussion a group of us had on our arrival in Thailand. All those who carried firearms swore they wouldn't have been alive without them. Those who didn't carry guns couldn't think of an incident when they had needed them! Although many people carried guns when they first started cruising, it appeared that those with the most experience had long since given them up as more of a problem than a benefit.

Penang is the oldest British settlement on the Malay Peninsula. Captain Francis Light, (an ancestor of our friend Mary Light) took over the island in 1786. With its longstanding multicultural mix of Chinese, Malay, Portuguese, Indian and British we found the island fascinating. What fun it is to travel around the humming city of Georgetown by bicycle rickshaw, passing the Chinese clan houses, or kongsi, and the temples with their rainbows of dragons, statues, paintings and carvings, particularly dramatic when on the roofs. Mosques, and Hindu and Buddhist temples abound, together with beautiful old colonial buildings—and to the boys delight a McDonalds restaurant!

Outside the city we relaxed in the cool, peaceful Botanical Gardens surrounded by jungle covered hills.

"Come and look at the monkeys," Colin called from the stream.

"They're just like children," I commented as we watched them diving exuberantly from the rocks with mum proudly looking on.

They were delightfully cheeky, swimming underwater and splashing their playmates, and as Andy took out the video camera to film them one darted over and started nibbling his foot! We had ended up buying the small Sony 8mm Handycam and were pleased with its ease of use. Being so light we took it everywhere, although still had to work out the dynamics of manipulating the equipment and time required to take photos, slides and videos simultaneously!

The butterfly farm was another photographer's paradise with its huge variety. The butterflies were very tame and the boys were able to hold and examine several. They were fascinated by their dramatic intricate markings and the vibrancy of the colours. They were also able to collect some wings of butterflies that had died, which made a fine addition to their journals.

We tried to get ashore early the next morning to complete some chores but it took forever to wave down a bum-boat, which was necessary to take as there was no safe place to leave a dinghy. All the blue ones passed us by, probably because both *Loralai* and ourselves had refused to

Colin in the Penang butterfly farm

pay $10 for the one minute trip to the dock the previous day! Finally a yellow boat picked us up and charged $3.

It took nearly two hours to get our Thai visas, two-month ones for the boys and me which was ideal but inexplicably Andy, as captain of the vessel, was only allowed one month. If needed he would have to return to Malaysia for an extension. Then off to the Post Office to mail the school papers where I gulped in horror at the $25 cost to mail two weeks of Colin's work. Usually I run into travelling Canadians who are only too happy to post it back home where the postage for correspondence education is free.

We had our first good wind for some time to sail north to the island of Palan Palan Dayang Bunting and loved its freshwater lake. It was a beautiful, cool spot and I did several bags of laundry whilst the boys swam and a family of otters came to visit. We had a quick stop for a duty free shop in Langkawi before we entered Thai waters, but we were fascinated

Jamie and Liza in Langkawi

by the designs of the local boats; some were even very similar to those of our British Columbia Haida Indians.

After entering Thailand we anchored between the two tiny islands of Ko Rok Nok and Ko Pok Nai. Their sparkling white sand beaches and turquoise water were so inviting we jumped straight overboard on arrival. The waters of the Malacca Straits had been murky; it had been a while since we had been able to dive in such crystal clear seas with such abundant fish life.

Nai Harn Bay on Phuket Island was full of yachts. As we cruised around looking for a spot to anchor, Skip and Denise waved us over to *Endymion*.

"Good timing, *Bagheera*, we're having a Christmas party tonight, for the 'lighting of the lights'. Any time after six and bring the kids."

"Wonderful. We'll bring along some nibbles."

It was great catching up with all our friends and the stories about the Kings Cup regatta. *Catriona-M* had managed just fine without our racing expertise, having won the event! I collected Duncan from Bangkok, here for the Christmas holidays, and we cruised up the west side of Phuket with its lovely sandy bays and wonderful beachside restaurants. Thai food was the best yet!

As most boats were in Nai Harn Bay we returned there for Jamie's seventh birthday. Andy made a rendering of 'Jaws' for the cake and there were ten kids for games, spinnaker pole jumping and to help Jamie test out his new bicycle ashore. His tricycle from Greece had long since been discarded and we had bought him a shiny red two-wheeler in Singapore. It had been greased and carefully taped in garbage bags for the trip and taken to the beach early that morning. Skip had videod the unwrapping ceremony, giving a lively audio account of Jamie's delighted reaction and very first ride. Jamie received considerable attention from the locals too; in fact within five minutes I had two offers for the bike for double its value!

With so many children even Santa came to the beach on Christmas Eve, and on Christmas Day after a relaxed family time opening stockings and presents *Bagheera* was invaded by the fleet, with enough people on board to sink her by several inches! Andy recorded it for prosperity on the video, including Skip swinging on the spinnaker pole from the bow and making a dramatic entry into the ocean. No light weight, Skip was horrified when we played it back to him two years later!

As the day cooled down seventy yachtsmen, including the Kearns family from Singapore, had roast suckling pig at a thatched restaurant on the beach. During dinner a minute's silence was observed in memory of John from *Quahlee*.

"How do you like boarding school?" Duncan was frequently asked.

"It's great," he replied. "I'm really enjoying being there."

We were relieved to hear it because like most teenagers he hadn't been terrific at corresponding! He was also enjoying the cool Vancouver climate and was finding it hard to adjust to the heat and humidity of Thailand.

Between Christmas and New Year we sailed up the east coast of Phuket to Phangnga Bay where limestone pillars of quite extraordinary shapes soar out of the sea.

It is a spectacular area for cruising and the boys loved exploring the overhanging, waterfilled caves. Fishermen, from the Muslim fishing villages on stilts, frequently came to *Bagheera* with catches of prawns and a variety of crabs. The boys were most envious of their slim, amazingly fast longtail boats, so called because of their long direct drive propeller

70' Asteriod sailing in Phangnga Bay

shafts attached to engines which swivel on their transoms. We continued to Krabi to extend Duncan's visa and spent the night at Phra Nang, a pretty bay but highly developed. We were told by some visitors, who were still in a state of shock, that the construction had just taken place. When they had visited twelve months before there was barely a guest house to be found. Koh Phi Phi island off Phuket was the same, scenically spectacular but the recent building boom had sadly run wild with apparently little planning or forethought.

"Patong is the place to be for New Year's Eve," was the word out amongst the fleet so we headed back up Phuket's east coast. It was an incredible evening on the town, a hive of activity and celebrations, with music blaring and firecrackers galore. Even a baby elephant skipped along the beach and Skip managed to end up with a python around his neck! There was great rejoicing at midnight, particularly amongst the yachtsmen. Then we went off to a Go-Go bar—where we found War-wick dancing on the stage completely surrounded by the gorgeous semi-clad girls! Meanwhile the boys had fun aboard the American yacht *Tamure* where all the kids gathered, and Dusty had arrived, tired, as he had sailed straight from Singapore single-handed, but so pleased to be back with everyone again.

On New Year's Day Dusty and Warwick came over to dinner. It was a belated Christmas celebration for them. Whilst in Indonesia Ines from *Quahlee* had bought the 'lads' washboards and had given them to me to complete the Christmas honours. Dusty and Warwick were delighted that they would now be able to clean their clothes to perfection and immediately started to play their washboards like banjos!

Christmas and New Year over, 'the fleet' settled down to serious business. Most boats were heading for the Mediterranean and to optimize the chance of having some favourable winds in the Red Sea they needed to get moving.

Yachts started heading out, the earlier ones intending to visit Sri Lanka and the Maldives on the way. Having cruised the Mediterranean at the beginning of our trip, we planned to head for South Africa. With so many fascinating places to see along the way, we had decided to take an extra year to do it!

This gave us time to explore some more of Thailand. We moved the boat around to the more protected anchorage of Ao Chalong, where there is a large live-aboard community, then headed up to Bangkok by bus, leaving Dusty taking care of *Bagheera*.

Our flight was remarkably cheap from Bangkok to the small town of Mae Hong Son in northern Thailand, close to the Burmese border. Andy and I went out walking early the next morning. It was so peaceful, the serene lake reflecting the picturesque Buddhist temple to perfection. Along the shore was a profusion of pink water lilies that were just opening their petals to welcome the day. Two hours later, when we took the boys out to breakfast, the scene had drastically changed. It had become a bustling, noisy town much busier with tourism than we had expected.

We took a tour to the hills where the little girls, in their black dresses with pink woven trim, coyly gave the traditional two-handed greeting. We passed Shan, Karen and Meo hill tribes but interestingly the village closest to the Burmese border is inhabited by Chinese who were originally part of Chiang Kai-Shek's army and who fled to Thailand after their defeat by the Communists. The Padaung, or long-necked people, are another group that live close by. The women traditionally wear metal rings around their neck in honour of an ancestor who was beheaded. At age nine the girls get their first wide collar and add a ring per year until they are married. A thirty centimetre long neck is highly prized, but has to have the rings to support it. With the custom dying out and only fifty known Pudaung left, the women are being somewhat exploited commercially. Along the road there were good views of Burma. Once these hills had been covered in teak forests, and the people had built their homes of teak, using the huge leathery leaves as roof tiles. Now there was not a mature teak tree to be seen.

We flew back to bustling, noisy Bangkok, but stayed in the charming restful guesthouse, Tavee. At $2.50 a night for a newly furnished room with designer sheets, it was a remarkable bargain. The boys particularly enjoyed the pet gibbon, (from the ape family) who loved putting his long furry arms around our necks. A short walk through a busy market brought us to the Chao Phraya River. The water taxis were the most interesting and least exhausting way of moving around the city, and convenient for the sights we wanted to see. The temples with their buddhas, such as the forty-six metre golden Reclining Buddha, were impressive, although discouragingly touristy with vendors in abundance. The Grand Palace, however, was beautifully maintained, with no vendors allowed on the grounds. The intricate workmanship and variety of architecture is so different to our western styles, and most dramatic with a magical skyline of green and terracotta roofs and golden spires. Our guide told us that each king designed his own palace. Each one looked very different from the others. Apparently this king had been a student at Cambridge University in England and had fashioned the stone facade after his college—with golden spires on its roof!

Finally the boys had a ride in a longtail. The vessel was about 60' long and only five foot wide, with a huge American Ford V8 engine and propeller shaft that protruded twenty feet astern. It moved along at tremendous speed down the narrow canals past the houses on stilts, and manoeuvred around other boats with amazing dexterity. We stopped at the colourful floating market, went to the snake farm and viewed the king's magnificently decorated barges. The colour of these canals, or klongs, left much to be desired. We came to the conclusion that the locals must have excellent antibodies as we saw everything done in the water from cleaning food, bathing children, brushing teeth to using it as a toilet!

We couldn't leave Bangkok without visiting the infamous Patphong Road, so Andy and I headed off one evening. We had hardly climbed out of our tuktuk, the three-wheeled taxis that zoom through traffic at breakneck speed, when some friends hailed us.

"There's no escaping, yachties are everywhere!" we joked.

There were Go-Go bars on either side of the street with a mass of vendors in the middle, all of them trying to get our business. We were finally lured into a bar that did not have an exorbitant entrance fee but as Andy obviously wasn't going to be good for business with me in tow they put us in the back row. The shows were 'interesting' but left very little to the imagination! Meanwhile I enjoyed chatting to the go-go girls who frequently sat down in the spare seat beside me. Gorgeous, with smooth golden skin and gleaming dark hair, they were just bubbly teenagers doing an accepted job, but we heard horrific stories of ten year olds going into prostitution for the locals. Sadder still was the statistic that one in six already had AIDS.

It was time for Duncan to return to Vancouver and, as our tenants were buying their own home, we decided that I should go too. We couldn't really complain. The tenants had signed a contract for twenty-five months and stayed over four and a half years. My step-daughter, Alison, did a wonderful job of managing our affairs but I felt that re-renting and possibly re-decorating was too big a burden to put on her. Ironically Duncan's Korean airlines flight which had been cheap from Vancouver, was the most expensive when booked from Thailand. My favourite Singapore Airlines which had been very expensive to book from Vancouver was the cheapest deal now for me! So Duncan and I returned separately.

I returned to Phuket ten days later having easily found new tenants. The house was in great shape—in fact most of my time was spent locating the items Andy had requested for the boat, in particular a new pump for our head! My only complaint, however, was that the changeover of tenants was happening in January. Unlike Duncan I found the cold and damp a rude shock.

Meanwhile, Andy had been making inquiries about completing some boat repairs after tangling with a floating branch in the muddy approaches to Penang and bending our propeller shaft. During the Christmas period friends had tried to help us straighten it by tensing various combinations of lines, but bent it stayed. Whilst only slightly distorted it was important to fix the problem before leaving Thailand as during our year in the Indian Ocean we would be remote from any facilities. Ideally this needed to be done out of the water so we took *Bagheera* round to the basin at the Siam Yacht Club. Unfortunately the tides and winds did not co-operate. Michael, the owner, offered his help to do the job in the water, which required removing the rudder, extracting the propeller shaft and blocking the hole with a wooden plug—very quickly! All appeared to go well and the shaft was taken away to a machine shop to be straightened. When it was reassembled, however, we found that the rudder had a lot of play. To our horror the lower bearing was missing. Andy couldn't believe it as he had tried to remove the bearing in Australia and it was firmly stuck. The water was too deep and murky, and the current too strong to hope to find it on the bottom but everyone searched the shore. To no avail, and being Chinese New Year nothing could be done for two days. To crown it all, on returning to the boat, I found a soy sauce bottle had cracked and the liquid had oozed through our tapes, cupboard and cushions!

A ten centimetre piece of teflon was needed to make a new bearing but there was none available in Phuket and a piece from Bangkok cost $250. A compromise was to machine out the spare teflon top rudder bearing we had on board and have a bronze outer shell made for it so that it fitted the larger, lower aperture. Measurements had to be done underwater. I waited apprehensively while Andy and Michael installed it underwater the next day.

"It seems to fit perfectly," Andy called up at last. What a relief!

While Colin and I did a final shop, Andy and Jamie sailed *Bagheera* north of Nai Harn to a water barge. The water came via a hose from a stream ashore and it was delicious to drink, cool and refreshing. It was the last time we were able to fill our tanks from a hose for many months to come.

We left at 3:00 A.M. on February 3rd. There were only a handful of us who planned to amble across the Indian Ocean. We talked to each other on the radio most days but met up only occasionally. We were now really going off the beaten track.

Crossing the
Indian Ocean

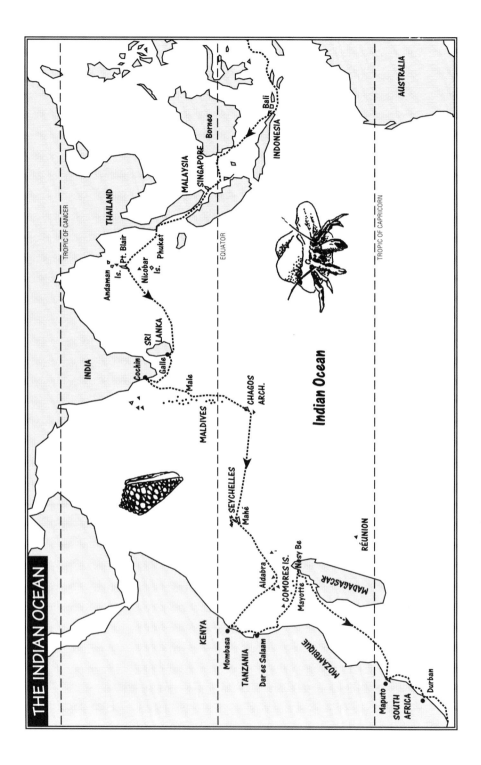

THE INDIAN OCEAN

TROPIC OF CANCER

EQUATOR

TROPIC OF CAPRICORN

INDIA

THAILAND

Andaman Is.
Pt. Blair
Nicobar Is.
Phuket

SRI LANKA
Cochin
Galle

MALAYSIA
SINGAPORE

Borneo

INDONESIA
Bali

Male

MALDIVES

CHAGOS ARCH.

Indian Ocean

SEYCHELLES
Mahé

KENYA
Mombasa

TANZANIA
Dar es Salaam

Aldabra

COMORES IS.
Mayotte
Nosy Be

MADAGASCAR

MOZAMBIQUE

RÉUNION

SOUTH AFRICA
Maputo
Durban

AUSTRALIA

7. The Andaman Islands and Sri Lanka

Port Blair
Galle and an island tour

Forming a crescent-shaped archipelago, the Andaman and Nicobar Islands, peaks of a sub-marine mountain range, separate the Bay of Bengal from the Andaman Sea. About three hundred in number, they stretch some 400 nautical miles between latitudes 6°N. and 14°N. The northernmost island being near the mouth of the Irrawaddy in Burma while the southernmost is close to Sumatra, Indonesia. The verdant islands are covered in dense tropical, evergreen and deciduous rain forest, with mangrove swamps or white sands at the waters' edge. In addition there are many mangrove-fringed or sandy islets that are surrounded by coral reefs.

We were heading for Port Blair on South Andaman, the administrative capital for both the Andamans and Nicobars. A Union Territory of India since 1947, it hadn't been easy to get permission to visit. It wasn't a problem for us, as the Andamans have a growing tourist business, but *Bagheera* was a different matter altogether. Having been sent from department to department in the Indian Consulate in Sydney, Australia, we finally found someone who was informative about the special application.

"Due to its unusual nature, your boat visa could take anything from three months to one year to process," the helpful lady told us. "Once granted it will be valid for three months."

We tried to explain that because of the weather patterns, particularly the monsoons, we didn't have that flexibility. To no avail, we were arguing against the unwieldy Indian civil service for whom, it appeared, procedure and paperwork was the prime concern.

Four months later in Darwin we received a letter from our Sydney friends, the Tandurellas, telling us that the Indian Consulate had phoned. Approval had already been given. However, not only did we have to collect the visa in person but it had already expired! Undeterred I went to the Indian High Commission in Singapore, requesting they issue another but I ran into the unwieldy process all over again. When I suggested they fax Sydney, they replied it would cost $75.00! I spent a frustrating two hours getting no-where on the first day and didn't make much more progress on the second. It wasn't until the third day when I arrived with Jamie and his school books that they realized I really meant business, and the visas were issued in no time at all!

With a ten knot breeze from the north-east, we had a comfortable three day trip from Phuket. It was our longest run since the Darwin Ambon race but the boys quickly settled into their routine. They did a three hour watch every day then filled the rest of their time with reading, listening to tapes, playing Lego and cards.

"Mummy, will you play a game of UNO?" was a frequent request from Jamie. He had become a fiend at this game and beat me every time.

There was very little traffic throughout the passage, just two big ships, and not a fishing boat to be seen. We entered Port Blair Harbour at 7:00 A.M., calling the authorities on the radio for clearance procedures. In perfect English they were most welcoming but insisted we needed to be towed by a tug! After explaining that *Bagheera* was a small yacht they informed us where we could anchor but they sounded confused. The officials arrived late morning and were extremely surprised at our permit. Apparently we were the third yacht ever to visit the Andamans, and only the second with permission. However, even though our visas stated that we could visit several of the other islands, they were adamant we could not take *Bagheera*, although we could go to some by local boat. It was disappointing, especially after all the trouble to get a visa. Being alone in such a remote place we didn't feel comfortable leaving *Bagheera* unattended.

"We're sorry, but it's too dangerous for you to go on your own," the officials said, seeing our frustration.

"But why?" asked Andy. "We're used to piloting through reefs."

"It's because of the tribal people; they're not friendly."

It wasn't until we visited the small anthropological museum that we

Jamie, Colin, Andy, Liza and Duncan at the Grand Palace, Bangkok, Thailand

We sailed over 50,000 nautical miles, the equivalent of almost 2½ times around the Equator

Duncan

Jamie

Colin

Eight metre high termite mound in Kakadu National Park, near Darwin

Lizard Island - looking down from Cook's Look

Festivities in Ambon at the end of the Darwin Ambon Race

Duncan with his latest catch

Some of our many visitors in Wangi Wangi

The awesome Komodo dragons

Komodo village

Serene Bali

Hindu festival – offerings being taken to the temple

Colin, Jamie and Duncan – playing a Balinese gamelan xylophone

Ubadiah Mosque

Old world Penang

Warwick and Dusty, single-handers with their Christmas washboards

THAILAND

Buddhist temple in Mai Hong Son

We loved Thai food

Thai greeting

understood the extent of the problem and reason for the restrictions. Many of the islands in the Andamans and all in the Nicobars are off-limits because they are populated by primitive tribes. We were fascinated that the four Andaman tribes—the Andamanese, Onges, Jarrawas and Sentinelese—are nigrito, while the Nicobarese and Shompens in the Nicobars are mongoloid. The islands have been populated by these tribes for thousands of years, some back to paleolithic times, and remained unexplored until the 1600s because of the hostility of these people. Due to this isolation many of the tribes still lived a stone age existence. They were hunter-gatherers, their tools basic, although some used iron found on wrecked ships, for arrowheads and harpoons. As recently as 1987, the Sentinelese shot poison arrows at government officials who were trying to make contact; the Jarawa on South Andaman are also known to be fierce. The Andamanese, who once inhabited the Great Andamans, didn't know how to make fire, and the Shompens have rejected all contact with the outside world, living in the dense forest of Great Nicobar.

Lying in the trade routes between Burma and India the islands were known to early traders. Ptolemy, a Roman geographer, recorded them in his map of the world in the second century A.D. The Mahrattas from India were the first to annex the islands, wanting them as a base to harass the trading ships of the Dutch, Portuguese and British in the seventeenth century. French Jesuits and Dutch pirates also visited and the Danish East India Company attempted to evangelize the people in the mid 1700s. In the late 18th Century the British tried to form a settlement but it wasn't until after the Indian Mutiny in 1857, with the building of a permanent penal colony on Port Blair, that they were successful. Except for three years of Japanese rule during World War II Britain governed the Andamans until Indian independence in 1947.

When wandering around relaxed Port Blair it was hard to comprehend the sense of dread the large numbers of political prisoners and criminals who were deported here felt, until we learnt that prisoners who came here seldom returned. They called it 'black water' because of the blood shed by the nationalists. The town, with its haphazard buildings with high corrugated roofs and old-fashioned shops, gave us the feeling of old world India, although subtle changes can be seen due to the increased tourism.

Traditionally most people have worked for the government. They all looked immaculate, the women in brightly coloured saris and the men in white shirt and grey trousers creased to perfection.

Port Blair

Hindu is the most practised religion and there were so many sacred cows wandering the streets that Colin started to count them.

"How many?" we asked him when we got back to the boat an hour and a half later.

"Three hundred and twenty-six and I'm sure I missed some!"

The immigration officials had told us that we could take an organized tour to see the sights, and we joined some Indians the next afternoon for an interesting $1.30 trip. The Chatham Saw Mill was our first stop. Lumber is one of the islands' primary exports, the lush forests covering over three quarters of the islands (about 7000 square kilometres) and sixty percent of the forests have been protected for the industry. Besides the commercially important teak and rosewood, mahogany and rubber have been planted to improve the economy. The mill is one of the oldest in Asia and the Forest Museum display shows how old and new methods are combined with elephants and bulldozers working together. The large mill was a hive of activity with a wonderfully pungent smell emanating from the cut wood. However, as we were shown the various stages of turning logs into graded planks, we were shocked by the lack of safety devices on the pre-World War II band saws and conveyor belts; the workers also wore no protection.

Although the run-down building of the Anthropological Museum didn't look promising, it was a treasure trove inside. Tremendous care had been taken with models of tribal villages and displays of everyday tribal artifacts. Photographs show various expeditions that had made contact with the tribal people, including a couple in both their tribal and western dress. This fragility of old traditions is evident in so many parts of the world. It was heartening to see the amount of literature that had been accumulated in the museum on the local tribal people, and to hear that the government's Protection of Aboriginal Tribes Policy has reserved 40% of the islands as tribal land. The 1986 population figures of 223,000 indicate about 15% were tribespeople although, as many of these people still shun outsiders, the numbers have been difficult to determine.

The boys enjoyed the Mini Zoo, which had some of the islands' unusual wildlife, and a saltwater crocodile-rearing farm. In the Marine Museum they compared the collection of corals and 350 species of marine life to what they had seen when snorkelling. Now that we were in the Indian Ocean there were several subtle differences in the fishes, corals and shells compared to the varieties we had seen in the Atlantic and Pacific.

Dominating the island's recent history is the Cellular Jail. Only three of the seven wings which extended spoke-like from the guard tower survived the 1943 earthquake but it is enough to give a feeling of the vastness of the place. Finished in 1910, it could hold 698 prisoners in solitary confinement and, without doubt, life in the hot, airless, small narrow cells must have been terrible. It is now a national memorial to the Indian Freedom Fighters who were interred there by the British before independence, and there are several galleries of their photographs. Artifacts in the site museum testify to the harsh treatment inflicted on these 'criminals', such as a device for holding prisoners whilst they were flogged, instruments used for torture in the death house and gallows, and information regarding food rations and work responsibilities.

The return bus stopped at the Cottage Industries Emporium. Here we found goods made from some of the island's more exotic woods such as paduak and marblewood. We bought a walking stick in the beautiful red paduak. It is of simple design and quite velvety to the touch.

Having seen the sights of Port Blair, it was time to leave for Sri Lanka. We went to clear-out with the officials the next morning. A helpful taxi driver took us into town and back, only charging us $4.00 for four hours. The harbour master was charming and insisted we stay for tea. Ninety minutes and three cups later, our documents still weren't complete, although they had been sent away and returned several times—for editing, for re-writing and then for typing. It was only when they were finally ready that the official mentioned that if we still wanted to visit some other islands we could go to the Commissioner to discuss it.

The thought of another three hours of officialdom was too much! Anyway we had been very content with our visit and would soon be in the Maldives for some diving. We also planned to stop briefly for a dive on our way out, on a reef further to the south. During our stay an Indian Navy Lieutenant had come to visit who had spent several weeks aboard Jacques Cousteau's *Calypso* the previous year.

"Don't worry about Jolly Buoy and Red Skin islands," he told us, "but the diving around the Cinque islands is spectacular."

We picked up some of the bread that had been recommended by the Harbourmaster. It was quite delicious and we were grateful for his directions as we would never have known it was a bakery from the store front. We could only find limited fruit and vegetables, however, and most had been picked very under-ripe. We called Jamie on the hand-held radio on returning to the harbour and he came to collect us in the dinghy. The children and adults waiting in the ferry alongside the dock were fascinated and couldn't take their eyes off him. As we left Jamie waved and with beaming smiles they all waved back.

We left at 7:00 the next morning; the winds were light and we ambled down the coast with the school books in the cockpit. When the Cinque Islands were clearly in view we altered course to the east so we would end up between them. It was at that moment an Indian naval ship appeared from astern. Slowing down after overtaking us, they started a loose, but purposeful, zig-zag course in front of *Bagheera* until we were on our way to the west and well clear of the islands. Then they peeled away, hooted, and headed back to Port Blair!

We spoke to Dusty on the radio that night; he sounded in good form. Most of the boats were now in the Arabian Sea, he told us, but they all had very light winds. *Wildfire* came up on the air from Thailand; *Asteroid* spoke from the Maldives. Then we had a call from the heavens! Our Singapore friend Sam Shaw was a captain for Singapore Airlines and he called from the cockpit when in flight to India.

"Ines has returned," he informed us. "She's planning to sail *Quahlee* back to Australia."

"Good for her," we replied. "Wish her a good trip from us."

With the winds from the north-east blowing ten to fifteen knots the sailing conditions were good, but the seas were very uncomfortable. The swells seemed to come from three different directions with strong currents causing an extraordinary vertical chop that slapped noisily against the hull. It was also stifling, particularly below. In Singapore we had purchased more fans and now had them everywhere—over each berth, the galley, the chart table and the main cabin for school. It certainly made a difference having the blasts of air, even though they were hot.

There was no traffic initially so watches were relaxed. We did some navigation exercises with the boys using the SATNAV (a satellite electronic navigation system). They enjoyed using its various functions—how far we had to go, what heading, our current position etc. As Colin plotted our position on the chart he also noticed how deep the ocean was here.

As we dropped further south we began to see more ships, but found that as they were off the shipping lane they were not keeping a very good look-out. One in particular seemed totally oblivious of our presence and seemed to alter course towards us every time we moved to avoid her. Of course it was in the middle of the night! We tried calling on the V.H.F. radio but there was no response. After taking evasive action Andy finally shone the search-light up into their bridge. They sure woke up in a hurry!

After entering the shipping lane between Singapore and the Suez Canal our watches became extremely busy. We sighted Sri Lanka on the morning of our fifth day out. With a favourable two knot current we made Galle before it was dark. Just before arriving in the harbour Jamie, who was on watch, called below.

"There's something in the water ahead, but I don't know what it is."

Andy and I rushed up just in time to see two sperm whales, that were almost as long as *Bagheera*, pass just four metres from the boat. They were moving fast, coming up for air and spouting furiously every few seconds.

"Do you think they saw us?" asked Jamie.

The same question had been in both Andy's and my thoughts. With our speed of seven knots, and theirs at probably twelve in the opposite direction, a collision would have been disastrous.

We followed fishing boats into the harbour. We had seen many of these dug-outs with their single outrigger several miles out at sea. Although they increased their freeboard by binding a plank of wood on each gunwale they were incredibly narrow, and the two or three crew could only stand sideways. We marvelled at their temerity, particularly when one came struggling in with a Marlin in tow that was almost as long as the boat.

Sri Lanka, formerly Ceylon, was one of the highlights of our world trip. It has so much to offer with an interesting culture, friendly people, wonderful beaches, spectacular scenery, cool hill country, fascinating ruins, game parks—and a variety of gems for Colin.

Interestingly, Marco Polo, in the late 1200s, wrote:

'On leaving the Island of Andoman and sailing a thousand miles, a little south of west, the traveller reaches Ceylon, which is undoubtedly the finest Island of its size in all the world.'

The island is like a tear drop that is almost attached to southern India by a chain of sandbanks known as Adam's Bridge. With its high central hills surrounded by a coastal plain it has a great diversity of climate and vegetation.

Sri Lanka is first mentioned in the epic of the Ramayana. It was the king of Lanka, the evil Rawana, who abducted Sita, the beautiful wife of Rama, taking her off to his island lair. Although it is not known if the legend has any historical basis, it is known that Buddhism, the dominant religion to this day, was brought to the island in 247 B.C. Although there were various raids and incursions from southern India, Sri Lanka was first settled by Europeans in the fifteen hundreds when the Portuguese arrived in search of the highly desirable spices. In the seventeenth century the Dutch displaced them as colonial rulers, followed by the British some one hundred and fifty years later. In 1948 it became an independent member of the British Commonwealth. Although changing its name from Ceylon to Sri Lanka in 1972 seemed to cause considerable confusion, the island had in fact always been known to the Sinhalese (the majority people of Sri Lanka) as Lanka and to the minority Tamils as Ilankai. The added Sri means 'auspicious' or 'resplendent'.

Galle is a large natural harbour on the south-west coast which, until the construction of breakwaters in the capital city of Colombo about 100 years ago, was the major port for the country. The entrance is dominated by a massive fortress that was built by the Portuguese and later modified by the Dutch. It is a natural stopping point for yachts heading west, and the authorities welcome them, providing mooring buoys and a dinghy dock. Water and fuel were of good quality and there were also facilities for garbage—although we seldom got our bags to the bin. They would be taken from us, with profuse thanks, as soon as we brought them ashore. It reminded us that one man's garbage can be another man's treasure, and after our bags were taken the first time I always found something to put in, such as the boy's outgrown clothing, that was worth finding.

One of our highlights in Galle was the yacht agent, Don Windsor. From a wealthy Sinhalese family, Don was widely travelled and highly educated and we spent many an evening being entertained and informed while sipping beer on his cool veranda, which served as an informal sailors' clubhouse. As a local agent he also arranged the necessary yacht paperwork and paid the harbour fees, exchanged money, secured special foods, wine and beer, and achieved miracles for those needing repairs and spares. Meanwhile his family made cushions and flags, and served delicious meals. Services were done for a 10% fee. Not only did we find this convenient, but elsewhere they charged 100%!

Don was also wonderful to the boys.

"Why don't you bring your bicycle ashore and store it here," he suggested to Jamie, and to Colin, "I've just had some gems sent over

Don Windsor (upper right) and his family always had open house for yachtsmen

would you like to go through them? You know Sri Lanka is famous for its gem mines."

Don was a jeweller before he retired, besides being a local politician and celebrity, and Colin's knowledge and interest in semi-precious stones increased dramatically while we were there.

The family on American *Delilah* watched over *Bagheera* while we took the train to Colombo to pick up a car and driver for an island tour. Arrangements were made by relatives of friends in Vancouver, who I met when I was home re-renting our house. The first stop was the Pinnewala elephant orphanage where many wobbly-legged babies frolicked in the water and played on the rocks. It was a picturesque setting in a wide river valley but before going closer we had to pay to take our cameras, with a surcharge for the video! To our surprise the babies were hairy. They were not as tall as Jamie and wonderfully cuddly, although very inquisitive, trying to get into our pockets with their trunks. Those in the water squealed with delight when one of the few mothers snorted a shower of water at them or gently pushed them over for a bath.

We were fortunate in having been invited to stay in the Ceylon Tobacco Company's airy bungalow with its lush garden, up in the beautiful hills above Kandy. The staff were delighted to have some children as guests, and without doubt our boys enjoyed being over-indulged. The best known of Sri Lanka's hill stations, Kandy is now the cultural and spiritual centre. That evening there was a show by the Kandyan dancers; their vibrant, colourful performance and dramatic finale of firewalking certainly lived up to their reputation. Kandy is also famous for its Temple of the Tooth, near the central lake, which reputedly houses one of Buddha's teeth. We went on a tour of the somewhat garish interior but there was a long line to view the tooth— apparently it is the size of a beer can although being in a gold casket you don't actually get to see it!

Sadly we were unable to visit the ancient ruins to the north due to the lengthy civil war between the native Sinhalese and the Tamils, who settled from southern India, many being brought in by the British to work the land. The Tamils want independence for the northern and eastern part of the island and there has been frequent fighting between the government forces and Tamil guerrillas. However, although there were heavily armed soldiers in many places and certain areas were off-limits, we never felt threatened. To the contrary, we found everyone extremely friendly and welcoming.

Heading out of Kandy we stopped to watch elephants at work moving logs, then entered the main tea-growing district. Sri Lanka is the world's largest exporter of tea, and it is the mainstay of the economy along with rubber and coconuts. Interestingly, tea was only introduced to Sri Lanka after most of the coffee plantations were destroyed by disease. The rolling hills were a brilliant green, with women pickers scattered up the slopes, big straw baskets on their backs. Picking only the top two leaves of the plant, they collect over sixteen kilos a day. Stopping at a plantation we sampled several different types of tea and learnt that only the dregs, the sweepings from the floor, go into tea bags!

Continuing on our way to Nuwara Eliya, a favourite hill station of the British in colonial times, Andy frequently called out to our driver, "Jaya, can you stop? Look, there's a fascinating bird," while I requested stops for a particular photo.

Jaya was exceptionally patient and seemed to be enjoying a tour that was somewhat out of the ordinary. However, as often as not on the popular routes, while we were appreciating nature a bus would screech to a halt behind us, with tourists pouring out at top speed convinced they were missing something of significance. It certainly scared away all the wildlife, and was very intrusive. In fact, once while Andy was filming he was physically pushed aside into the ditch!

Jamie was most impressed by the Grand Hotel in Nuwara Eliya, with its high ceilings and large rooms, although it was somewhat run-down with the lack of tourism in recent years. Andy and I also enjoyed a drink at the very colonial British Hill Club, after persuading them to lend Andy a tie which was mandatory in the bar.

A van was needed for the rough drive up to the Horton Plains. The dew was glistening on the immaculate market gardens on our way to the high plateau and breathing in the cool, clean air, we enjoyed a shiver or two, the pre-monsoonal weather in Galle at this time of year being particularly hot and humid. From Farr's Inn the walk to World's End was spectacular through a mass of temperate wild flowers—deep purple violets, bright blue lilies and cerise rhododendrons—to the stunning abrupt drop of 1800 metres to the coastal plains. Our driver had insisted we start early to get a clear view and as we were leaving the mist was beginning to swirl in.

Our stay that night was at Rose Villa, the home of a retired Sinhalese tea planter and his wife who enjoyed the company of visitors and had much to offer. They had cats, dogs, a monkey and newborn budgies, and were also growers of rose plants. They showed us the fifteen hundred different varieties in their garden, many of which were in bloom. The fragrance was unbelievable, the hospitality magnificent, and with all the fresh food for our meals coming from their garden, we left with reluctance. How easily we could have spent a week with them.

The boys were thrilled to be going on an open-jeep safari in Yala Safari Park situated on the south-east coast, but even before we started an elephant wandered into our hotel during lunch. The safari itself was action-packed with elephants, water buffalos, mongoose, crocodiles, wild pigs, goannas, many colourful birds—and surely that was a leopard disappearing into the distance!

Ratnapura is the gem centre of Sri Lanka.

"We need at least half a day there for Colin to see everything," announced Jaya. Jaya had been amazed how many times we had stopped along the way to look at gems, fossils, rose quartz, etc.

He suggested visiting the mines first. In haphazard pits with open huts roughly covered in palm fronds, men stood almost waist high in muddy water. Filling straw pans with rubble, they bent over to methodically wash the contents hoping to find some sapphires, rubies and garnets. The conditions were gruelling but the workers were welcoming, frequently offering the boys the pan to shake for themselves. The boys didn't find any precious stones but there were lots of other interesting rocks—great souvenirs for a boat!

In contrast the gem museum was pristine with an attractively displayed collection of stones from Sri Lanka and around the world. The problem for me was that it was too sophisticated as it showed all the complex colours the gems could be. In my simple mind sapphires should be blue and rubies red—but it intrigued Colin and didn't confuse him one bit! We didn't buy any jewellery here but it certainly stimulated our enthusiasm. Before leaving Sri Lanka we obtained several interesting pieces from Don Windsor as gifts and a brilliant blue sapphire pendant and ring for me.

I also purchased a new stone for my engagement ring. I was very partial to the old stone, a citron topaz with an interesting stripe, but on the boat it had become badly chipped. I had first taken it to a jeweller in Galle to see if it could be refinished.

"There was no point," he announced, "it's just glass!"

Thinking he was deceiving me so I would buy a new stone, I went to Don. He confirmed it; the St. Thomas, Virgin Islands jeweller had cheated me and if I had continued leading a regular lifestyle I would probably never have known!

As we were leaving we looked up at the impressive Adam's Peak, the

2224 metre high mountain that is famous for the huge foot-print on its top. There are differences of opinion as to whose footprint it might be, some claiming it as the place where Adam first set foot on earth when cast out of Heaven. Others say it belongs to Buddha, to St. Thomas the early apostle of India, or to Lord Shiva. There are also those who ignore the footprint completely and call it the butterfly mountain as it is here that butterflies are reputed to go to die.

We returned to Galle to the tragic news that my sister had died. She had been diagnosed with cancer over a year before and had fought the disease most courageously. Within three hours I was on my way to Colombo and England, Don Windsor having organized and guaranteed payment for my air ticket. I gained great comfort from being with so many friends and relatives, and how glad I was to be with her husband and three sons. After living overseas, they had moved into our family home on the River Thames at Twickenham, just outside London. The memorial service was held at our local family church—where we were both christened, where she was married and where, such a short time ago, we had held funeral services for our parents.

Coincidences and fate never cease to amaze me. John on *Quahlee* could so easily have died in the depths of Indonesia where it would have been a nightmare for Ines, and if my sister had died just two days later we would have been out of contact, having left for India and the even more remote Maldive Islands and Chagos archipelago.

8. India and The Maldives

Cochin, Peryar Wildlife Sanctuary North Malé Atoll

Cochin, on the south-west coast of India, is the name for a cluster of islands, towns and backwaters that surround a harbour. Fort Cochin occupies the southern promontory on the seaward side of the bay, with Willingdon, an artificial island, to its east. Bolghatty Island and Vypeen Island are to the north, while the town of Ernakulam on the mainland stretches down the eastern side of the bay. The area is picturesque and historically interesting with its combination of Dutch, Portuguese and English colonial buildings. As well, it is the largest port in the state of Kerala handling over five million tons a year.

Huge dipping fishing nets, which stretch high up over the water, line the shores of Fort Cochin and Vypeen Island making a spectacular harbour entry. This method of fishing is an ancient tradition of Chinese origin dating back to Kublai Khan's era in the thirteenth century. All day long the fishermen lower, then raise these nets which are suspended on long wooden poles lashed together, about twenty-five metres in length. They go down in the water for half an hour then up again to be checked. On the shore, a series of suspended rocks acts as a counterweight so only a few men are needed per net. The catches were meagre while we were watching and the fishermen had to move quickly to get the fish out of the net before the gulls had a feast! However, it seemed a most relaxing way of life, with plenty of time for gossip and meditation.

The fishing nets, Cochin

We needed some rest ourselves as the two and a half day trip hadn't been one of our best, not because the weather was bad, although the north-west wind could ideally have held off for another day, but because Andy and I both became ill.

It being my birthday just after my return from England, Andy and the boys had spent a day in Galle looking for presents. It was stiflingly hot and incredibly humid, but wanting the birthday to be an extra special one they persevered in the mid-day sun, and they all suffered heat stroke. Colin was very sick the day I arrived, while Jamie had a temperature of 40°c on my birthday. Thankfully, with fluids and rest they soon recovered.

The next day we provisioned, filled up with fuel and water, took delivery of our new main cabin cushions made by Don Windsor's niece, bought some last minute jewellery and left late that night. The following morning Andy awoke with a high fever, but felt very cold and could hardly move. We discussed returning to Galle but he was sure it would pass. In all our years in the tropics he had never suffered heat stroke.

I gave him fluids, bathed him with wet towels, and turned the fans on high to cool him down. Fortunately it was calm as we motored north and he was able to sleep in our comfortable forward cabin. The boys and I spelled the watches. Colin was particularly responsible on deck and even managed some schoolwork, while Jamie excelled in the galley. We had some excitement along the way; a huge school of dolphins came to play and stayed with the boat for well over an hour.

Later that day I started to sneeze and within a few hours had a streaming cold and blinding headache. Simultaneously, a north-east wind filled in. The seas built as the winds gained strength, giving an increasingly uncomfortable motion as we pounded into them. Andy, uncharacteristically affected by the adverse conditions, wanted to turn around and head for the Maldives, four days to the south and a comfortable trip down-wind. I, on the other hand, felt that as the wind was only blowing 20 knots and Cochin Harbour was but a day away, we should continue north. One day at sea feeling ill was far better than four I rationalized. It was also much closer to medical facilities and I was becoming concerned about Andy's prolonged high temperature, lack of co-ordination and emotional over-reactions. After listening to the weather forecast and realizing, when he got up, how sick he still was, Andy agreed to continue to Cochin.

Having met some people in Malaysia who had just come from Goa, further up the west coast, we knew the ropes for entering India, in particular the requirement of an itemized list which is supposed to include every article on board and its value! To simplify matters, I had decided to categorize by cabin, but with all our personal possessions, the boat equipment and spare parts, the list still looked impressively long. At least it seemed to satisfy the Port Authorities and Customs officials who came on board.

Professing to be feeling much better after a long, quiet night's sleep, Andy went ashore to finish the clearing process the following morning. It was a protracted procedure in a very hot office with only a hard bench on which to sit. He returned three hours later looking drained. Not only had the officials been unnecessarily long winded and difficult but the exertion had also completely exhausted him.

Bolghatty Island had been recommended as an anchorage so we took *Bagheera* over later in the afternoon. We crossed the harbour with several 'open lighters', their cargo piled high. At first we were amused by their tiny patched pocket handkerchief sails that looked extraordinarily out of proportion for the size and load of the vessels. However, in the brisk breeze of the afternoons the sail worked perfectly and they easily overtook us. Later we had trouble keeping up to a very laden vessel in our dinghy!

"Isn't that a yacht over there?" said Colin peering at the anchorage in the distance.

These lighters moved amazingly fast

Looking through the binoculars we could see it was a trimaran; to our surprise it was registered in Vancouver. The owner, a single-hander, was just leaving as we arrived, but came over for a quick visit by dinghy.

"I haven't seen another yacht for weeks," he told us. "What a pity I have to leave. Incidentally, they're very helpful at the Bolghatty Palace if you want to go on a tour of the area. They will also arrange a trustworthy guard for your boat."

This was great information as we wanted to travel inland but, as in the Andaman Islands, had been concerned about leaving *Bagheera*.

The palace was originally built in 1744 by the Dutch, then became the home of the British Resident at the court of the Raja of Cochin after 1799. Sadly run-down but still with the charm of a gracious old manor house, we found it a restful place to eat, and also enjoyed the walks in its spacious, peaceful grounds.

Jamie, however, was most disappointed in its size. "That can't be a palace," he exclaimed. "It's nothing like Buckingham Palace!"

The staff at the 'palace' were most helpful in arranging a tour of the older part of the city. How fascinating it was strolling through the streets behind the docks that are lined with old merchant houses, warehouses and courtyards piled high with ginger, peppercorns, betel nuts and coir. With the air filled with aromas from the wonderful variety of spices and the men shouting as they pushed the rickety heavy carts out of the ditches, it was the epitome of an eastern scene that has probably changed little over the centuries.

A trading port since at least Roman times, Fort Cochin is thought to be one of the oldest European settlements in India. It first saw the Portuguese flag in 1500, then three years later Alfonso de Albuquerque came with a dozen ships and the original Fort Cochin was built. The settlers included five friars and by 1510 St.Frances was completed—the first European church in India—although it is said that St. Thomas the Apostle first brought Christianity here in 52 A.D.

Within a few years the original wooden building was replaced with an impressive Spanish facade in stone which still stands today. It was here that Vasco da Gama, the Portuguese explorer who was the first to sail around South Africa to India, died, in 1524, when he was Portuguese Viceroy of the Indies. He was buried in the cemetery, although his remains were removed to Portugal fourteen years later.

"Look at the all the religions that have been practised in the church," I commented to Andy. They included Roman Catholic, Dutch Reform, Anglican, and Church of South India.

"How well they reflect the colonial struggle for India," he replied.

Mattancheri to the south of Fort Cochin, looked even older. It is here that Jews came in the sixth century B.C., then again in the first century A.D. when they were fleeing Roman persecution in Jerusalem. The White Jews of Cochin flourished as a sizable community serving also as a haven to Jews from the Middle East and later from Europe. We visited the synagogue in Mattancheri's Jew Town that was built in 1568, and admired the paved floor of hand painted willow-patterned tiles.

"They came all the way from Canton in China," our attentive guide informed us. "Then the synagogue was full, but now the congregation has almost vanished," he told us sadly, "with few of the old blond Jews left. Many emigrated to Holland and England in the last two centuries. Others went to Israel."

Also in Mattancheri is the Dutch Palace which was actually built by the Portuguese, although the Dutch did make some improvements. It was rajahs, however, who used it the most as a palace and it was they who had the wonderful mythological murals painted in the bed chambers, one containing the entire story of the Ramayana, the Hindu's sacred text. The palace also has traditional Keralan flooring that looks like polished black marble, but is far more exciting in composition, being a mix of burned coconut shells, charcoal, lime, plant juices and egg whites!

It was dinnertime as we were making our way back to the boat and enticing aromas emanated from the restaurants. It was Colin who saw the sign.

"It said 'air-conditioned'," he commented, looking at us hopefully. "Wouldn't it be great to be cool?"

Even when you are on a budget you do have to pamper yourselves occasionally, especially when you've been sick! There were white starched tablecloths and it was the perfect temperature. We all ordered steak, fries and salad; nothing like some western food to settle the stomach. The meal was inexpensive, huge and cooked to perfection. With regular food and an energizing temperature we suddenly felt healthy and fit again.

Kerala (the land of the coconut palms) is a green lush narrow strip along the coast with hills known as the Western Ghats forming a natural inland border. The state has always been renowned for its independence from the rest of India and in 1957 it claimed to be the first state in the world to elect a communist government, against non-communist alternatives. The town of Ernakulam is clean, uncrowded and prosperous, and everyone was very friendly and welcoming on our trip inland.

Our driver arrived in an old-fashioned Indian built Ambassador Mark 4, and we purred along through beautiful terrain to Periyar Wildlife Sanctuary up in the hills. At the beginning the vegetation was lush and there were palm-thatched villages with the occasional incongruous church built in colonial style, then there was mile on mile of rice paddies and palms before we reached the hills of Western Ghats with their tea covered slopes, rubber, coffee, cardamon, pepper plantations and tropical forests.

Periyar Lake is a reservoir created by a dam on the Periyar River, built in 1895. It is at the heart of the park and the best place for viewing the wildlife. We had arranged to stay at 'Lake Palace', a hunting lodge in an island setting. The ferry was crowded but once there it was wonderfully serene, and as we shaded under the wide-spread jacaranda trees a herd of elephants ambled down the beach.

The hotel organized a boat trip the following morning, and we saw several more elephants at the water's edge, the young squealing and snorting as they sprayed water with their trunks and swam.

"The Indian elephant is smaller than its African relative," our guide informed us, "particularly the ears. Also, the females have no tusks, nor do some of the males."

It was a very relaxing way to go on safari and we were treated to sights of a variety of animals from the huge buffalo-like herbivores called gaur to sambur, the largest deer in India, also wild boar and monkeys. The binoculars were in constant use for the many varieties of birds, but there was not a glimpse of a tiger, although Periyar Sanctuary was declared a Tiger Reserve in 1978.

It was again a picturesque ride going back to the coast. We stopped to watch some trained elephants at work moving logs onto a truck, and to admire the ladies doing their laundry along the river banks, the colourful saris being laid out neatly to dry along with the men's white lungis, amidst much chatter and laughter. There were sacred cows all over the road, many with curved horns painted blue.

"Maybe I'll count them again," remarked Colin.

"Why don't you just say infinity," replied Jamie who had just learnt the concept. He wasn't far from the mark.

The boys wanted to buy some souvenirs before leaving so we hitched a ride across the bay on a cargo lighter. The sailors were most welcoming and full of fun, their faces characterfully lined from their lives in the sun. The boys bought sandlewood elephants and brass trimmed teak boxes, and I finally chose a peacock blue sari from an amazing variety of brightly coloured lengths.

A final shop for bread and eggs, we had already been to the vegetable market and filled up with fuel from drums, and we left for the Maldives. It was choppy motoring out of the harbour particularly as the fishing boats were coming in with their catches and all wanted to take a look at us. After rounding Fort Cochin, having had a last look at the long row of the huge dipping nets, the water flattened out and we could ease our sheets for a comfortable sail south.

The next day the wind died but previously there had actually been some rain. It was blissfully cool but yet again I got caught all lathered in soap when the squall abruptly came to an end. It was at times like these that I would have loved a water maker, especially now that they were getting so small. However as long as we had rain our catchment systems worked well, and I was seldom to crave an additional supply—although it would have been nice to relax our strict rationing occasionally, such as having several litres for a washdown instead of a cupful!

After motoring for several hours the engine started playing up, revving by itself, then spluttering to its death. Andy found there was bad contamination in the Cochin fuel and had to change filters continuously and bleed the engine. The cooling system also developed problems and the subsequent lack of raw water in the exhaust system melted a hole in the plastic water trap. Then the log lost its impeller, so we couldn't tell our distance travelled or speed—not a good day! Fortunately there was a diversion, a group of killer whales chose that moment to visit.

With their distinctive black and white markings they were quite magnificent in the deep blue water, but at twelve metres long, the length of our boat, they seemed enormous as they played right under the bow. They also made us think of home as they are commonly seen in British Columbian waters and the boys had loved watching them in the Vancouver Aquarium.

"But I thought they only liked cold water," Colin commented.

"No," said Andy, "this is the second time I have seen them in the tropics."

In fact, the group that we encountered in the Indian Ocean were pelagic orcas. Whereas the ones back home have been studied in depth and are known to have their local territories and diet of salmon and seals, little is known about the lifestyle of the ocean going killer whales and many people have since expressed their envy of our sighting.

The Maldives promised a special magic and we were not disappointed. The archipelago is about six hundred kilometres south-west of India and it consists of almost twelve hundred coral islands, some two hundred being inhabited. Each island is surrounded by a coral reef that encloses a shallow lagoon and these are collectively grouped into atolls, or atolu, a Maldivian name which has since entered the English language. There are twenty-six atolls in all and they stretch seven hundred and fifty kilometres from north to south, straddling the equator, and one hundred and eighteen kilometres from east to west.

We were heading for North Malé atoll, almost half the way down the chain, as we had to clear-in with officials at Malé, the capital.

The westerly winds were light and we were being increasingly set to the east by the strong current. We trimmed our sails, coming closer and closer on the wind, and finally ended up beating, zig-zagging as the wind was from ahead. In the black of night it seemed to take forever to reach the entrance; at one point we couldn't seem to get nearer than 2 3 nautical miles! At dawn while the sky was still tinged with pink, the breeze filled in, giving us an exhilarating sail through the sandy islets into the vast blue lagoon.

The island capital is tiny, barely more than two square kilometres despite land reclamations, with its newest, tallest building only five floors high. Its skyline was dominated by a golden dome, aglow in the sun, that we were to learn, was the Grand Friday Mosque.

"It's definitely a Moslem country," Colin had already observed. He had heard the loudspeakered tape recording of the Muezzin calling the faithful to prayers. We had been to other Moslem countries during our travels—Tunisia, Turkey, and Morocco, besides the recent visits to Indonesia and Malaysia.

Although Buddhism had been widely practised, in 1153 A.D. the sultan of the Maldives embraced the Islam faith and ordered the country to become Muslim. Today, no other religion is permitted, and Islam is fundamental to all aspects of life. It is a liberal form, however, and women do not have to observe purdah, the wearing of clothing that conceals them completely, when they go out. As in Indonesia there are also local beliefs, with the evil spirits from the sea, land and sky being blamed for everything that is not explained by religion or education. Spells and potions are provided by the local hakeem, or medicine man, while getting a divorce is even easier; all you say is 'I divorce you' three times and the marriage is over!

It was too deep to anchor outside the breakwater so we drifted around until Customs and Immigration came out to see us. They were most welcoming and advised we could go into the commercial harbour.

"Although it's crowded you'll be fine, but keep over by the fish market for the best depth," they told us. "At the moment there's plenty of water in the channel."

We tied alongside a power boat, it was next to the fish market which as the afternoon progressed became a hive of activity. The fishing boats, most picturesque with their distinctive high, curved bows, were laden with pelagic bonito and tuna. Obviously they knew something we didn't; we hadn't caught a thing on this ocean trip!

Motoring alongside the wharf by dinghy, we had to be careful to avoid the many stern anchor lines. The fishermen nodded or smiled, they were used to foreign yachts here, and a young lad held up a bunch of fish by their tails for the boys to admire.

The town is neatly laid out, with streets made of coral rubble and buildings brightly painted. A quarter of the Maldives' 200,000 population lives in Malé. They are small in stature, and are a mix of Aryan, Dravidian, Arab and African. It is thought that the Dravidian population from south India came as early as the fourth century B.C., with Aryans from India and Sri Lanka arriving some five hundred years later. The Arab traders en route to the Far East were frequent visitors as were many other nationalities.

In the early 16th century the Portuguese decided they wanted to profit by this trade. In 1558 they killed the Maldivian sultan and took over the country. The rule only lasted fifteen years. Other than this the Maldives has been independent. Although a British protectorate from 1887-1965, Britain did not interfere in its internal affairs. In 1965 the country gained full sovereignty. It is now the smallest state of the United Nations.

The Maldives has had a couple of recent colourful incidents. The first was in 1978 when the president fled to Singapore reputedly taking with him the contents of the treasury. The second, a year before our visit, was a coup by local businessmen using Sri Lankan mercenaries. It was put down by an Indian task force. One learns while travelling that there are constant conflicts happening all around the world, and we always tried to keep up with current news by listening to the B.B.C. World Service.

The Arabs called the Maldives the 'Money Isles' as there were large quantities of the cowrie shells that were used as an international currency. Besides the cowries we found many other varieties of interesting shells due to some recent dredging. With the boat apart, for Andy to complete the engine and log repairs, it had seemed best for the boys and I to retreat ashore, so we had plenty of time to search. Although it is forbidden to collect live mollusks in the islands the officials gave us permission to collect those that had been long buried. The boys were delighted with so many new varieties, especially the gastropods, the mollusks with a single shell.

"Look," said Colin holding one up triumphantly. "It's a textile cone. I was just reading about them last night."

Textiles are variable in colour and pattern; Colin's find was deep brown and white with horizontal pyramid markings, eight centimetres in length. It was indeed dramatic but I was glad there was no live body. One of our reference books informed us that an octopus stung by a textile cone is likely to die within twenty-four hours, with a remote chance of humans dying from cardiac or respiratory failure from their venom. We looked and dug further with enthusiasm and found several more cones, including the *Conus Maldivas* with its zebra-like bands spaced with gold.

Our Turkish-American friend Tanil and Australian Annette on *Kelebek* had ordered some t-shirts here a month previously and had asked us on the single sideband radio if we would pick them up. It was a pleasant atmosphere as we wandered the streets whilst trying to find the store, although interestingly there were very few women about and when I was taking a photo of the young girls who were coming out of school, they immediately hid their faces.

Many of the shops were geared for tourists. The goods, particularly the clothing, were brightly coloured, attractively designed and inexpensive. The *Kelebek* custom designed t-shirts were an exceptional deal—20 for $60.

"Will you do some for us too?" I asked.

"How long will you be here?" was the reply.

"About ten days."

"I'm not sure. It's Ramadan now you know."

We had been in Turkey during the Islam month of Ramadan. The people had really slowed down and had become quite irritable due to the required fasting between sunrise and sunset, which includes eating, drinking, smoking and sex!

On our way back to the boat we stopped at a hardware and fishing store. "Can we buy one of these fishing boxes for our shells?" requested Jamie.

It was an excellent idea and we bought three, one each for the boys and one for the family collection. Previously new shells had rattled around the cabins until I packed them away in boxes to be sent home. The fishing boxes provided sorting trays and the boys were subsequently able to compare their finds, keeping only the best samples and quickly returning those alive to their natural habitat.

Repairs completed and having obtained permission to visit the islands, we headed out. We were only allowed to cruise in North Malé Atoll but it is a huge lagoon, about 30 by 20 nautical miles, and full of many smaller atolls. We could see the sandy islets sparkling white in the brilliant blue, way into the distance, and it was an utterly beautiful sight.

We first went to Furuno, just a few miles to the north. The resort was closed for renovation so we had the beach to ourselves, except for hundreds of highly mobile, characterful hermit crabs, and the anchorage was almost deserted. It was blissful diving into the water, although very hot in places. Fish were abundant around the boat, but at the drop-off of the reef the diving was amazing. We had never seen such large, brilliantly coloured fish in such quantities. I will never forget swimming with Jamie, holding his hand, and at times not being able to see him for fish.

We went to several anchorages, some having an island, although the maximum elevation was only three metres, on which there were mostly resorts, and other sunken atolls that appeared varying shades of blue under the surface. Many hours were spent snorkelling daily, and at most other times, when we weren't doing school, the boys seemed to be in the water. A particularly popular activity was roaring around behind the dinghy on a huge rubber ring, that had been a Christmas present from Singapore, or just jumping on it from the boat. There was only one other yacht, whose owners left their boat in Furono to fly home to a family emergency in the States. Most other yachts had called in here earlier in the year on their way to the Red Sea.

Although the economy has been based on fishing, since the early 70s tourism has become a major source of revenue. Now there are over sixty resorts with many more planned. We were able to visit some of the 5-star facilities that cost guests an arm and a leg. It was most enjoyable sitting in luxury over a coffee or beer reading the newspapers that are flown in every day. In Kurumba we met some people who offered us their shower. With such clean hair I didn't go diving for a couple of days!

We also called in at Furukolufushi, one of the two club Meds, distinctive with its sweeping thatched roof. They weren't very keen on us visiting initially as they were just about to serve lunch. As Club Meds are 'everything included' I think they thought we were going to dig in for free! However, they did suggest we come back later. The boys were able to join other kids in a t-shirt printing craft programme and were thrilled with their parrot and angel fish designs.

Except for Furuno, one could seldom anchor in depths of less than 90 feet, a heavy strain for our electric windlass with our all-chain rode, and when it finally burnt out it presented Andy with another repair challenge—which of course he solved admirably although it took many hours of labour. There's no doubt, that when sailing off the beaten track there are times when one has to be very practical and resourceful.

After a week we returned to Malé. The weather on occasion had been quite stormy. With the south-east monsoon imminent it was time to head south. As we entered the commercial harbour, one of the resort commuter boats beckoned us over, indicating we were welcome to tie alongside. We accepted their offer and went ashore to clear out with the officials and order some duty free beer and wine. The wine should have been delivered that afternoon but it didn't arrive. Then we realized it was the Moslem Holy Day and, of course, Ramadan.

However, we did find an excellent supermarket. They even had Spanish canned pimentos that were cheaper than in Spain. It was amazing what odds and ends we were able to find in the side streets, although the biggest challenge was sugar. On our return to the harbour we found some melons had just arrived by ship; it seemed the whole town turned out to buy them, as little fruit can grow on the infertile sandy islands.

That evening the skipper on the tourist boat presented us with a bill—$125 for tying alongside!

"I think we'll have to be creative with this," commented Andy. As everyone in the Maldives had been so friendly it was quite unexpected.

"What about all the rides we've given them ashore?" said Colin indignantly.

"And you've lent them lots of your tools, Daddy," added Jamie.

"We've even entertained them," I commented.

Despite being a modern, fast, multi-passenger boat that took guests to the resorts, its crew had been going back and forth on a waterlogged sunfish dinghy hull. They had therefore been very grateful for the rides the boys had given them in our Zodiac. We decided to give them a return bill—$150 for dinghy rides ashore. Our duty free arrived and we cast off without further mention from either side. Unfortunately, the water in the channel wasn't deep enough for us to leave for several hours, but there was no further interaction, maybe because, we noticed, their dinghy had finally sunk! It could have marred our visit to the Maldives but in fact it had provided us with a good laugh.

As we departed, to head back to the ocean, Colin commented wistfully, as he did with so many of our visits, "Do you think we'll ever be back here again?"

"Who knows," said Andy. "As the oceans rise with global warming the islands may not be here much longer; you noticed how low they all are."

"We also heard that the whole island chain is sinking," I added. "If this is so, they might disappear in as little as twenty-five years. However, we're now going to Chagos which is reputedly just as idyllic. It's about as remote as you can get in the tropics, with wonderful shells, fishing and diving, and it has no population—except for cruisers."

9. Chagos

Salomon and Peros Banhos Atolls

We had a frustrating trip down to the Chagos group as there were southerly winds and a strong current pushing us east. In fact, for a while we were heading for Australia! It meant that we missed Gan and the surrounding islands which are said to be the real, unspoiled Maldives. However, with a tack and the wind backing we fetched the Salomon group three and a half days later for another wonderful landfall.

As dawn broke, tiny sandy islets dotted with palms floated up on the horizon, then the atoll began to take form. Entering the pass, we were greeted by a large pod of frolicking dolphins who jumped and spun beside us in the translucent turquoise water.

Small, but protected, Salomon consists of ten islands that surround a lagoon, about four nautical miles in diameter. Slowly we made our way across to Tanil and Annette on *Kelebek* who were with five other yachts. It was the most beautiful of anchorages, with white sand beaches and lush green vegetation beyond. It wasn't hard to understand why the uninhabited and inaccessible Salomon has become a mecca for yachtsmen, with many returning for increasing periods of time.

We anchored off Takamaka Island.

"What a wonderful name," I commented. "It would be great for a boat."

It was so easy having no officials to deal with. Immediately Tanil and

Annette motored over in their dinghy and came straight on board. We hadn't seen them since Christmas in Phuket and spent all morning catching up.

"It's fantastic here, excellent diving and fishing, and heart of palm for the asking," Tanil told us enthusiastically, "and down at Boddam at the other end of the atoll some of the trees at the old abandoned settlement still bear fruit."

"We brought some heart of palm and fish for your lunch," said Annette holding up a bag.

"Marvellous, why don't you stay and join us?".

It was an idyllic week at Takamaka. The diving on the reefs was spectacular, although we never saw quite the density of fish as in the Maldives. There was a huge variety of shells—cowries, cones, harps, helmets, clams, tritons, augers, miters, tuns, bonnets, drupes, conchs, top shells and murexes. A bag was soon over the stern with the shells whose bodies I'd been unable to remove. Our shell books were constantly in use and the new boxes quickly loaded with specimens, although as always we were conservationist in our collecting and returning of molluscs to their natural habitat.

The vegetation ashore was dense, the palms angling out over the beach. Tanil took us to the far side of Takamaka and showed us the best size tree for the sweetest heart of palm, the tender centre of the coconut palm. These trees grow in such abundance in the islands that they have to be cut back constantly to keep the trails open. It was hot, hard work cutting it down, but a rewarding task, providing a delicious vegetable that lasted for several meals. We had it cold with a vinaigrette dressing and hot with a bechamel sauce.

Annette also showed me how she made yogurt and gave me some culture, so yogurt was added to our diet and was good for additional sauces besides. There was no problem with milk as we had purchased many cases of 'longlife' milk in Sri Lanka. This heat-treated milk is a boon for sailors. We have been using it since the sixties in the Caribbean, however the taste has improved over the years and, if chilled, it is hard to tell the difference from fresh. It can now be found all over the world with various levels of fat content.

As the fish conveniently ran between the sandy spits at dusk, we barbecued almost every night. Jamie would cast his line and always had a perfect crevalle jack within minutes. He didn't bother to reel it in, it was so easy to haul it up the beach.

A perfect fish every night!

We'd build a fire of wood and coconut husks, making sure there were no coconut crabs inside, then eat by the glowing embers, watching the sun go down, the palm fronds silhouetted against the deep orange sky.

On other nights we varied the menu; Andy shot a huge grouper with his spear gun and we found a colony of the spider conch *lambis lambis* so made a large pot of chowder. Others came to join us, frequently Americans Peter and Sandy on *Rai Riva*. There were also French, German and South African yachts with us in the lagoon.

A group went to the outer reef early one morning at the bottom of the lowest spring tide. There were few lobster inside the lagoon but we hoped to catch some leather or green lobster on the drop-off at the edge of the reef as we'd been taught in French Polynesia. It was a rough walk over the coral. The sea urchin spines were so long we had to look carefully so they didn't go through our reef shoes.

"If you get a piece in your foot," I told the boys, "you should pee on it at once!" As they gave me one of those looks I explained, "It takes away

Idyllic Takamaka Island

all the pain because the acid dissolves the calcium spines." This treatment was learned from West Indian fishermen and it really works.

I had taken the video camera along, hoping to record a successful trip. We'd not found any lobster since buying this camera. I also wanted to get some practice as I was still struggling with filming and simultaneously talking into the microphone. My eyesight also didn't help as I had to remove my glasses and couldn't focus the viewfinder enough to completely compensate for my deficit. Seeing that Andy had found some lobsters I went over to film him.

As he turned around holding his catch he suddenly started waving it around.

"He must think this is photogenic," I thought, but it was awfully hard to focus.

Then he called out, "Why on earth are you filming a lobster without a head!?"

"I didn't know," I replied sheepishly.

"Thank goodness I'm not short sighted!"

"It's better than being bald!"

The hunt was successful, although Andy dashing forward after a receding wave to peer into the chasms over the reef edge didn't fill me with joy. I had an uncharacteristic flash of our vulnerability here in such a remote location.

The Chagos Archipelago is all that remains of the British Indian Ocean Territory. Scattered over an area of 54,389 square kilometres the total land area is only sixty square kilometres. Salomon and Beros Banhos atolls lie to the north with Diego Garcia, the largest island, to the south, across the Great Chagos Bank. The group was first discovered by the Portuguese, then settled by the French in 1776 who used it primarily as a leper colony. The Archipelago became British in 1814 at the Treaty of Versailles. In 1970 the U.S. leased Diego Garcia, with its old war-time RAF airfield, as a military base.

The only current population in the Chagos group are the U.S. military, with a handful of British administrators. The Military patrol the other islands periodically and we heard they are generous with the yachtsmen, bringing welcome goodies such as steaks, produce and ice cold Coke. They didn't come during our visit but later we heard that a lady who had suffered a stroke had been flown home from the Diego Garcia. Her husband had to continue single-handed.

Even a tropical paradise can be unpredictable and we awoke one morning to sheet rain and high winds. We had heard the front was coming and had moved down to the former settlement of Boddam at the southern end of the atoll, which has a more sheltered anchorage. As the wind clocked around from the south-east to north, we had to keep a diligent watch in the water as there were many coral heads that came close to the surface.

"I think everything's full now," called Jamie who was in charge of watching the rain fill our tanks. "The main tanks, all the jerry cans and your washing tub as well, Mummy." It hadn't taken long with such a heavy downpour.

"The rain is so beautifully cool," he continued, standing with his arms spread wide. "I just don't want to come below."

With everything battened down it was hot and humid in the cabin.

"We must get on with school," I reminded him.

The boys had been working hard. With Duncan being in a regular school and joining us at the end of June, they were determined that when he arrived they too would have finished their school year. I was delighted with their motivation, looking forward to the time off myself!

As the front passed we were able to go ashore and explore the old ruins of the settlement. A British flag was flying at the pier and several of the old buildings were recognizable, such as the church, the manager's and administrator's houses, shops, a school and the old cistern that still provides many a yachtsman with water and a shower. We picked some limes from the old trees, and some fruit called bilimbies, which were incredibly sour. A sign on one building said Yacht Club, put there by a yachtsman several years previously. Visiting sailors had written their yacht's names on the inside walls. Those more ambitious had also painted a picture of their vessels and we persuaded Andy to do a rendering of our *Bagheera* spinnaker cat.

Away from the sea the crumbling buildings were dank, many taken over by the undergrowth. Shivering, partly from the damp, but also from the eeriness of the derelict buildings, I commented, "It's strange to think of this thriving community just packing up and leaving."

"They were from Mauritius and in the copra business, I understand," said Annette.

"Maybe it wasn't profitable," said Andy, "although it's hard to believe with this dense growth."

The archipelago was originally peopled by Portuguese fishermen, in addition to lepers sent from Mauritius. By the beginning of the 20th century there were over four hundred and fifty families in residence. Due to the nature of leprosy, which remained endemic, the men died sooner than the women, resulting in a majority female population. A matriarchal society developed, with the women setting the rules. It became accepted practice for women to have extramarital relations while their husbands were out fishing!

The islands were called the Oil Islands, due to the oil extracted from the copra, the dried meat of the coconut. The people worked for a French company and were known as Ilois. In 1970 when the U.S. took over Diego Garcia as a base, one of the conditions was the removal of the population from the archipelago, so the two thousand Ilois were sent back to Mauritius. The story is a sad one as some of these people were fifth generation islanders; eventually they were given compensation by the British government.

We had a last evening with new friends at Ile Anglaise, and found the mixture of cruising plans incredible. One boat was heading north-east to Thailand, another south-east to Australia. Those heading west were bound for the Seychelles, the Suez Canal, Madagascar and Tanzania, while one couple, having found the ultimate paradise, had decided to stay in Salomon for several months.

There was no wind for our trip to Peros Banhos, an atoll larger but less protected than Chagos, twenty miles to the west. We motored in seas that were calm, unusual in the Indian Ocean, and the boys could do school work in the cockpit.

Our landfall was Petite Ile Coquillage, one of the many islets which dot the atoll's rim. Although the diving was good it was the island itself that we enjoyed the most. There were hundreds of tame baby terns, also noddies and frigate birds, and several good specimens for the shell collection. Colin was particularly thrilled with an orange-mouthed helmet shell.

On arrival at the Moresby Islands on the far side of the atoll, Andy went straight over the side with his spear gun. The boys and I barely had our shells out to categorize before he returned.

"What's the matter?" I asked. "Have you forgotten something?"

"No, the water is really murky and there are several sharks around that I don't recognize." It was uncharacteristic for Andy to show concern about sharks.

"Doesn't sound great for shooting a fish!" I replied. "Don't worry we can treat ourselves to some of the steaks I bought in Sri Lanka."

We had replaced our 12 volt refrigerator in Australia with an engine-driven system with holding plates. This allowed us to have a freezer section at the back of the fridge and we were really enjoying the flexibility it gave us. Before then, however creative we had been with canned and dried goods, our meals had always been mushy. Now with frozen meat, and a locker full of fresh vegetables from both India and the Maldives, it was just like eating at home.

Heading out to Ile Diamont, another of the atoll's islets, we were beset by squalls, so decided on the more protected anchorage at Ile du Coin in the south. During the night we were awakened by a particularly vicious squall, with wind gusting from the north-east, putting *Bagheera* on a lee shore and dangerously close to the reef. It was one of our worst nights at anchor. As the wind strength increased Andy went forward to let out more anchor chain but looking astern from the cockpit I fleetingly glimpsed a coral head. Andy took in the chain again but was concerned we would drag, so one of us kept watch all night, with the motor ready to reduce the strain on the anchor in the strongest gusts.

Tanil was very cheerful on the radio the next morning.

"We've just cleared the pass at Salomon," he told us. "There's a great breeze and we're really looking forward to having a barbecue with you tonight."

"I think we're leaving. I don't want another night like the one we've just had," replied Andy dourly.

"The weather looks terrific now and I gather Ile Rouquet is the place to go. Although it doesn't look so sheltered on the chart it's very protected," replied Tanil undaunted.

"It was great here last night, *Bagheera,*" a voice interjected. We had spotted one other yacht anchored in the distance the previous day.

"Can't we stay?" pleaded Jamie.

"Daddy," called Colin excitedly, "you should see the sky. It completely cleared while you were talking on the radio."

"I can't believe it," said Andy peering up the companion way.

"Okay *Kelebek*, it looks as though we're on for a barbecue."

"What's this," chipped in Peter from *Rai Riva* who was still anchored in Salomon atoll, "the Captain's decision being overruled?" he teased.

"It's terrible I agree, but damn it, they're right!"

"Don't worry," sympathized Peter, "I'm generally overruled by the dog!"

It was a great day. While the boys did school Andy caught up on sleep and then we went ashore and discovered the ruins of another settlement. Along the beach and covered with creeper, these buildings didn't seem eerie at all and we found callaloo, a big-leaved vegetable, and cut down more heart of palm. Colin even found a first, a fusiformis conch. It wasn't a very dramatic conch shell in either size or colour but it is always exciting to find the first of a species. We were just entering the known limits for this variety.

The anchorage at Ile Rouquet was beautiful, a long white sand spit, with the sea a bright turquoise in front and a deep blue behind. In the distance two yachts were passing to the south of the atoll on passage to the Seychelles from Salomon; one had a traditional rig with all her sails flying. It was a fairy-tale scene with the colours so brilliant and the yachts dancing along the sparkling surf by the reef.

Kelebek and *Bagheera* left for the Seychelles the next morning after a relaxed evening and a good night's sleep. Earlier *Rai Riva* had left from Salomon so was only a few miles behind. The weather was perfect, with winds from the south-east blowing 15 knots, although there were some standing waves during the day and some very bouncy ones at night. We headed south to avoid the equatorial doldrums and maintained good winds all the way.

As usual, we quickly became acclimatized and into the routine. The boys continued with their schoolwork, Jamie mastering his three and four-times table, and I finished reading him C.S. Lewis' 'The Lion, the Witch and the Wardrobe'. We caught a small yellowfin tuna, one of my favourites, and a barracuda.

"It's surprising to find a barracuda in such deep waters," remarked Andy, "and I think we had better put it back. They are so smelly to clean and at ten pounds it could have ciguatera."

Ciguatera is a toxin that proliferates when a reef is damaged, moving up the food chain through coral eating organisms, then to the fish which prey on them. The toxin accumulates in the human body causing serious itching, tingling and vomiting, and can be fatal. We had been aware of it during all our tropical sailing, particularly in French Polynesia and avoided eating any fish which inhabit the reef.

As usual, we ate well with so much time to prepare food whilst underway.

"We're really having an international meal," I joked one night. "There's beef from Sri Lanka, onions and garlic from India, canned pimentos from Spain that were bought in the Maldives, oyster sauce from Thailand, rice from Australia, and heart of palm from Chagos."

"And Sprite from Singapore," added Jamie.

"And how about beer from Indonesia and wine from South Africa," said Andy.

The weather charts concerned us as we approached the Seychelles, as a deepening low had shown up on the weather maps from Australia. Although a thousand miles behind us, it was closing in and we didn't want to be caught in a cyclone at sea. Every day it grew deeper but to our surprise for three days it wasn't noted on the American weather charts sent out from Diego Garcia, although the French ones from Réunion also showed it quite clearly. It would have been too late for yachts to have taken evasive action had they relied solely on the American weather service. Once again it was brought home to us how much weather forecasting relies on an individual's interpretation of the masses of data received and how important it is to use every source of information when at sea.

As the winds veered to the south-west we had to beat up the island of Mahé to the capital, Victoria. The low was now classified as a tropical storm but was still five hundred miles away, so we had reached shelter in plenty of time. It was after 3:30 p.m. when we arrived at the harbour and too late to clear in. We anchored off the lighthouse, then indulged in luxurious hot showers and fresh sheets as we could fill our tanks with water and do laundry the next day—what bliss!

10. The Seychelles

Mahé, Praslin, La Digue and Aldabra

Although it was Sunday, Security and Health came out to clear us. Immigration came later, after we had moved into the harbour. The small yacht club was most welcoming and with no banks open they suggested we eat and drink on the tab. There was only one shock, a $10 a day fee for anchoring. If we had been just two feet longer it would have been $20. (Recently I read it had gone up to $100!)

Kelebek and *Rai Riva* arrived the next day. *Rai Riva* had planned a landfall in Mayotte, an island between Tanzania and Madagascar, but with the threat of the cyclone had decided to alter course for the Seychelles.

The boys and I were ashore as they approached. I called Andy on the handheld radio from town.

"*Bagheera, Bagheera*, this is Rikki-tikki-tavi."

"Go ahead, Rikki," Andy replied.

"Andy, we'll be a bit longer as I've only just changed money. We're now in pursuit of ice cream!"

"Okay, see you later."

"Rikki-tikki-tavi, this is Baloo," quickly followed.

"Go ahead, Baloo," I replied, recognising Tanil's voice.

"Rikki, Baloo is drooling at the thought of ice cream. He would like a very large tub."

"Any particular flavour, Baloo?"

"Any would be wonderful."

Tanil's refrigeration had broken down some weeks previously; after a hot trip at sea, they were panting for something cool.

For anyone not familiar with Rudyard Kipling, Rikki-tikki-tavi was the mongoose in The Jungle Book and Baloo (pronounced Bar-loo) was the bear. Incidentally, Bagheera, the black panther, is pronounced Bag-eera.

Victoria is a small, charming town, with the courthouse and post office giving an air of colonial days. In the centre stands a distinctive clock tower, a replica of the one on Vauxhall Bridge in London that was given to Queen Victoria in 1903.

The people dressed flamboyantly, with a sophistication found in so many of the places that have a French background. Also typically French was the lack of racial inhibition and there was every colour and feature imaginable arising from a background of African, Indian, Arab, Chinese and European. Today, both English and French are official languages for the 70,000 inhabitants, with a French creole the Lingua Franca. The dialect is very similar to that of Mauritius in the south Indian Ocean and Martinique in the Caribbean.

The cyclone progressed quite slowly but with barometric pressure down to 970; it was a low one. Two days later it hit, but gusts were limited to 45 knots in the protected harbour, with frequent vicious squalls of rain. Several boats dragged their anchors. On the radio they advised that no-one should go out to sea. Its track was unusual as it passed the Seychelles to the south, then headed north-west, going as far north as 3°s. Then it turned back to the east deluging the Seychelles again, although this area is theoretically out of the cyclone belt.

Unable to cruise the outer islands we made the most of our time in Mahé. We travelled around in a Mini Moke, lent to us by friends who worked for Barclays Bank. Dramatic in scenery, with the white sand beaches and green vegetation, there are also spectacular views from the volcanic hills that run through the centre of the island. Tea plantations covered some of the hills, although copra and cinnamon are the traditional agricultural exports.

We visited the Craft Village, located in a peaceful plantation, and went on to the botanical gardens. The gate to the area housing the giant tortoises was open and we wandered inside. The tortoises were so used to people they were very tame and, like their Galapagos cousins, liked having their heads rubbed. It was only when we were leaving that the cleaning lady came rushing back, somewhat flustered when she realized we had been inside. The giant tortoises are indigenous to Aldabra, another island governed by the Seychelles, that we planned to visit on our way to Kenya.

We also saw the huge seed of the coco de mer tree. The nuts on the female tree are famous for resembling voluptuous feminine buttocks; appropriately the male flower is somewhat more phallic!

As the drizzle continued we looked to indoor pursuits and saw three films in two days, our first since Australia. Two were aboard *Rai Riva* after which the boys continually asked, "Can't we get a TV and video too. We could watch movies every night!"

Andy reminded them, "The problem is that you need a multi-system TV when travelling. 12 volt ones are hard to find and are generally big and expensive. Besides, one of the joys of cruising is getting away from 'the box'!"

It was still overcast and stormy when we headed out to the island of Praslin. It was not a pleasant trip in the lumpy seas, Colin was seasick and I felt terrible. *Kelebek* left at the same time but they headed south having an even rougher ride into wind, but thrilled that they had seen a huge whale shark very close to the boat.

Praslin is the second largest island in the Seychelles, about twenty nautical miles northeast of Mahé. We anchored off Chauvre Souris and took the bus to St Anne's to have our official yellow document signed by the police—security being tight on the islands. The pace of life here is much slower than in Mahé, with little traffic and no towns. With the white sands, trailing flowers and sleepy atmosphere, it felt rather like the Ile des Pins in New Caledonia, one of our favourite spots on our travels across the South Pacific.

The police had noted on our document that we had to leave by seven o'clock the next morning, but as we hadn't had time to see the main attraction of Praslin, the Vallée du Mai, we decided to stretch the time a little and depart that afternoon. About nine o'clock we set out by bus to visit the park, which is high in the granite mountain ridge in the centre of the island.

"Oh no," said Andy suddenly.

"What's the matter?"

"Everyone duck down. The bus is stopping at the police station!"

The park has wonderful trails through dense undergrowth, and we were treated to a fleeting glance of two of the rare black parrots. Much of the valley is taken up with the broad leaved coco de mer palms which have been the cause of much discussion over the years. Gordon of Khartoum thought it was the tree of good and evil knowledge used by Adam and Eve but, because of its nut, most interest has been in its supposed aphrodisiac qualities. Not only is the shape of the mature nut intriguing but the tree also has a titillating method of propagation as it only takes place when the flower of the female tree is close to the long, dangling catkin of the male!

Also part of the fascination of the coco de mer is its longevity. Some of the trees in the park are up to 800 years old. They only bear fruit after twenty-five years and the nuts take seven years to mature. Nuts were selling for around $100; I'm not quite sure what one would do with them!

We departed for La Digue mid-afternoon. Riding around on our rented bicycles, with Jamie bringing his own from the boat, we found the island delightfully unspoilt. We were interested to see that vegetables were being grown, but only for local consumption.

I had been shocked by the price of the produce in the Victoria market, cabbages for example were $12 each! Most fruit and vegetables were flown in from South Africa. It appeared the government had put the local producers out of business by making it law that growers sell only to the government, and setting buying rates that made growing unprofitable. Government corruption seemed to be rife in many areas, with foreign aid being cut off as a consequence. We met one of the doctors funded by Britain. His contract was not being renewed.

"The British government has decided that if the President can afford his own private jet, the country can afford to pay medical personnel themselves" he told us.

The family were moving to Bundaberg in Australia, and were not entirely happy with the arrangement.

"We loved Bundaberg," I reassured them. "In fact, we thought about buying some land there. But tell us about the politics of the Seychelles; from all accounts it's been pretty explosive."

"Yes, for a country that was so passive for so long it's really made up for lost time in the last twenty years."

Uninhabited until the 17th century, the Seychelles were first discovered by the Portuguese, with the British making the first recorded landing. Pirates and privateers also stopped at the islands to rest and replenish supplies. In 1742 Mahé de Labourdonnais, the governor of Mauritius, sent a party to check out the area and they named the main island after him. The French and their slaves started arriving during the latter part of the 18th century. The Seychelles became British in 1814 after the Napoleonic wars and the Treaty of Paris, when Mauritius came under Britain. However the French culture remained dominant including the language. In 1902 the Seychelles became a crown colony that was administered from London.

All was apparently peaceful until 1964 when political parties were formed. There were two, the Seychelles People's United Party under France-Albert René and the Seychelles Democratic Party under James Mancham. Both leaders were lawyers. Mancham's party was made up of planters and business people while the SPUP was socialist. When independence from Britain was given to the islands in 1976 there was a coalition of the two parties, Sir James Mancham being the first president, with René the Prime Minister.

Mancham immediately set about advertising the Seychelles for tourism, flitting around the world to entice the rich, and he was very successful. However the SPUP felt the islands were becoming a rich man's playground with not enough money going to the poor. Just one year after independence René carried out a coup, taking over the islands while Mancham was in London attending a conference of Commonwealth leaders.

Resistance movements were formed in Britain, Australia and South Africa and there were several bungled attempts to regain the islands.

"One group even tried to come in as South Africans on a rugby tour," the doctor continued, "but Customs discovered weapons in their baggage."

There was also an attempted coup by majors in the Seychelles' army. Although the coups were foiled, tourism had almost dried up.

"Rumour has it that René is going to introduce a two party political system again. He'll have to if he wants to get any foreign aid."

He was right. In 1992 elections were held with René winning and Mancham in the minority—although Mancham contested the results were rigged! Tourism is again flourishing and one of the government's primary goals is self-sufficiency of food production.

Traditionally fish has been the staple diet of the Seychelles and stopping at the shipyard in La Digue, we were impressed by the standard of boat building; the fishing boats were massive and well-constructed.

They were made out of takamaka wood which grows in the Seychelles in abundance. Now we knew where the name of our favourite Chagos island came from. The carpenters asked us if we had bought some tuna, informing us that there was a processing and canning plant on Mahé. It was a great tip, we bought two cases very inexpensively. The tuna was flavourful and succulent and it lasted us until South Africa.

Boat building in La Digue

It was time to go back to Mahé to stock up on everything and get our clearance from the officials. *Kelebek* had been heading for Mayotte but was also returning to Mahé as their engine water pump had given up. They brought over a mahi mahi for dinner. After helping Peter and Sandy on *Rai Riva* celebrate their twenty-fifth wedding anniversary, we went off with Lyn in the Mini Moke to shop. Later we had a visit from a shell collector who swapped some of his local finds for some of Colin's shells. We found out later that he had gone away with some rarities which Colin had found in Chagos.

Andy cleared out of the Seychelles but also obtained permission to visit Aldabra. We went north about Mahé into very rough, uncomfortable seas. Despite having put on an ear patch twelve hours in advance I was seasick—ugh! Usually this method is infallible for me. During the night it became quite cold and we had to break out sweaters, shivering after the constant 32°c.

Once off the bank the waves lengthened, giving an easier ride, but at nine o'clock the following night the autopilot jammed—of course not on the course we had in mind! With the wind on the beam Felicity, our wind vane, coped well. Andy had added a small skeg aft of the rudder in Australia, to add directional stability in quartering seas and it did a great job in stopping the back of *Bagheera* from skittering around. He had also increased the length of the wind vane's paddle in Singapore which made it very powerful.

The seas built again and became very lumpy with a 25 knot wind that increased to 30, gusting 35. At nine o'clock the next night the 'sail' broke on the windvane. As I hand steered Andy rigged our small emergency Autohelm 800, but as he was working on it we became worried about a clunking sound from the rudder below. Andy was convinced it was the lower bearing that had been made in Thailand. We had visions of the bronze shell grinding away at the hull causing a leak that would be hard to sustain.

When we turned on the Autohelm 800 the clunking increased so I went back to hand steering, nursing the rudder along in an unpredictable, jerking motion. Meanwhile Andy suspended upside-down in the lazarette, and fibreglassed a thick re-inforcing collar around the base of the rudder stock tube. Later we found considerable wearing had occurred. With the motion and fumes he came as close to being seasick as at anytime during our trip.

As he surfaced looking green I repressed an, "I want you to remember how it feels." It didn't seem quite the right moment!

Meanwhile, as all this was transpiring, the boys were in fine form. Full of energy in the mere 28°c, they had got out the Lego and were cheerfully chatting and building away. What a contrast in worlds just a few steps apart, battling the blustery elements on deck to a peaceful domestic scene below.

As we came up in the lee of the Aldabra the seas gradually flattened out. We anchored by the settlement; there was no sheltered anchorage, just the protection from the reef, as long as the wind stayed in the southeast. It looked pretty ashore with the long white beaches, casuarina trees and palms.

Aldabra is one of the largest atolls in the world, stretching twelve nautical miles from east to west, with four large islands surrounding a lagoon. Like the passes in the Tuamotu Atolls in French Polynesia, Grand Pass, the main entrance to the lagoon, can be dangerous with currents running as fast as ten knots. The lagoon itself is also shallow so there was no possibility of entry for Bagheera, although we were able to explore it by dinghy.

The atoll is inhabited only by scientists, and then for just three months a year. The warden and meteorological officer came on board to check our papers; all was in order. They told us very few private yachts had stopped here, under thirty in total they guessed. In fact, when we looked in the visitors' book ashore, which went back over the years, we were actually the twenty-seventh ever recorded.

We planned to go ashore the next morning but it was gusting over 40 knots and we were rolling badly, making it unsafe to launch the dinghy from the deck. The boys were really disappointed but soon became absorbed in school work.

"I've finished Paper 27," declared Colin triumphantly. "Now I've only got eighteen days left of school."

"How many days do we have before Duncan arrives?" asked Jamie.

"Just nineteen," I told him.

"Oh, we're going to be doing an awful lot of school. But I'm sure we'll get it done," he concluded with his usual optimism.

Meanwhile we put out a stern anchor, pulling ourselves around so we headed into the swells.

It was really calm for a change the next day. The boys rushed up on deck to pump up the dinghy and we raised it on the mainsail halyard, using the anchor windlass to get it over the side. Andy and I put on the outboard using a tackle, with pulleys rigged on *Bagheera's* wind generator post on the transom to lower it down. These systems had greatly eased the need for brute strength.

"Look at all the turtles in the water," said Colin excitedly as we motored between the reef and the beach.

"You can also see their tracks up the beach; they go ashore to lay their eggs," added Andy.

The warden and meteorological officer were most welcoming and helped us carry the dinghy up the beach. It was very neat and tidy ashore and they showed us the generator, canteen and library. Their research books were fascinating and soon we were all absorbed. Some students from the Smithsonian Institution arrived back for lunch. They were travelling on a large yacht and studying coral. French researchers also arrived. They were introducing ladybirds (ladybugs) hoping they would control the mealybugs which were sucking sap from the trees that were the giant tortoises' main food source. They were breeding the ladybirds in tanks. The plan was to release them in the south so they would blow to the north, hopefully covering the whole atoll.

Much to our delight there were giant tortoises everywhere, although they were very shy, instantly tucking their heads under their shells at the slightest sound. They are smaller than their Galapagos counterparts and it fascinated us that these two locations, the only places where species of the giant tortoise are found indigenously, could hardly be farther apart.

At the turn of the century, the Seychelles tortoise was almost killed off by British and French sailors seeking a meat supply, but now there are over 200,000 of them. They almost suffered another fate twenty years ago when Aldabra was fancied by the Americans for a military base. Fearing run-ins with conservationists, the U.S. decided on Diego Garcia and had the people there removed instead!

After enjoying the birds—ibis, heron, frigate birds and flamingoes which migrate here in their thousands, and with the white-throated rail the only remaining species of flightless bird in the Indian Ocean—and having been privileged to watch some turtles mating in the lagoon, we set sail for Africa.

"Wow!" said Jamie impressed. "We'll be going to a new continent."

"Actually, you have been to two African countries before, when we were in the Mediterranean," I reminded him.

That was hard for him to relate to. He had only been three years old when we were in the Mediterranean and after thirty-five thousand nautical miles it seemed far removed from Kenya. He went below to get the school atlas.

Africa,
The Comores,
Mayotte and
Madagascar

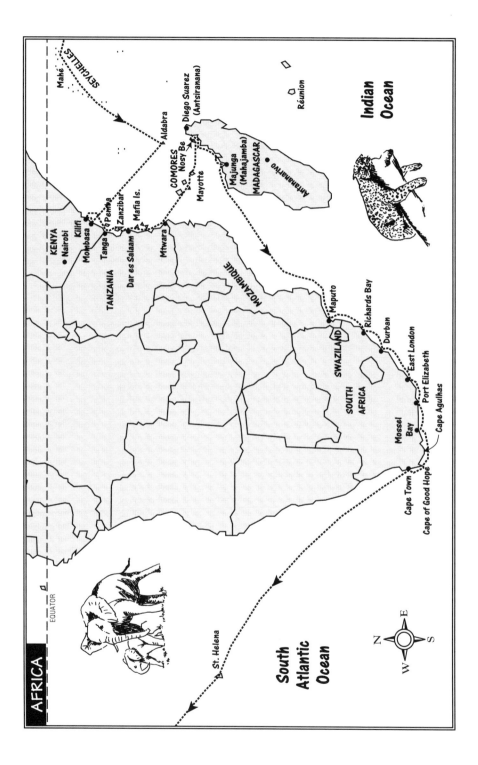

AFRICA

EQUATOR

SEYCHELLES
Mahé

Indian
Ocean

Réunion

Diego Suarez
(Antsiranana)

Aldabra

COMORES
Nosy Be

Majunga
(Mahajamba)

Mayotte

MADAGASCAR

Antananarivo

KENYA
• Nairobi
Kilifi
Mombasa
Tanga • Pemba
Zanzibar
Dar es Salaam
Mafia Is.
TANZANIA
Mtwara

MOZAMBIQUE

Maputo

Richards Bay

SWAZILAND

Durban

SOUTH
AFRICA

East London

Port Elizabeth

Cape Agulhas

Mossel
Bay

Cape Town

Cape of Good Hope

St. Helena

South
Atlantic
Ocean

N
W — E
S

11. Kenya

Mombasa, Kilifi, Nairobi
On Safari

To minimize the loads on the rudder bearing we sailed sedately for Kenya, setting only the genoa, the large foresail. 'Felicity' did a splendid job on the helm for this downwind trip with a new paddle, and although slower than our usual 150 nautical miles a day, it was a very comfortable ride.

It is usual to find a strong north setting current near the east African coast. The boys were looking forward to calculating it but, frustratingly, we didn't have a viable fix on our satellite navigator for five hours.

"I don't think there is very much current," I said finally, long after the boys had gone to bed. "The lights of Mombasa don't seem to be closing very fast."

By the time we reached the harbour entrance it was 3:00 A.M. and we calculated there had been only two knots at most.

"At least that's good news for our trip south," Andy commented.

It was not an easy entry as frequent squalls obliterated the dim leading lights and it was very cold, comparatively speaking. We anchored off the Mombasa Yacht Club. So many warnings had been given about theft in this part of the world that I felt all easily removed deck items should be taken below.

"It's almost light," said Andy, who was tired and ready for bed. "I'm sure it will be okay."

"But this is when we are most vulnerable. Being newcomers they'll think we don't know any better," I replied.

I put a few small items away then grabbed Jamie's boogie (surf) board. It had scant monetary value but of all the items it would cause the most upset if taken!

I had just stripped off for bed when search lights illuminated the cabin! It was the Marine Police.

"Why did you sneak into the harbour?" they shouted.

"We tried making contact several times on the VHF radio on Channel 16," I called back, having ducked, grabbed a towel and draped it around me, "but there was no reply." They seemed satisfied, telling us to use Channel 12 in future as Channel 16 wasn't manned, but decided to come aboard anyway to complete the official paperwork. It took quite a while and then they wanted to chat, by which time their shift was almost over, they informed us. We finally dropped our heads on the pillow at dawn.

During our trip from the Seychelles, we had started talking on the Ham radio to Tony Britchford who runs an informal net out of Kilifi, a small town about fifty kilometres north of Mombasa. A retired airline pilot, Tony enjoys the interaction with yachtsmen and he and his wife, Dorothy, are extremely hospitable and helpful to those in the area.

It had been great to talk to someone ashore about our rudder bearing problems and haul-out facilities.

"There's a railway at the Mombasa Yacht Club," Tony told us, "but last I heard it had been taken over by an old vessel with a family living on board. I doubt they'll ever move. Swinford's Boat Yard up here in Kilifi also has a railway but it is too small for you," he continued. "You could go against the wall, however, to take out the rudder."

"Sounds good, but do you have any suggestions about getting a piece of teflon? It's very hard to come by; we couldn't get it in Phuket," replied Andy.

"I think I have a piece in my garage," came the unexpected response. "I'll check later."

That evening he confirmed he not only had some teflon but it was a 15 x 15 millimetre block, more than big enough to machine out into a new bearing.

"It's all yours," Tony concluded.

"I can't believe it," replied Andy incredulously. "No-one has a piece of teflon, let alone the right size, just sitting in their garage!"

Mid-morning Tony arrived in a borrowed dinghy. He sported a huge wicker basket, a veritable Pandora's box. There were enormous apple mangoes, pineapples, local charts, a money exchange form, paludrine pills for malaria as Kenya is chloroquine resistent, an enormous pile of mail that had been collecting for three months with a friend of a friend in Mombasa and the block of teflon—which was indeed just what we needed.

All seemed wonderful until we opened our letters and found that our dear friend and frequent *Bagheera* visitor, Mary Light, had died. We first heard the news from our Vancouver friends, the Sellers, with whom we had sailed the South Pacific.

The boys were very upset.

"I do hope she got my picture," said Colin finally.

The next letter opened was from my step-daughter Alison, who told us she had taken some flowers to Mary in hospital.

'Mary was asleep when I went to see her,' she wrote, 'but I noticed that your rainbow picture was up on the wall, Colin.'

Mary was such a vibrant, unique personality and we felt a terrible sense of loss. At least, unlike my sister whose death had seemed so unfair, Mary had lived a long life, dying in her late 70s. But it was hard to accept her death in such a vacuum, so far from our mutual friends in Canada and Australia.

Mombasa is Kenya's second largest town and the oldest. Its history stretches back almost 2000 years when a Greek merchant living in Egypt reported that there was a lively trade between the Arabs and the local people here, with the Arabs trading ironwork, cloth, and olive oil for ivory, rhinoceros horn, cinnamon and slaves. Mombasa was also mentioned by Ptolemy, the Greek astronomer and geographer, in his 'Geography' in the 2nd Century A.D. It is now the largest port on the coast of East Africa, serving Uganda, Rwanda and Burundi, besides Kenya itself. With its half million population, the town now spreads beyond Mombasa Island, which is connected to the mainland by an artificial causeway, but despite its growth it has maintained a low-level profile, and has much the same oriental character as a century ago.

Fringing the dhow harbour is the old town, a labyrinth of narrow, winding streets lined with shuttered houses and open-fronted shops. Most are built of wattle and daub with occasional coral cement. We stopped to admire the massive intricately carved Swahili doors, balconies of lattice work, etched glass windows and old signs. Ethnically diverse the Arab and Asian influence is particularly evident with several mosques and frequent Hindu and Sikh temples. The distinctive styles of dress, from the women's brilliant 'kanga' outfits and head-to-foot 'buibuis' to the men's hip wraps and 'kanzu'gowns add character to the town.

To the boys' delight there were street vendors everywhere, selling carvings, gems and jewelry, soapstone, clothing, locally woven fabrics and prints.

"Come and look at this malachite chess set," called Colin.

"Look at these carved animals," cried Jamie.

There was much of interest and I made a note to stock up on presents and souvenirs, as the prices were very reasonable.

"Are you tourists?" more than one vendor asked us hesitantly.

"No, we're just here on our boat!" I answered.

"On your boat, how interesting."

Again, being tanned and not quite as trendy as tourists we weren't treated as such. Soon we were chatting like locals and I was getting valuable information about the markets while the boys were looking around without being harassed. Even those vendors who were quite persistent could be forgiven here, as their big smiles and enthusiastic "Jambo" greetings were most infectious.

Overlooking the old town and dominating the entrance to the dhow harbour is the massive Fort Jesus. It was built in 1593 by the Portuguese but saw many different occupants from Portuguese to Arab, various sultans of Oman, and the Sultan of Zanzibar. The British converted the fort into a prison. In 1960 it was architecturally restored and now houses the National Museum of Kenya, which supervises the excavations along the coast, besides having collections of Chinese, Arab and Persian ceramics, ancient maps and 16th Century weapons and tools.

That night was race night at the yacht club and we were made to feel most welcome. It was interesting talking to people who had lived in Kenya for decades, although many were very concerned about the deterioration of the country. We left for Kilifi early the next morning in a lumpy sea, but picked up a favorable two to three knot current which shortened the twenty-five nautical mile trip north.

Tony stood by on the radio to help guide us in through the offshore fringing reef, by identifying landmarks we could discern on the shore. With the frequent squalls it was hard to identify the beacons. At one point we thought we must have gone too far and furled the sails heading back into the huge swells, but in a lull we spotted the towers and came in safely, passing under a new bridge that was being built by the Japanese. We anchored off Tony and Daphne's on the north side of the inlet and landed by dinghy on the small beach below their property.

It was lovely to relax on their veranda with the ice clinking in our gin and tonics. Fragrant tropical flowers enveloped us and the birds gave us a voluble welcome when they came to roost as the sun went down.

Daphne took the boys inside and they came out beaming, their arms full of books.

"Mummy," said Colin excitedly, "they've got all the Asterix series, and there are several we haven't read before."

We went up to the house again early the next morning to phone Duncan in Canada about his travel arrangements but the phone wasn't working. It happened several times during that week. It was frustrating as I was also trying to make arrangements to go on safari. We were, however, able to make arrangements to go alongside the wall at Swinford's by using the V.H.F. radio. It was necessary to wait a few days for the lowest spring tide.

The time was put to good use with schoolwork. Finally Paper 29 was completed; there was just Paper 30 to go, six more days work left to do.

"It'll be a cinch," said Colin, "as it's just review tests." He didn't feel that way by the end of it!

Ashore the boys looked for fossilized shark's teeth on the beach, collected some tiny tadpoles and took the Britchfords' dogs for long walks. At first the dogs barked ferociously as we climbed the steps to the house, but the morning we took ashore a tape machine, to record their barking to scare off future would-be intruders, the dogs came bounding down to meet us not uttering a sound. It was the same for the rest of our stay!

Daphne drove everyone into the small town of Kilifi, whisking us around to her favourite market stalls where we loaded up on produce, particularly the huge succulent apple mangoes, almost a meal in themselves. She then took us to the butcher for beef filet, which was all of $1.50 a kilo!

One evening we entertained on board and enjoyed the company of cruisers from *Whimbril* and *Rainbow*, Americans who had come through the Suez Canal from the Mediterranean and were heading east.

The trip to Mombasa by bus was a crowded, noisy affair. The women were in brightly coloured sarongs, many with babies slung on their backs in another piece of cloth. The man next to us was holding two live chickens. The old lady behind was topless; she sat tall and serene. Jamie and I were squashed tightly against the window as yet another person tried to get at least one buttock on the other end of the seat. We were at the near side and as more luggage was thrown on the roof, and more people hung onto the bus outside, the angle of heel was becoming alarming. I had a moment of claustrophobic panic as it hit me that if the bus went over, Jamie would be smothered by a mass of humanity, not to mention two frantic chickens. At that moment, to my relief, Andy pointed to the door. It was time to try to get out.

I booked a safari trip with Best Camping, a budget company which had been recommended.

"The price is certainly right," I told Andy when we all met for lunch. "It's $1,500 for all five of us for a ten day trip and that includes the train ride to Nairobi. From the itinerary it appears we spend several hours each day viewing game, except for the drives between the parks."

"We're definitely camping?" asked Jamie. "Hooray!"

"And will we be in a van with a pop-up roof like all the pictures?" asked Colin, as excited as Jamie.

"It sounds a great deal," agreed Andy.

"Well hopefully the tents won't leak, and I have to warn you the food doesn't sound exactly 'haute cuisine'," I told him.

"I'm sure I can survive for ten days, I'll feast my eyes instead on all the gorgeous students who are along on the trip!" replied Andy.

Finally the tide was right for *Bagheera* to go against the wall so we headed across the inlet. *Rainbow* also wanted to do some bottom work and went in first. Then disaster struck. Even with only six foot of draft she was aground. She could wriggle her way in but there was obviously no hope for us. Andy was distraught.

"We can't leave the boat without the work done," he said. "There isn't another spring tide high enough for a month and we need to be away south by then. We just won't be able to go on safari."

This didn't sit well with me!

"There must be another solution. Why can't we dig a ditch for the keel?"

Ashore we spoke to Philip who runs the yard.

"I can certainly provide shovels and get some manpower," he promised. "The only trouble is, I have to go away for the weekend."

"Remember Colin is here," Charlotte, his wife, reminded him. "He's my brother," she told us, "and very competent."

We had an excellent lunch the next day at the boatyard, with passion fruit ice cream that was 'out of this world', and met several of the local white population, most of whom were retired. As the tide went out, all was 'action stations' as everyone we could round up started digging away furiously. Ideally, we needed an extra three feet of depth, as the tide height was already on the decline. All went well until we hit rock. A conference ensued and then an investigation. Fortunately the rock was intermittent, and with a slightly different angle we could still get the right sized ditch, about forty feet in length.

And it worked! Our fin keel is only about three feet long so several lines were tied to the ancient stone wharf to secure *Bagheera* from tipping forward or aft, with longer lines to buildings and trees to hold the boat against the wall. As the tide went out there was no doubt that the boat was well supported, although looking at photos in our album with the boys nonchalantly playing underneath now fills me with horror!

Another hour with shovels and we had a pit deep enough to enable us to lower the rudder. While I taped around the waterline and gave a quick coat of anti-fouling paint to the bottom, Andy completed the inside reinforcing of the fibreglass around the bearing housing before the tide came in again.

"How's it going?" I asked, as he surfaced from the lazarette for air.

"Great, I have to congratulate myself on the job I did when we were underway. It was beautifully done!"

Tony picked me up at 6:30 the next morning, to take the rudder to Mombasa so the teflon could be machined to fit.

It was an interesting trip, past plantations with long straight rows of

Bagheera at Swinford's Boatyard, Kilifi

fleshy leafed sisal plants, with the occasional surviving baobab 'upside down' tree standing out bizarrely. The plantation, Tony informed me, was the biggest on the coast. Kenya is the second largest sisal producer in the world after Tanzania, although the demand for this fibre crop is subject to considerable fluctuation. There were also mango orchards and cashew nut groves, and we passed through the traditional moslem fishing town of Takaungu, supposedly the oldest slave port of the Kenyan coast. Mtwapa Creek cuts deep inland with magnificent cliffs. Many years ago there was a hand-hauled chain ferry. Its crew were renowned for their sea shanties and are said to have inspired Paul Robeson in his ballads.

The Mombasa machine shop was extremely efficient and made a perfect 'top hat' bearing exactly to Andy's drawings. They needed a couple of hours so I went off to collect our mail and change money, then to Best Camping to pay the rest of the deposit, as they didn't take credit cards. We were back at the boat exactly at noon.

The bearing was a perfect fit in the hull and we were all set to move out as the tide rose. At the last minute the engine gave problems; there was no water coming out of the exhaust. Just in time Andy managed to clear the air lock and we wriggled and bumped our way down our channel into deep water. What a relief!

After school the following day Charlotte took the boys and her son to the Bamburi Quarry Nature Trail. Created to look like a mini game park on what was once a limestone quarry and cement works, the area now has vivid green shrubs and forests stocked with a variety of wildlife. The boys had a wonderful time seeing eland, oryx, waterbuck, bush pigs, wart hogs, buffalo and monkeys, to name a few, but returned later than expected. Once on board we hoisted the anchor and motored at top speed over to Tony and Daphne's. They were hosting a film night and we had been given strict orders that we mustn't be late.

We anchored in the dark beside *Whimbril* and *Rainbow*.

"Quickly get ready," Andy called from the bow, "we'll just make it in time. Can you get my shoes and a clean shirt." All the while he was paying out the anchor chain.

"Okay, we're all set. Let's go," he said coming aft.

We were the last to arrive but not unacceptably late and had an excellent evening watching Jeffrey Archer's 'Not a Penny More, Not a Penny Less'. It was after 11:00 P.M. before the group off the boats headed back down to the beach.

Jamie was ahead and suddenly called out, "One of the boats is right over on its side."

Although it was dark we could see the outline of other yachts at anchor. You've guessed it, the yacht was *Bagheera*! It was so shallow we could wade over to the boat. Although we had anchored a long way out, knowing there was a long sand ledge before the drop off, *Bagheera* had drifted inshore into the shallows.

It was incredibly awkward climbing around on board. Even when heeled right over whilst sailing, the boat was never over this far. With wet bare feet we skidded on the fibreglass on deck and on the woodwork below. The boat was over on its starboard side, our galley is to port. The top lockers in the galley were open; with shock-cord fiddles across, nothing ever came out at sea but at this angle several jars had fallen to the floor. A gooey mess greeted us of instant coffee mixed with ketchup, mustard and Worcestershire sauce.

Thinking we had dragged anchor, and that with diminishing spring tides we would be unable to float off at the next high water, Andy assembled willing volunteers. We formed a chain up the beach to remove jerry cans of fuel, water, extra propane and anything else of weight we could find.

The alarm was set for 5:00 A.M. It was going to be a short night. The boys were invited to sleep elsewhere, fortunately, as Andy and I had a very uncomfortable time on board. I ended up in Colin's aft cabin with the fishing reels in the middle of my back, and had vivid dreams of being pushed along by a rhino—no doubt caused by all my research into safaris!

At 5:00 A.M. *Bagheera* was still well and truly on her side, but the water was beginning to rise. At 6:00 the mast was beginning to lift. By 9:00 A.M. we were afloat in plenty of water and feeling a little foolish as we pulled in our 'miles' of anchor chain. Then we had the task of loading everything back on board. Again everyone rallied round and all came for coffee afterwards.

"I've always enjoyed Jeffrey Archer for the twist at the end of his stories," I commented. "It's ironic that it was after watching a film of one of his novels that this should have happened to us. It was so unexpected in such a familiar and easy anchorage!"

We still managed to finish Paper 30 during the afternoon. School was now officially 'out'. I cleared a cabin and lockers for Duncan, no small task with our souvenir collection. That evening Charlotte gave us all a wonderful dinner at the boatyard. Hopefully life was back to normal!

The next day Tony kindly took us to Mombasa to pick Duncan up at the airport. Jamie and Colin could hardly contain themselves. When Duncan finally appeared, we were amazed by how much he had grown;

he easily topped me and was barely an inch shorter than Andy. It was wonderful to have him back, and he was full of news and loaded with letters and gifts.

Three days later we were off on safari. The train for Nairobi left in the evening and there was great excitement opening up the berths, with their crisp white sheets and blankets, but Andy, who had to sleep in the next compartment found his bed already occupied! The train was somewhat run-down but delightfully old-fashioned, with an excellent four course-meal in the dining car.

Colin was the first to awake the next morning.

"There are elephants and giraffes outside," he cried excitedly.

The animals were ambling along totally unconcerned by the train; we felt well and truly in Africa.

Having booked in at the Fairview Hotel, we set off to explore Kenya's capital city. Nairobi got its name from a stream called Usao Nairobi which means cold water in Masai. It is supposed to have one of the best climates in the world and was very pleasant for touring. The first stop was the National Museum where there were excellent taxidermy animals and birds, of particular interest to us before going on safari. There was also a good display of cultural artifacts and wonderful paintings by Joy Adamson, of 'Born Free' fame.

Then off to the 'Carnivore' restaurant for a lunch which certainly lived up to its name with enormous hunks of meat brought from the barbecue pits to the tables, on Masai swords. There was beef, pork, lamb, sausages, chicken, ham, spare ribs and hartebeest with a variety of salads and sauces to go with them, followed by strawberries and cheesecake!

We found the wild animal orphanage a little disappointing given the fame of Kenya's animals, but the boys loved climbing on the old steam engines at the Railway Museum. The displays gave an informative insight into Kenya's history since the beginning of the colonial period.

Although there had been much interest in the Kenyan coast due to its trading history, the interior developed quite differently, being settled by over seventy different tribal groups, with a large diversity of people who spoke almost every major African language. It was primarily the warrior-like Masai who deterred the Arab slavers and traders, and European missionaries, from going inland, despite the rest of Africa being explored. By the late 19th Century, however, the Masai were considerably weakened by civil war, white man's diseases and famine.

In 1884 a young German arrived in Dar es Salaam, headed out in a caravan and got several tribal chiefs to sign a document ceding almost all of East Africa to Germany. The British were not happy about this, particularly as it included land controlled by the Sultan of Zanzibar whom the British had promised to protect. The following year at a conference in Europe the British were given Kenya, with Germany getting what is now Tanzania. Later, Uganda was also made a British protectorate, however the British had to show occupation. To join Uganda to the coast a 921 kilometre railway had to be built. It took almost six years with a cost of several million pounds and hundreds of lives of Indian labourers but its completion transformed the future of Kenya.

The headquarters of the colonial administration was moved from Mombasa to Nairobi. To encourage settlers, the government took over all land considered uninhabited, much of it extremely fertile, and sold it to settlers to recoup some of the costs of the railway. In 1902 there were a dozen European farmers. Life wasn't easy. Initial experiments in sheep farming and wheat growing failed disastrously but settlers gradually found out what grew well, in particular coffee, tea, cotton and pyrethrum. By the 1950s, there were 80,000 whites, and the local tribes were increasingly resentful of what they saw as a massive land grab.

The Masai and the Kikuyu were especially affected and, with the whites unwilling to make concessions, ceremonies spread through the tribes with oaths being taken to kill the Europeans. In 1953 the Mau Mau rebellion erupted. When it ended in 1956 13,500 Africans had been killed and just over 100 Europeans, of which 37 were settlers.

The rebellion caused many white settlers to leave and prompted the British government to provide grants and loans to buy out the European farmers and return the lands to the tribes. The first African elections were held in 1957. By 1960 there was an African majority and the Kenya African National Union was formed. When Kikuyu Jomo Kenyatta was released from detention, for his part in the Mau Mau uprising, he became leader. In 1963 K.A.N.U. won the General Election and led the country to full independence. Under Kenyatta's presidency, Kenya developed into one of Africa's more stable and prosperous nations. However, there was much criticism that control of the government and much of the economy was in the hands of the Kikuyu, to the detriment of the other tribes.

Kenyatta was succeeded by Daniel Moi, a member of the Tugen tribe, chosen by the Kikuyu as a suitable front man for their interests. Under Moi the country declined. There was much corruption and like the Seychelles, excessive government monopolies. With the continued division of the lands, agricultural production fell abruptly. In 1975 Kenya was self-sufficient but by 1980 it was importing half of its cereal needs.

Signs that the 'Jewel of Africa' was on the decline were everywhere, from the pot-holed roads to the game parks, and the fertile land that was lying unused. Rumour had it that almost all grain now had to be imported. In particular, the people, whether black, white or Asian, had several controversial issues to discuss in private. We were told that many who had voiced criticism of the government had been removed and there had been various conspiracies and attempted coups.

Kenyan politics in recent years parallel those in the Seychelles, and much of the rest of Africa. With the fear of Communism removed, donors of overseas aid increased their requirements and specifically demanded an effective multi-party system of government. Elections were held at the end of 1992. Due to infighting within the opposition, and such strategies as the government having $250 million printed to line pockets before the election, Moi was again voted into power, although with only one third of the vote.

'Best Camping' picked us up in a mini van from our hotel; a New Zealand couple were already on board. We headed for Amboseli a game park on the Tanzanian border at the foot of snow-peaked Mount Kilimanjaro, the highest mountain in Africa (5895m.). Having settled our gear in the large tents we went straight off for a drive. With the sparse scrubland the animals were easy to see and they were everywhere—elephants, zebra, wildebeest, baboons, many varieties of antelope and buffalo. Our guide drove the van up to them slowly, and the animals seemed amazingly close as we stood with our heads out of the pop-top with its all-round viewing. With the engine turned off we could really attune ourselves to the calls of the birds and the rustle of the animals through the grass as they nonchalantly went on grazing. Even the boys were silent, totally awed by the abundance, beauty and fascination of nature.

A large campfire was burning on our return to the camp site and we joined the other travellers who were gathered around. What an enjoyable group. To our surprise there were very few students, most were professionals who had decided to take a few months away. Even the food was remarkably good.

The next day there were three drives and we started to become more discerning. There were Thompson's and Grant's gazelles, Masai Giraffes and Burchell's zebra and we also saw reedbucks, lions, little dik-dik antelopes and a variety of birds, including huge malibu storks. The dawn drive was best for the sheer numbers of game; there were fewer on our late morning one, although this included a refreshing swim at Kilimanjaro Lodge. That evening we were able to take the classic shot of a huge bull elephant, with Mount Kilimanjaro as a backdrop.

It was a hot drive the next day and even hotter after tents, mats and food had been piled into our van, besides two extra passengers. Andy was beginning to mutter, always hating a crowd. However the grassy campsite beside Mount Kenya was very pleasant and the native dances that evening entertaining. There was mime, acrobatics and dancing, all performed in bright costumes and headdresses, to the music of a very versatile, enthusiastic accordionist.

Mount Kenya, which straddles the Equator, is Africa's second highest mountain. All we saw was a series of jagged peaks on our way to Samburu National Reserve. This time our campsite was by the broad, sluggish Ewaso River. Crocodiles and hippos are common and even before we had pitched our tents a crocodile had consumed a dik dik right beside us!

In this hot dry park the game gathers by the river, in the shade of doum palms. Disappointed with the numbers of animals, (although we had watched a wonderful display of two juvenile elephants playing, butting and wrestling each other with their trunks), Joseph, our guide, decided to head off to the hills in search of Klipspringer, which inhabit high rocky cliffs. We seemed to be in the middle of nowhere and hadn't seen any other vehicles for awhile when suddenly a voice shouted, "Andy!"

"Good heavens, Liza," said Andy, who at that moment was the only family member looking out of the pop-top, "it's your nephew Andrew."

We did know my nephew was on safari somewhere, but hadn't expected to run into him way off the beaten track in Samburu! He was travelling with Dominic; they had been friends since childhood, both growing up in Nigeria. Now in their mid-twenties, they were revisiting Africa and doing it in style. There were just the two of them, in the same size mini bus as all nine of us, and they were also staying in expensive hotels!

"I can't believe it," Joseph muttered to us all the way back, "your nephew travelling like that and you travelling like this!"

The validity of his words was driven home when we returned to the muddy campsite. There were no tables, dinner was late, and sparse when it finally arrived. Andy and I even had to share a fork. There were few pickings for the baboons who eyed us hungrily. After dinner we walked down to Andrew's hotel. Jamie's eyes nearly popped out of his head on entering the diningroom. There was table after table of absolutely every kind of food, mouth-wateringly presented, of course!

As is common practice, the hotel had put out food to attract game and on a tree on the far side of the river lay a leopard contentedly gnawing away at a piece of meat, until a babble of baboons came along and harassed him away.

The next morning was beautiful and fresh and the game were out in abundance, including the birds. We saw many of the varieties of animals common to Samburu but rarely found elsewhere, such as the narrow striped Grevy's zebra, the brown tortoiseshell patterned reticulated giraffe, and the shy long-necked gerenuk, an antelope that stands on its hind legs searching for succulent leaves.

It was pleasant having drinks with Andrew that evening, relaxing in the comfortable chairs in the hotel.

Suddenly Joseph, our guide, rushed in saying, "You have to leave now, the hotel locks its doors at 7:00 P.M." It was 7:04 P.M. and Joseph did a lot of fast talking to get us out!

It was a long drive to Lake Nakuru but there were magnificent views of the Great Rift Valley, a fault line that stretches 6500 K.M. from Jordan in the north, through the Red Sea, and then down through Ethiopia, Kenya, Tanzania, Malawi and Mozambique. A massive chasm, it is apparently one of the few natural features that can be identified from space.

Due to poor drainage, the valley floor is covered in shallow lakes which have become very alkaline because of their high rate of evaporation. They are known as soda lakes and the water, which is almost soapy to touch, provides the perfect environment for microscopic algae and diatom growth. Insects and crustacea eat the algae which in turn are consumed by fish, which in turn attract vast quantities of birds.

"Often Lake Nakuru is covered with thousands of flamingoes, both the deep pink and pale pink," Joseph told us. "Sometimes there are just as many of other varieties, such as ducks, pelicans, storks and cormorants."

It was very peaceful down at the lake. Although not covered in birds, there were plenty at the water's edge with a predominance of pale pink flamingos and the large beaked pelicans. Peacefully grazing on the bright green surrounding grassland were several species of game: waterbuck, cape buffalo, wart hogs and gazelles, and a sighting of some jackals just as we were leaving.

We stayed at a hotel in Nakuru, Kenya's fourth largest town and farming capital. Before taking us into the dining room Joseph gathered the group around him.

"It is essential," he told us seriously,"that you do not talk about politics or anything to do with the government whilst you are in the dining room. There have been some troubles," he added in explanation.

There had been some violent rioting against the government in Nairobi that day, we were to find out. Government officials had chosen our hotel as a meeting place to discuss their strategies. They were all having dinner as we walked in!

Later we met a Canadian who was in charge of a Canadian foreign aid road-building project. The Canadians built the roads, the Kenyans were responsible for maintaining them.

"It's so disheartening," he told us, "none of the roads we have built have been properly looked after. Now, with our latest project, we find many of the materials have been stolen or substituted with inferior products."

At 6:00 A.M. we left for Masai Mara, stopping en route at spectacular Lake Navaisha. Lying in the shadow of an extinct volcano this is the highest and purest of the Rift Valley lakes, and its shores are lined with lush farmland, vineyards and yellow-barked acacia. It was here that Joy Adamson raised the lioness, Elsa, made known to the world in her book 'Born Free'.

Joseph also talked to us about the Leakey family's discoveries both in Olduvai Gorge in Tanzania and around Lake Turkana in Kenya, which earned East Africa the name of 'the cradle of mankind'. These excavations have revolutionized theories of the origins of human evolution by the discovery of several hominid skulls, one of which was estimated at almost three million years old. Previously it had been thought that one of the Australopithecus species was the ancestor of homo sapiens, modern humans. These later African discoveries led to the belief that this newly discovered species, named Homo Habilis, was the ancestor, with the other two species being extinct side-lines.

It was a rough dirt track into Masai Mara National Reserve, the extension of Tanzania's Serengeti. At one point we went far off the track. "It's smoother on the grass," explained Joseph.

During a break for refreshments some Masai came over. Standing tall and regal, decked in brightly coloured cloths with ornate beads around their necks and wrists, they carried considerable presence. They were tending their cattle, the mainstay of the Masai lifestyle whose diet is traditionally milk, blood and meat. The hides of the cattle are used for bedding, sandals and mats, while homes are made from the dung. Later we were to go into a Masai village, and I have to admit that I found the small, divided smokey dwellings more than a little oppressive, but the people were most welcoming.

Unlike Amboseli where we always kept to the tracks, in Masai Mara Joseph made a new trail through the golden grass every time. It gave a wonderful feeling of discovery and aloneness although we wondered how the park could survive with the constant devastation. We were early for the annual southerly migration, when thousands of animals gather to migrate to the Serengeti, but the herds were beginning to form and there were unbelievable numbers of wildebeest (gnu), hartebeest, zebras, antelope and elephants. We also saw leopards, cheetah, wild dogs, and hippos snorting in the river, and a lion and lioness having a great love-fest!

"We've seen thirty-six different types of animals," announced Duncan, who had been counting from the Game Record card he had been given to fill out. "All we really need to see now is a rhino." However, rhinos eluded us in Kenya, their numbers having been horrifyingly reduced by poaching.

The staff at the campsite did a good job in driving and cooking, despite

Duncan trying a cape buffalo skull for size — it was very heavy

the lack of supplies from Nairobi. As always, it was sad saying goodbye to new friends, the group on safari had been diverse and stimulating. Back at the Fairview hotel we met Andrew and Dominic and made plans for Andrew to meet us in Kilifi, so that he could join us to cruise down the African coast. Andy had an interesting if sleepless night on the train back to Mombasa, as his Kenyan sleeping compartment companions discussed their frustration over the current corrupt, one-party political situation. We were surprised but delighted to find that Tony had come to meet us at the station.

I did a huge provisions shop in Kilifi for only $250; it was great having Duncan's and Andrew's muscles to bring it to the boat. With the extra help, the cans were quickly labelled and it was soon stowed away. We had a final party on board to say goodbye to our Kilifi friends before leaving for Tanzania, and gained an extra passenger. Tony asked if he could join us for the two day trip down to Tanga.

"Some boats that I've been talking to on the radio for months will be there," he told us. "I would love to get together with them."

We were pleased to be able to repay some of both his and Daphne's unbelievably generous help and hospitality.

12. Tanzania, The Comores and Mayotte

Tanga, Dar es Salaam, Pemba, Zanzibar, the Mafia Channel and Mtwara

Heading south from the calm haven of Kilifi, we discussed with the boys the possibility of some uncomfortable trips ahead. Generally, since leaving the Mediterranean, we had been heading downwind. Our sails fully out we were on an even keel, although rolling wasn't unusual. Now we would not only have to sail into wind, when we would be heeled over, but would also be battling into a strong current, so our trips could be rough and slow.

Being prepared for the worst, of course it didn't happen this trip. There were only five knots of wind so we motored and found that by keeping close to the reef and when possible by going inside it, that there was very little current.

There had been almost no marine traffic and Tony commented in particular, "There are so few dhows now on the water, it's really sad how they're dying out."

The Arab dhows had been sailing this coast for centuries, bringing goods to and from the Persian Gulf and India. Varying in size they are either planked or dug-out wooden vessels that have a rudder, mast and triangular lateen sail. Traditionally they were completely dependent on the wind although now some have engines. Hulls are generally broad and designs rugged to withstand frequent bumping along the reefs. Some have woven, coconut fibre matting fixed to their sides to reduce splashing.

They are very attractive sailing vessels with huge sails supported on a sprit which protrudes far forward of the bow.

During our brief stop in sleepy Shimoni, pretty with its thatched roofed houses, we completed the formalities to clear out of Kenya. Officials are not impressed if one arrives without clearance papers from the previous country and may refuse entry to a boat without them. Returning to the boat we noticed a couple of dhows on the beach. They were leaning towards each other, their skeletons entwined, a poignant reminder of days fast departing.

We entered Tanzania at Tanga, a town founded by the Germans in the late 19th Century, and now the second largest Tanzanian port and centre for the export of sisal. The boys immediately identified our three radio correspondents at anchor. We had last seen *Oriana* and *Wisp* in Thailand, *Rai Riva* in Chagos; all were Americans. We were able to get together after we had cleared-in, although as the customs official was visiting his daughter in hospital it took us awhile to locate him.

It was a wonderful feeling of camaraderie, sharing adventures and places in the Indian Ocean that have been little explored by yachts, and finding out details of stories that had been half told on the radio whilst at sea.

There was an Indian dinner at the yacht club the next night. All the women were invited to arrive early and to be 'dressed.' I took ashore my Indian sari and it was wound around me and flung over my shoulder in the traditional way, while my hair was pulled back into a plait. The ladies took tremendous trouble and I looked quite the part, except for having red hair! The formal evening was certainly different for us. The guests were beautifully attired and everyone most hospitable and welcoming. Mouth watering aromas attracted us to tables piled high with heavily spiced food.

"I really enjoyed wearing a sari," Sandy from *Rai Riva*, commented on our way back to the boat.

"Yes," I agreed, "it feels so cool and elegant, and is so practical—except when you have to wade out to the dinghy," I added, as I hitched the material up around my middle.

Sunday was relaxing, lazing in the cockpit then sailing on a borrowed laser dinghy and windsurfer. As the afternoon breeze filled in Duncan and Andrew skimmed back and forth across the bay, both in their element.

Oriana invited us over to see their intricate Maconde carvings. Made of black wood, known locally as ebony, they were beautifully fashioned with a baby's-bottom smooth finish. They sold all over the world for large sums of money. The Maconde tribe lives in southern Tanzania and northern Mozambique. It was in Mtwara in southern Tanzania that Ed and Bernice had purchased their carvings and they gave us valuable information about how to buy them direct from the carvers.

Tony drove us all into the town the next morning, having borrowed a car from a friend. It had a sleepy colonial atmosphere. The market was wonderful, with goods even cheaper than in Kenya. For some reason apple mangoes here were out of season, although a few miles north they had been abundant everywhere. We bought some finely woven sisal bags to carry our purchases. They were remarkably cheap. In fact everything was inexpensive except a visit to Ngorongoro crater. We had entertained the idea of a visit to this reputedly spectacular scenic area that teemed with almost every type of game found in East Africa, but with stiff fees for entering the park and high prices for accommodation, three days would have cost far more than our ten day safari in Kenya.

"Besides," I rationalized, although disappointed, "all we really need to see are rhinoceros, and now that we know they have a successful breeding programme in South Africa hopefully we'll see them there."

I baked and prepared food all afternoon as the party that night was aboard *Bagheera*. We finally went to bed at midnight having been highly entertained by Ed's fish stories. It had been a whirlwind three day get-together. The next morning we all headed off in different directions.

It was a rough few hours sail over to Pemba Island, with constant spray coming across the deck. The boys stayed below most of the passage and when on watch I sat at the top of the steps, getting what shelter I could from our small companionway dodger. It was one of the few things I would have changed on the boat. Andy had claimed this type gave better visibility. I didn't like it as it gave little protection, and I frequently ended up sitting in a puddle of water.

"I can't understand your complaints," Andy would say, "It's never a problem for me."

"You haven't got a woman's anatomy!" I would reply. Fortunately, as we seldom sailed to windward, we didn't have spray over the deck very often.

About six months ago Andy finally 'saw the light'. Could it have been something to do with the British Columbia climate? (Proofreading this he claimed he finally gave into my nagging!) In any event we are now the proud owners of a regular coachroof-wide spray cover and Andy is its greatest advocate!

Pemba lies to the north of Zanzibar but it was never as important, and there was little to be seen of a colonial past. We were told there are remains of a palace on the east coast that was destroyed by the Portuguese. After the expulsion of the Portuguese, Pemba was taken over by the rulers of Lamu in north Kenya, then by Mombasa and finally by the sultans of Zanzibar. It is now part of Tanzania. Cloves are the mainstay of its economy.

Our landfall was Wete, the most northerly of the island's three towns. It was old-fashioned, laid back and friendly, many of the stores being general purpose with everything imaginable on their dusty shelves. There were few signs of tourism except for a government hotel.

During lunch in the cockpit we watched a container being unloaded from a freighter.

"Surely they're not going to put a container on that tiny wooden lighter," I exclaimed.

"It's amazing," continued Andy after the container had been unloaded and the lighter, with just a tiny outboard motor, was staggering in to the town dock. "I hate to think what would happen if the wind came up."

Similar to South East Asia, everywhere there was an incredible mix of the old and new; when the container reached the shore the cargo was mostly unloaded into ox drawn carts. Later a passenger ship arrived from Zanzibar and for several hours the goods and passengers were brought ashore by sailing dhows.

We met some wonderful people whilst cruising down the coast but they were the poorest we had ever come across. Most lived almost totally off the sea but they always invited us to share their meagre fare, usually shellfish that had been skewered on sticks with meticulous care. Except for coconut palms there was almost no cultivation by these villagers. Their homes were palm frond lean-to dwellings and many were perched high up on clam shell middens that had built up over the centuries. Their clothing was wraps of bright cloth, with babies slung at their sides.

There were shells in abundance, especially murexes, conchs, cowries and clams, and Duncan found our first bull helmet. Its glossy mouth a brilliant orange with light bands and dark 'teeth' it was one of our most dramatic finds. As always we chose the best specimen, then returned the other mollusks to their original habitats.

Zanzibar, infamous from the slave trade days, was run down and dirty, but there were occasional glimpses of its past glories under the Arab Omani Sultans. Zanzibar's exotic history compares to 'The Thousand and One Nights' and it has lured travellers to its shores for centuries, some to trade and indulge, others to plunder. Its heyday was during the nineteenth

Pemba Island

century when it became the world's largest producer of cloves and had the largest slave market on the east African coast. At this time monopolizing all the trade of East Africa Zanzibar wielded enormous power.

As recommended by *Oriana* we went to find Juma at the tourist office. He took us on a walking tour and as we wove our way through narrow winding streets lined with shops, bazaars, mosques, and white-washed houses with carved, brass studded doors and intricate terraces. We began to get a feel for the fascinating place this must have been. He took us to the once grand Sultan's Palace, and the huge Shirazi Mosque, and to the area of the Old Slave Market.

"Nearly 50,000 slaves came through here every year," Juma told us.

We dined at the water's edge, watching the dhows sail past *Bagheera* as the sun went down. It had been a wonderful day with friendly people, and this scene was so peaceful and serene.

"Do you think it's safe to stay anchored off here?" Andy asked the restaurateur to whom we had been chatting all evening.

"You should be absolutely fine," he answered. "I wouldn't recommend you go into the dhow harbour as it's so crowded, but outside you will be safe and tonight it will be a calm night."

It was what we wanted to hear. The next anchorage was a good five miles away and we were feeling too content to move.

As we had been warned of the severe theft problems in the harbour, we rigged a variety of alarms in the cockpit. In the middle of the night we were awakened by Jamie who called out in his sleep. As I went to reassure him, Andy took a quick look around the deck. All was intact.

Ten minutes later, when we were just verging on sleep, there was a thud that jerked the whole boat.

Andy leapt up through the forward hatch 'roaring' loudly as he pounded aft. Although well hidden in a sail bag, wrapped to disguise its shape, the would-be thieves had found our large outboard on *Bagheera's* stern pulpit, and the jolt had been caused when they broke one of the brackets with a crow bar.

Andy's antics had the desired effect and as the thieves bolted they capsized their dugout, with the coral anchor falling out and anchoring their canoe. In their panic they abandoned the boat and swam for the shore.

Reaching out with the boathook Andy was able to hook the anchor line then tied the canoe to *Bagheera*. He kept watch on deck and just before dawn another dug-out approached but quickly fled when Andy shone the search light on it.

At breakfast we surveyed the boat to see if anything had been taken.

"No equipment has gone that I can see," said Andy.

"I know what has," said my nephew finally. "There was a big plastic bag on deck last night."

"And it was sitting in the old washing tub," I added.

"You mean all the thieves got was our garbage and the washing tub that has a hole in it!" laughed Duncan.

We called the Marine Police on the radio and they came and took the dug-out ashore; later that morning we saw it on the police station steps, with the outrigger sawn off. These dug-outs are important family possessions. We knew the owners would pay to get it back but hoped we had made a statement about stealing.

Ed and Bernice on *Oriana* were particularly pleased. When they had been in Zanzibar they had also had a thief on board, although by the time they realized it, he had assembled a huge pile of their belongings in the cockpit. Much of the clothing had come from a locker right beside the berth in which they were sleeping. If Jamie hadn't called out, if it hadn't

Traditional dhow in Zanzibar

been such a calm night and if the thieves had not broken the bracket, we may not have awakened ourselves.

Dar es Salaam, the capital and largest port for Tanzania, has an attractive entry with palms, colonial buildings and red tiled roofs on shore; while sailing dhows mingle with freighters on the water. A city of one and a half million people, ashore we found it a busy town and none too clean.

As we headed up the coast to the yacht club after clearing with the officials, we were hailed by a rather rusty Greek ocean-going trawler. At first we weren't sure of their intentions.

"What are they waving?" I said to Andy.

"It looks like boxes."

As the vessel drew alongside the crew greeted us like long lost friends.

"Our relatives live in Canada," they called out. "We would like to give you some fish."

To our delight they handed over not only some frozen fish but also three large boxes of prawns!

The yacht club was attractive and friendly and offered us space in their freezer for our unexpected gift. Some Canadians came over to introduce themselves; they were attached to the Diplomatic Service and large Canadian Aid Programme. Not only did they show us around and take us both to the produce and souvenir markets the next day, but they also entertained us at their base nearby.

We also saw a family who had left Chagos when we did. Theirs had been a harrowing trip, first due to bad weather and then to a very close call. They had been lacking some charts between Chagos and Tanzania. At dawn one morning, just as the light was improving, the father had caught a fish. As he wound it in he realized to his horror that he could see bottom and was looking at coral heads. Seconds later and they would have been hard aground. Frantically gybing around and pulling in the sails he headed east and then south and had a very anxious time, particularly when darkness fell, wondering about the extent of the mid-ocean reef and if they had finally cleared it.

The islands in the Mafia channel, off the Tanzanian coast to the south of Dar, proved to be wonderful cruising, definitely one of the most beautiful and unspoilt areas we found on our trip. There are several islands, reefs, and safe anchorages, with white sandy beaches and scrub on the shore. Careful 'eyeball' navigation was needed, as there are no aids to navigation and charts date back to surveys done in Colonial times. The steps up our mast were put to frequent use, the visibility in the water being greatly increased when viewed from the spreaders about thirty feet up.

We spent many an hour snorkelling and wandering the reefs looking for shells. Although there are few permanent inhabitants on the small islands, there were fishing camps on most. A relaxed barbecue takes on a different tone when surrounded by fishermen, and at times their aggressive curiosity was a little overwhelming. However they were also full of fun, having a good laugh when we used tin foil, and wanting to try everything we cooked in it.

The overnight leg down to Mtwara on the mainland was another uncomfortable trip but it made a great difference having extra hands for watches. Andrew and Duncan did a night watch together. Andrew sensibly took a seasick pill. Duncan, who had almost never suffered at sea, declined and was really surprised when he felt terrible. Not only had he lost his immunity but the motion close-hauled is very different to the slow rolling one he had been used to. Also, the conditions were rough with winds of 15 to 20 knots, gusting 25 not infrequently—but teenagers have to find out for themselves!

As we neared the entrance we could easily identify the channel and there were even a few buoys to guide us. However, with the strong currents which changed with the tide, and sharp drop-off into deep water, there was no obvious place to anchor. We finally decided on a spot close to the shore which worked well for the boat but was tantalizingly close for the locals. At 1:00 A.M. we had another 'visitor'. We heard him as he tried to climb aboard at the bow right by our berth; Andy's imitation of a pack of hunting dogs in full cry soon frightened him off.

We went to clear the following morning. All went well until the officials asked for our 'money change paper'.

"Oh, we handed that in at Tanga," said Andy, who didn't know what they were talking about. Apparently it was a sheet to show you had been changing money at the bank at the official rate—we hadn't been into a bank once!

It was hot and dusty ashore in a town that was very spread out. Apparently it had been designed to be a large town but with new government policies and economic strife the development never materialized. As Andrew and I went to the market we were struck by how very poor the people appeared. There was little produce to buy, just a few withered vegetables and green bananas. Even in the Indian run grocery store there were few canned and dry goods. We left with almost nothing and later found the spaghetti we had purchased was full of weevils.

That afternoon we all took a taxi to the Catholic Mission, *Oriana's* contact for Maconde carvings. The mission provided schooling for over 600 children to the age of eight and the major source of revenue was from the carvings sent to Germany to be sold for very high prices.

The head of the mission was most welcoming. He had some beautiful carvings in his office, the figures intricate with most moving expressions.

"The carvings are made in native workshops, scattered all over the area," he told us, "but I'll be happy to get my driver to take you around. There are also some carvers here and you are welcome to take a look." We couldn't believe his generosity.

The workshops were poles rigged with palm fronds for shade; generally several men would be working and chatting together. It was amazing to watch the carvers cut the incredibly hard wood with the bluntest of saws and most primitive of tools, producing intricate carvings with a myriad of detailed figures, all piled on top of one another in a tall column. Made out of one piece of wood they could take up to three months to fashion. All the traditional carvings have a story, they told us. When the figures are on their sides they are sick, when upside-down they are dead, and when the right way up they are well and happy. The stories were of family or community events. Many were related to superstitions and religions, both western conversions or ancient animism. It was the devils and evil spirits that were Andrew's and Colin's favourites.

As we were taken around to look for carvings, it was pitiful to see how people lived in comparison to Kenya. Apparently Tanzania was largely ignored by the Germans and the British during their eras of rule in the 19th and early 20th centuries as it had no exploitable resources and little fertile land. It was not an auspicious start for Julius Nyerere, Tanzania's first president, when the country gained independence in 1961. Committed to radical socialism and self-reliance, he decided to follow the Communist Chinese model of moving the population into collective agricultural villages, with much of the economy nationalized. This and several modifications of the schemes failed to work. Socialism had in a very few years turned a self-sufficient country into one where thousands were starving to death.

As we staggered to the boat with our purchases, Andy having gone off to get diesel, I suggested to the boys, "I wouldn't mention the weight of the carvings when you're talking about them. Daddy's going to have a fit when he realizes how many we have on board!"

The local ebony is so dense that it sinks like a stone when put into water, and each carving weighed a 'ton'.

"Don't worry, I'll remind him that I will be taking mine off soon," said Andrew, who sadly would soon be leaving us.

It was only when we reached South Africa that I realized the combined weight of those that were left. As I moved the carvings from the port to the starboard side for packing, it started to feel as though I was walking uphill. Extra weight never seemed to affect *Bagheera's* performance, however Andy never let us get the waterline too high having regular tantrums when we collected too much!

The trip to Grand Comore was our worst on this leg, although we had anticipated having these conditions all down this coast. We bounced and thrashed our way back and forth, with the wind 'on the nose' and a strong south-easterly current against us. We all felt sick, except Andy, and developed the routine of taking a pill an hour before our watches. At least I didn't have to do much cooking; crackers and cereal was the diet for most of us, with plenty of liquids. In the end *Bagheera* logged 309 nautical miles through the water to cover 190 over the ground.

After two days we arrived at Moroni at dusk. It was an attractive landfall at the Arab-looking town, the fading colours of light reflecting

A sample of our Maconde carvings

from the distinctive white arched Mosquée de Vendredi, with its tall square minaret silhouetted on the surrounding buildings. Behind rose the green slopes of Mt. Karthala volcano.

The boat ship-shape with sails furled and cover fastened, we went to explore the harbour. A sea wall was being built, but there was only a shipping channel, not an anchorage, so we had to moor outside. It was a very rolly night and I woke feeling seasick the next morning. Later the officials told us there was a deeper 'hole' in the inner harbour so we thankfully moved in.

In the morning light the waterfront looked almost Mediterranean and we were lured ashore by the smell of fresh bread. The winding streets of the old town were fascinating, rather like Zanzibar but whitewashed and cleaner. The women were very colourfully dressed, with a shawl flung over their heads, in deference to the Muslim religion. Some had a strange yellow paste on their faces, a pack to stop aging and wrinkling they told us.

Few people spoke English so we communicated in our 'school' French. The official languages are French and Arabic, although the patois is a dialect of Swahili. The people are a mix of backgrounds, most descending from African slaves who mixed with groups passing through, such as the Arabs, Persians and Malay-Polynesians.

Andrew packed that afternoon and I helped him with a final clean of his shells. I'd experienced opening a bag with clothes reeking of rotting mollusk and wouldn't wish it on anyone! We had a farewell fish dinner on board, with Duncan making a trifle for dessert.

The next morning we picked up our Madagascar visas at the consulate. They had wanted unbelievable numbers of copies of paperwork, but it seemed to have worked. Andrew's flight left that afternoon; he just made it after a protracted and delicious French lunch.

It was sad watching him depart; we had so much enjoyed having him on board. It had been an interesting trip, certainly not your 'milk-run' cruise.

"Thank you so much," he said to us. "It's been wonderful in every way—but I will enjoy being able to have a daily shower!"

It had been a joke throughout his visit. Like all our visitors he really missed the availability of unlimited fresh water and whenever we heard there were showers ashore he was always the first to be ready.

In contrast to our previous trip, we had a calm run to Mayotte with light winds and initially very little current. When the current did become strong it was from the west thus helped us along. At dawn the wind filled in and we had a spectacular sail past the lush island of Mohéli, skimming along in its lee at over seven knots. It was a beautiful fresh sunrise with the new moon gradually fading, then quickly it became a very hot day. We anchored off Iles Choizil in Mayotte the next afternoon.

"Look," said Jamie, staring at the chart. "Mayotte is like a seahorse upsidedown!"

Mayotte is geographically the oldest island in the Comores and it has a lagoon and encircling coral reef. It has been likened to Bora Bora, although its hills are more rounded and much lower. Unlike the other Comores Islands which became independent from France in 1975, Mayotte decided to stay with France as a Collectivé Territoriale. In consequence, while the other islands have had traumatic political regimes, Mayotte has been stable and the people better off economically.

We went ashore at Dzaoudzi, the former capital, which is an island connected by a causeway, that people have likened to a small rock of Gibraltar. It had a sleepy French atmosphere with attractive stone buildings and flowering trees. I couldn't resist some French goodies when we passed a bakery and delicatessen, although was shocked at the prices.

"You're to savour every mouthful!" I ordered during our lunch of croissant, baguette, patés, and cheeses that were matured to perfection.

Kelebek had advised us to use a local agent called c.t. for clearing in; he certainly made it very easy and changed money for us besides. He was unable to help us with propane, however. Being a French territory, they used a bottle exchange procedure rather than filling one's own. We now used large 20 lb. aluminum containers, which last about six weeks, but to exchange an empty bottle for a full one. One had to own one of the small type the locals used. We had long since got rid of ours from Europe and to buy one here cost a fortune. We contemplated decanting the liquid propane from one bottle to another but this would have involved having a special fitting made up.

We were fortunate, however, that *Bananas*, a large catarmaran from South Africa, was in the harbour. They had plenty of extra propane and when they came over for drinks that evening kindly brought us a full 40lb bottle.

"Just give it back to us in Durban," they told us. "There will be no problem with that, you're bound to be there before New Year." In fact all went according to plan but little did we know what we would encounter on the way there.

13. Madagascar

Nosy Be, Nosy Komba, Mitsio Group, Diego Suarez, Nosy Kisimani, Nosy Iranja, River Baramahamay, Nosy Valiha, Nosy Lava, Moramba Bay, Majunga, Baie de Baly

It was a lovely sail away from Mayotte, *Bagheera* gliding through the water, the ripples tinged with pink as we passed through the reef at sunset. The wind died completely the next day, so we had to motor but as the sea was flat calm the boys were able to pick up several different organisms from the surface of the water with their nets.

"Look at these," Colin showed me excitedly as I came on deck for my watch. He had quite a collection of delicate, brilliantly purple-coloured snail shells.

We arrived at the island of Nosy Be early the next morning and were welcomed on the radio. Friends of *Kelebek's* from *Monte Cristo* took us ashore. After clearing with the officials who were very friendly and easy going, we went straight to Air Madagascar.

I had been anxious to get to Madagascar as I had been unable to book Duncan a flight from Nosy Be, our landfall, to the capital Antananarivo, to connect with his flights to Nairobi, London and Vancouver. Originally we had planned to rent a car to take him to 'Tana', as the distance was just a few hundred kilometres. Then we learnt that the roads were virtually impassable and that the trip would take a minimum of three days if we were lucky.

"There are no seats available to Antananarivo that I know of," the manager told us, "but your son could fly out of Diego Suarez, in the north, then on to the capital from there."

"Could you phone Antananarivo to see if there is a waiting list?" I asked.

"That is very difficult from here. Generally the telephones do not work but I will try," he ended.

We left encouraged, at least we could get Duncan to Tana to catch his connections.

The next day the flight from Diego Suarez was confirmed and the following day we were given the name of a lady who worked as a 'universal aunt'. She would meet Duncan's plane and take him to his hotel at the airport. She would also collect him the next morning and make sure he was on the flight to Nairobi.

We heaved a sigh of relief and set about enjoying our last few days with our eldest. We had already found Hell-Ville (Andoany) pleasant, with great French food that was inexpensive. The town was named after Admiral de Hell, a governor of Réunion. The cannons and colonial buildings give an old world charm, in fact little appeared to have been done to the town for a long time. There was always a hive of activity on the wharf when we went ashore, where the little wooden ferries from the mainland discharged their passengers and livestock. The people were smiling and welcoming, especially to the boys.

Nosy Be is the biggest island lying off the Madagascar coast and with its long sandy beaches is written up glowingly in the government brochures as the ultimate tropical island paradise. Most of the tourists, however, seem to remain in the few hotels (which includes a Holiday Inn); we saw almost none in town. Sadly, with the drastic economic state of Madagascar, Hell-Ville is very run down, and with common local habits such as defecating in the street, it struggles to compete with other Indian Ocean facilities, such as in Africa and the Seychelles.

Surrounding Nosy Be are several smaller islands, most now being nature and marine reserves. We headed over to Nosy Komba, between Nosy Be and the mainland, particularly to see the lemurs. Due to its split from Africa over two million years ago a unique set of plants and animals have evolved in Madagascar that appear no-where else in the world. One of the best known animals is the lemur, a primate that belongs to the same family as the bushbabies and pottos of Africa, and the tarsiers and lorises of Asia. Zoologist Gerald Durrell became particularly fascinated with these unique animals and took some back to Jersey in the English

Colin in Nosy Komba

Channel Islands where his zoo specializes in breeding rare and endangered species.

Nosy Komba is a delightful little island, the virile coconut palms overhanging the wide sandy beach, with outcrops of rocks at the water's edge. Due to visits from hotel groups the people were used to strangers and most smiled and went about their daily business, whether doing their laundry, panning large woven trays to remove the husks from the kernels of rice, or tending to their fishing boats and nets.

As *Kelebek* had suggested, we went up to Martin's for lunch, wandering by the palm frond homes and passing a group of women who were hanging out white lace tablecloths they had stitched and would be selling on the mainland. It was a relaxed simple meal of fish and rice; the boys were delighted that they had several tortoises wandering around the garden.

It was so early the next morning when we went to see the lemurs that we woke these fascinating creatures up, but they quickly clambered towards us, especially when they saw our bananas.

"They are so cuddly," giggled Jamie as one clambered onto his shoulder.

"What interesting dark faces and beady eyes, and gorgeous white tufts around their heads," I added.

"Just like you Daddy when Mummy hasn't given you a hair cut!" commented Duncan.

"Look at that beautiful tail," said Colin. The lemur was sitting up on a pole and her chestnut tail was hanging down, almost a metre long and fluffed out like a bottle brush.

There are about thirty species of lemurs; these were black lemurs. Only the males were black in colour, the females were light brown, some even chestnut. We moved away from the tourist platform up into the forest and more lemurs swung down to greet us, moving with ease and dexterity. Soon Duncan had two on his shoulders, Colin another, and Jamie was squirming away from an onslaught as he had the hand of bananas; without doubt this fruit was a favourite.

"Did you like the lemurs?" asked the man at the gate when we had finally torn ourselves away, long after our large supply of bananas had run out.

"Oh yes," chorused the boys.

"They are sacred in our community, so we protect them," he continued. "Sadly many species are now endangered. We also used to have animals like the pygmy hippo and a flightless bird that was over three metres high, and giant tortoises, but they are gone now."

"You should go to Aldabra," said Jamie, with a young child's lack of inhibition. "There are hundreds of tortoises there!"

"You have been there too? You are very lucky."

It is good to be reminded every once in a while, otherwise it is easy to take this life for granted.

A tourist boat was obviously coming in later as some souvenirs were laid out along the route to the lemur park. Colin was attracted by the crystals, and carvings that were in a rose coloured palasandra wood. He liked a mask in particular and I was able to buy it later for his birthday.

Kelebek had been urging us to join them when we chatted on the radio each morning. After a quick trip back to Hell-Ville to check with Air Madagascar, and finding that Duncan still couldn't get on a flight from Nosy Be but was definitely still confirmed from Diego Suarez, we set out to join them in Nosy Mitsio, an archipelago about 30 nautical miles to the north-east. *Kelebek* was in a beautiful anchorage but it was blowing hard and we were on a lee shore.

"It's a real problem up here," said Tanil. "With the diurnal wind pattern half the day this is a perfect anchorage, then the wind turns through 180° and we end up to windward of the island."

The locals took full advantage of it, however. Although we had

160

initially commented on their primitive sails, that were like pocket handkerchiefs and could be efficient when the wind was behind them, we soon realized this is all that they needed. They sailed downwind in the morning (or night) to their destination and downwind that evening (or the next morning) to return!

Kelebek had a delicious fish dinner awaiting us and the next day Andy shot lobster and Duncan a 'sweet lips' and 'glass eye'— such appetizing names for fish!

The boys were keen to explore the island, especially after Tanil told them about the caves on the far side. When we visited these caves, even they were silent when we peered into the darkness at the dug-out canoes or 'pirogues'. Each of the pirogues had a skeleton inside. The way they were propped up made our skin crawl, as their big eye sockets seemed to be looking right through us. These were burial caves where a fishing tribe left their dead.

Amongst most Madagascar tribes, ancestors are held in great reverence. Apparently it is often the custom to exhume and re-bury the dead several times to keep them as content as possible. Despite considerable effort by both the Protestant London Missionary Society and the French Catholics to convert the population to Christianity, outside the cities old superstitions have much more influence over every-day life. These traditions are governed by 'fady', the system of local taboos that vary from one village to the next. Fady can be as obscure as not being able to talk next to a certain tree, or as unfathomable as a type of food being the main diet in one village and taboo in the next. Fortunately tourists appear to be excused from most superstitions, otherwise we would constantly be putting our foot in it.

When we took Duncan up to Diego Suarez for his flight we would be leaving from Antsahampana, the closest port on the mainland to Nosy Be. Andy was concerned about leaving the boat there unattended so the next day we headed south to check it out. It was difficult discerning the channel but the local fisherman were friendly and helpful and we finally made it up to dock, where the ferries left for Nosy Be. It was obviously too shallow to leave *Bagheera* there for a couple of days but we were able to find out that the ferry left from Nosy Be at 7:30 the next morning and that there were several mini-buses heading north. We returned to Hell-Ville, feeling organised only to be told that the ferry left at 6:00 A.M.!

It was a rude awakening at 4:45 A.M. but we were on the the dock by 5:45, fortunately, as the boat was punctual. It was a car ferry so we went on as foot passengers, but to our surprise when it docked on the mainland it was a long way from town. By the time we realized this, there was just one taxi-brousse left.

Taxi-brousse is the least expensive and most popular way of travelling around Madagascar. The name covers a variety of vehicles but they all have certain attributes in common, we were soon to find out. Firstly they are all in an unbelievably dilapidated state, and secondly their drivers have no limits, either with their driving habits or with the numbers of people they encourage to get on board.

Our taxi-brousse was a Peugeot van which one entered from the back. It had seats down each side that held four people comfortably, five at a pinch. After fourteen people had squeezed in, Andy, with his character-istic dislike of crowds, started to get up.

"Where are you going?" I asked.

"To get on the next bus, this is too crowded."

"I think this is the only one."

"It can't be."

"Daddy, the others have gone."

"I can't believe it. How far have we to go."

"Two hundred forty kilometres."

"I suppose I'll be able to put up with it for three or four hours."

I didn't think it prudent to mention it would probably take all day.

By the time we departed there were twenty-seven inside the bus, including several babies, five on the roof, including Duncan and the luggage, and five in the cab with the driver. In fact, the driver drove most of the way with his head and shoulders out of the side window.

The roads were unbelievably bad, full of potholes where tarmac existed; usually it was hard, uncomfortable muddy ruts. We stopped frequently to exchange passengers or for passengers to disappear into the bushes. There were never less than twenty-six in the back, for a few miles it went up to thirty.

While Andy wore a glazed expression of resignation, the rest of the bus load seemed perfectly content. Even the babies and young children settled down with never a cry or complaint, and our boys were having a great time, with Colin having joined Duncan on the roof and Jamie moving up into the cab.

One couldn't help but admire the serene dignity of our fellow travel-lers and how pleasant and polite they were. As in Africa the women were dressed in colourful lambas, or sarongs, that were intricately patterned. It's amazing to see all the ways these pieces of cotton material were used. They could be a dress, a wrap, a blanket or a shade for the sun. It can also be wrapped around as a carrier—for a baby, for food, for groceries, even for lifestock. The Malagasy women are small and delicately boned, and look most elegant in their lambas.

The people are a fascinating cultural mix. Despite the proximity to Africa, the first inhabitants of Madagascar, thought to have arrived about 1500 to 2000 years ago, were Malay-Polynesians who crossed the Indian Ocean from Indonesia and Malaysia in coastal outrigger twin-hulled canoes. The majority of the Madagascar population is descended from these first migrants although gradually there were more arrivals—Arabs, African slaves, Indian and Portuguese traders, and British, Dutch, and particularly French colonials.

The Malagasy are now divided into eighteen tribes that are based on old kingdoms. Although remarkably homogeneous in language and culture, the physical and racial diversity is still great, with some that are pure Polynesian while others look more African or Arab. Most people, however, are a remarkably attractive mix.

Like so many third world countries the population is increasing rapidly, having doubled to twelve million since independence in 1960 and expected to double again in the next twenty years. Almost every young woman had a baby slung at her side, although population growth has also been from migrant Europeans (mainly French), Comorians, Chinese and Indians.

This increase is particularly concerning when one sees the state of the land. Although potentially fertile, the slash and burn style of agriculture and disastrous economic management after the French left has led to the country having to import food, including the staple, rice. As we travelled to the north we were shocked at the arid, denuded hills that were until recently densely forested. The only trees to be seen for mile upon mile were mango, which had been kept for the fruit. Apparently the country has lost over 85% of its natural forests, and large tracts of Madagascar's surface are burnt every year to provide land for cattle and crops; without fertilizers and with the loss of top soil the cleared land is often infertile after a few months. We had heard of famine to the south; many of the people in this region also appeared to be living at a very low level.

One bus change and ten hours later we arrived at Diego Suarez. All of us, including Andy, were in good spirits! We took a taxi to the best hotel in town, only to find it had doubled its price two months previously. Despite the peeling paint and cracked sink it was comfortable enough, and we had an excellent dinner, being entertained by local musicians.

"Look! That's just like the musical instrument I bought in Nosy Be," said Duncan.

It was a cordophone with a large gourd as a resonator, an instrument that was probably influenced by the French, although with the gourd it looked very tropical. Colin had chosen a 'valiha', a bamboo tubular sound-box that was ornately decorated in pen and ink and surrounded by different length strings. This instrument is still played in Indonesia and Malaysia.

The hotel told us where to enquire about a taxi for the return journey.

"It's twice the price of the taxi-brousse but well worth it," declared Andy. On our way we took Duncan to the airport. Air Madagascar couldn't find his name but accepted his ticket. Having sudden pangs of anxiety I asked if there were extra seats. I was given a firm, "no," by the manager but assured with typical malagasy charm that everything would be fine. We left Duncan boarding the flight for Antananarivo.

The return taxi took only six hours. After darkness had fallen the only indication that we were passing a community was the smell of fires and cooking; only one town during the entire journey had electricity. As the hours wore on we noticed our driver's head beginning to nod so started talking very loudly; the poor man almost leapt out of his seat. We kept up the conversation, throwing in a few words in French to keep him alert, until he pulled into a very pleasant hotel in Ambaja.

He came to collect us the next morning for the 9:00 A.M. ferry from Antsahapano, but no boat appeared. As the morning wore on, more and more people arrived at the dock with mountains of luggage. Finally everyone piled into a tiny vessel. Its engine was noisy and frequently 'hiccupped', and the crew bailed with a large bucket the entire voyage, but no-one but us seemed concerned. We were used to commanding our own destiny at sea!

"What a trip!" exclaimed Andy to Tanil and Annette, who we visited on the way back to *Bagheera*, "but at least we got Duncan off safe and sound."

We had a day of respite, cleaning and getting ready to leave, before the bombshell dropped the following morning. Charlotte came up on our 8:00 A.M. radio 'sched' transmitting from Kilifi.

"*Bagheera* this is *Wisp*. How do you read me? Over."

"*Wisp* this is *Bagheera*. You're faint, Charlotte, but go ahead."

"Liza, Tony told me to tell you Duncan didn't arrive in London. We'll do anything we can to help."

Needless to say we were devastated. I had asked my brother-in-law,

Christopher, to phone Tony in Kenya to confirm Duncan's safe arrival. When he hadn't phoned, Tony called him. I could just imagine Christopher and Andy's sister, Lyn, waiting expectantly for Duncan to appear at Heathrow airport and the worry that would have ensued when he didn't show up. How their imaginations would be running wild regarding all the family's safety. They hadn't heard from us since Andrew had left in the Comores, and without doubt he would have given them vivid details of our being boarded by robbers in Zanzibar and Mtwara.

Fortunately I had booked Duncan's plane ticket in England when I was there for my sister's funeral, so Christopher was immediately in touch with the travel agent. Meanwhile, Tony contacted our friends, the Cahills, in Nairobi, to see if they had any suggestions. Having three children who commuted to England to school they were familiar with the airlines, and we hoped they could track him down. I also rushed ashore to the Air Madagascar office but it was the same old story, the telephones didn't work to the capital. I tried all the major hotels but they couldn't help me either.

"It's ridiculous," I exclaimed in frustration to Annette, "how do they arrange any business here? You know the only communication we have with the world is by the ham radio to Kilifi. Thank goodness propagation is good, two days ago we couldn't hear Charlotte at all."

"We sat glued to the radio; all we could do was wait."

At mid-day Charlotte had some news. "Duncan wasn't on the flight from Antananarivo to Nairobi," she told us. "The Cahills are trying to get him on another flight. They say the flights are frequently overbooked. Their son was bumped off the British Airways flight from Nairobi to London last night."

"Do they know where Duncan is?" I asked.

"I don't know. Tony's wife spoke to your friends, but I got the impression he is fine."

"I do hope he has enough money," I said to Andy. I had given him $150, thinking that more than ample, now I worried I should have given him more.

The next day we heard Duncan was flying out on Air France from Réunion to Nairobi. What was he doing in Réunion we wondered; it was in the opposite direction to Kenya.

That night the Cahills took their son to Nairobi's airport for his flight to London, and when he had passed through security he went to find Duncan; fortunately they had met at dinner in Nairobi. Amazingly the two boys met and then went to the glass window where the parents were waiting. Duncan waved his boarding pass to confirm that he had a seat on the British Airways flight to London, otherwise the Cahills would have taken him home.

Two days later Duncan was safe and sound back in Vancouver, quite excited by the whole adventure!

It wasn't until he joined us in South Africa for Christmas that we learned the details. There was no-one to meet Duncan in Antananarivo but he found his hotel, although there was no reservation in his name. He was early at the airport the next day but they had overbooked the flight with government officials so they bumped him off, claiming he hadn't reconfirmed his flight, despite it being reconfirmed in Nairobi, Dar es Salaam, Mayotte, Nosy Be and Diego Suarez. He was put up in a hotel that night but wasn't given any food, then flown to Réunion the next day. As he was now out of Madagascar the airline disclaimed any more responsibility. It is unbelievable that this could be done to a fourteen-year-old. Réunion is also one of the most expensive places in the world.

Fortunately for Duncan other people had also been bumped off the flight and a kind Belgian couple took Duncan under their wing, paying all his expenses. Duncan kept a record so we were able to pay them back. It was only due to the efforts of the Cahills and the English travel agent who specialises in Madagascar tours that the situation was resolved. When I booked Duncan's flight to South Africa for Christmas I made sure he was met at every stop along the way!

We could now leave. While I stocked up, Andy took jerry cans for fuel. When full, the cans are extremely heavy and he took a taxi back to the boat. Some yachts carry carts to transport the cans, something we will consider for our next trip when we have fewer kids on board and more space! We were still self-sufficient in water. After relaxing for a morning with the lemurs in Nosy Komba we headed south in the afternoon to a lovely protected anchorage on Nosy Kisimani.

Early the next morning *Whimbrel* called on the radio; she was about 1500 nautical miles away.

"We have reached Chagos," they told us excitedly. "It's just as you told us, utterly beautiful."

"Are *Belair* and *Archangel* there yet?" I asked. These were Bermudian and Canadian friends from our South Pacific crossing. Both boats had been in New Zealand for awhile but were now heading for South Africa.

"No, but we understand they should arrive soon."

We were back to spring tides so went for a walk on the huge sand spit when the tide was out. In many ways it was more like a temperate beach with clams everywhere but the boys found plenty of 'widgers' and shells under the rocks. Because of the silt from the rivers there was not much coral. We left for Baie D'ambavatoby in the early afternoon. Jamie made cookies as we motored, Tanil and Annette came and joined us for tea on arrival.

Annette and I weren't feeling very well, both had grumbly stomachs, sore throats, headaches and back pains. Later, Colin gave me a wonderful eucalyptus back rub. Ashore there were cone shells and cowries galore, and some particularly interesting varieties of the poisonous textile cones with very clear markings. There were no fish to be caught, however. I had a sudden craving for fresh foods, probably because I was sick; lately I had been finding a lot of weevils in our dry goods, despite using airtight storage jars. This hadn't exactly stimulated the taste buds, especially with my husband's comment, "Just some extra protein, no problem!"

The next day was Saturday, September 8th, an ideal day to re-start school—I had been putting it off since the official Tuesday the fourth! The boys were quite excited and motivated. Jamie had been avidly reading Asterix and Calvin and Hobbs, besides some of the children's series we had on board, and his reading skills had noticeably improved. He was starting Grade 3. In the British Columbia schooling programme the instructions are written at the appropriate grade level and Jamie forged ahead by himself, far more independent than he had been at the end of Grade 2.

There is a lighthouse and fishing village at Nosy Iranja and a beautiful sandy spit joining two islands. After a wander, we followed *Kelebek* to the River Baramahamay, going ashore to the village at its mouth. Considering how unusual it was to have two yachts anchored off, the villagers, including the children, appeared remarkably disinterested, but we had noticed this before. It was part of their culture it seemed and a pleasant contrast to Tanzania where we were followed by curious locals everywhere.

I swapped some bars of soap for eggs. The ladies immediately opened the packaging, holding the soap to their noses, their faces alight with warm smiles. Again the people seemed to be living at a minimal level. We were particularly fascinated by their primitive forge. It could have been from the iron age, with a man sitting three metres high pumping the bellows that were vertical, hollowed-out logs. The charcoal was white-hot. They were melting pieces of scrap metal from a car and making simple tools and cooking pots.

Nosy Valiha, to the south was a small island but there were four communities with two hundred people. One man talked to us in French. There had only been one yacht there before, he told us, and that had been British. We found quartz crystals ashore, to Colin's delight, with lovely, varying amethyst tones.

The coast had become very arid when we reached Nosy Lava. Being a prison island we thought we wouldn't go ashore, although some of the prisoners came out to talk to us. When *Monte Cristo* had stopped here, some of the inmates had apparently swum over to the boat saying, "Could you please give us a ride to the mainland, it is a long way to swim!

The wind was now from the south-east during the night and early morning. The north-easterly wind filled in late morning which gave us a very pleasant ride to Moramba Bay, a wide sheltered bay, a lovely setting with big rocks, sands and baobab trees.

The baobabs are extraordinary-looking trees; with their thick pot-bellied trunks and short crop of branches on top, the name 'upside-down tree' is very appropriate. Legend has it that they enraged the Almighty by wandering around the countryside, refusing to stay in one spot. As a punishment, God immobilised them by plucking them from the earth and somersaulting them so that their roots were in the air and branches underground. Strangely enough, due to their awkward shape, when there is a group of trees they almost look as though they are having a social get-together. Who knows what happens in the glow of the moon? Madagascar is, after all, a land of the spirits!

We went ashore to clean the huge yellowfin tuna which we had caught during the trip. Andy pointed out the black parrots and as we looked up at them we became aware of other beady eyes in black and white faces cheekily peering down at us. There were several of these sifakas, cousins to the lemurs, and they were obviously fascinated by us, frequently swinging to other branches to get a better view. It was idyllic, a great spot to spend a few days and celebrate Colin's birthday.

We wished Colin happy birthday the next morning only to be told by Tanil and Annette that we were a day early!

Such is the cruising lifestyle; we rarely knew what day of the week it was. In fact I had looked at my watch but with all the time changes I must have sometime changed the date once as well as the time.

I gave the boys the day off school anyway and after they had completed their journals they went ashore, totally content on the beach building forts and racing their home-made pirogues. It gave me extra time to

The forge

prepare for Colin's birthday, make some decorations and bake a cake for Andy to decorate. Although, for the first time, there were no other children for a party, it was a lovely birthday for Colin. He was thrilled with the presents we had been collecting for him along the way—the 'chop' seal from Kuala Lumpa, crystals and gems from Sri Lanka, a game of solitaire with pieces carved from different stones from Madagascar, African and Madagascar carvings. Tanil and Annette had special presents for him also, a hand-made collecting bag for shells, a painting of our present anchorage which Tanil called Colin's Cove. We had pizza on *Kelebek* for lunch and barbecued on the shore for dinner. While we were cooking, a fisherman came by offering us prawns and crab; we had given him some hooks and a line earlier in the day. We finished our meal with the birthday cake, ornately decorated as a spider conch shell.

While visiting a village the next morning, we were frequently asked for aspirin. We had a good supply on board so Andy went back to the boat to get some. Being so remote and poor the locals had difficulty getting any medication. Andy also brought back some bars of soap and fish hooks. The villagers were delighted with our gifts and gave us cool green coconuts to drink. After we had been with them awhile I took out the camera; their smiles instantly disappeared and they all looked away. Some of the children started running off. I quickly hid the camera and the smiles returned.

Late that afternoon we left for Majunga (Mahajanga), a large town about a third of the way down the west coast, arriving at 7:00 the next morning. While Andy slept we did school; my reward for keeping awake was a wonderful lunch at the colonial Hôtel de France. Later, although the town had obviously seen better days, it was delightful, travelling by rickshaw to the port captain's office, along the wide promenade.

On the way we stopped to look at a massive baobab tree that is reputedly over 700 years old. Needing to stock up, I went to exchange money the next morning but the bank insisted that on Mastercard one had to exchange a minimum of $300. Knowing that I couldn't possibly spend that amount with the local cheap prices and limited selection, I asked if the bank took Eurocheques. Luck was with me, approval had been given the month before. Eurocheques are taken in most places in the world with the exception of North America. Cheques are guaranteed up to the value of £100, approximately $150, so are quick to exchange. In Europe, shops as well as banks accept the cheques—very convenient in comparison to cash withdrawals on Visa or Mastercard, which can sometimes take an hour or more for approval. Direct debit credit cards have hopefully speeded up the process.

Annette and I made a final visit to the market, stocking up on produce which we carried in colourful local straw baskets. I bought a few extra goodies for the boys. The trip to Maputo in southern Mozambique would take a good week and I always liked to have a few diversions to help the time pass quickly.

14. To Mozambique and South Africa

Maputo
Richards Bay

The Mozambique coast is reputed to be beautiful but we had been warned that it might not be safe to cruise there, due to recent murders and kidnappings aboard two South African yachts that had been anchored off the north coast. The country was in turmoil; there had been a violent civil war since gaining independence from the Portuguese in 1975. National statistics were horrifying; with a gross domestic product of only $80 per capita Mozambique was now one of the poorest countries in the world. There was a literacy rate of 14% in the 14,500,000 population with only 103,000 students enrolled in Secondary school. Of the labour force 80% were employed in agriculture, yet only 4% of the land was cultivated, with the rest mostly too infertile. What little industry had survived after nationalism, declined in production an average of 7% a year between 1980 and 1989. Even the new hydro electric power plant on the Zambezi River that was so vital to the economy had just been sabotaged. The boys couldn't believe that there were a mere 62,000 telephones in the entire country and only 35,000 television sets!

The course to South Africa was south-westerly meaning that we would be close-hauled for most of the trip. We motor-sailed hard on the first day, trying to get around Cape St. André, but it was so uncomfortable in the big seas that we decided to stop for the night at Baie de Baly. It had been a long 70 nautical miles.

We made a quick trip ashore before leaving the next morning. The beach was black sand and rocks. Two men were fishing with several children running around. They looked very poor and their catch was meagre. We gave the men some fishing hooks; they were so pleased and offered us their few small fish in return. Not wanting to offend, we drank from a coconut instead, as they had plenty of those.

The wind was blowing even harder when we set off, increasing to a steady 25 knots as the day progressed. We put a reef in the mainsail and increased the revs on the engine, but with the wind on the nose, big seas and more than a knot of current pushing us north, progress was slow around the Cape. Not only was the boat bouncing around and uncomfortable, but I had been smitten by constant diarrhoea. I couldn't think what had caused it as I hadn't eaten ashore for a couple of days but Imodium, which generally sorts me out very quickly, had no effect.

The next morning *Kelebek*, who had left shortly after us, radioed to tell us that they weren't making any headway and were turning back for Mayotte, planning to go south again after the full moon when the winds were reputed to be lighter. Meanwhile my upset stomach continued; I staggered up on deck for my watches but the rest of the time I was completely debilitated and could only lie down. Fortunately the boys had settled into the motion and Jamie was now reading as much as Colin. During the day they kept me entertained; during the night when alone on watch, I was beginning to panic. I'd never had a prolonged stomach upset before and with all medical facilities at least five days away, and dubious or unknown at that, what was I going to do?

It suddenly dawned on me that I had read about these symptoms. I knew it wasn't in our medical books but where else would there be pertinent medical information? It had to be in one of the Lonely Planet Travel guides. Leaning over Andy, who was sleeping in the main cabin, our forward berth being like a roller coaster, I pulled the guide for Madagascar from the book shelf. I could find nothing pertinent but there was a section on 'Mally Belly', a Madagascar fever that is like a 'flu virus that commonly lays people out for a couple of days. It sounded exactly like what Annette, Tanil and I had suffered from earlier. But, when I turned to the health section in the 'East Africa, a travel survival kit' I found what I was looking for.

'Bacillary dysentery comes on suddenly and lays you out with a fever, nausea, painful cramps and diarrhoea but, because it's caused by bacteria, responds well to antibiotics.'

What a relief to have my symptoms described exactly. The antibiotic Bactrim was recommended for treatment—we even had that on board. From that moment I started to feel better! The next day Andy developed similar symptoms so immediately went on antibiotics also.

Bagheera was making only about 125 nautical miles a day. As we crossed the Mozambique channel we hoped to get into a favourable current. The South Equatorial current swings to the north up the Tanzanian and Kenyan coasts, after coming across the Indian Ocean and rounding the north end of Madagascar, giving us the adverse currents of our previous trips. However, the current swings south past Mozambique, as the Mozambique current, then becomes the Agulhas current by South Africa. Like a huge river, sometimes over 100 miles wide and at others only twenty, it surges down the coast, but we had to come right over to the African coast before finding it. The current was strongest only fifty miles outside the 100 fathom line and then only in a very narrow band.

On the radio we heard a yacht that was about two days ahead of us. The current had helped them travel seventy nautical miles that day and they also had a north easterly wind. A day later we also had the wind on the quarter and had a wonderful relaxed day of sailing, with two knots of current helping us over the ground. We could always feel when the current was strongest as the boat surged around with a jerky motion, but the added speed was a real bonus.

"We covered almost 200 nautical miles in the last twenty-four hours," Colin told us excitedly.

"Unfortunately it looks as though the weather is going to change," commented Andy. "Look at this weather fax picture that has just come from Réunion; it clearly shows that a front is about to come through."

"Darn, I was getting used to being comfortable again," I moaned.

The wind from astern died at 2:00 P.M. and by 3:00 a southerly began filling in. By 5:00 it was blowing 20 knots and building. It was getting increasingly uncomfortable with *Bagheera* pounding into the huge square seas created by the wind against the current. Instead of crashing on through the front we decided to ease sheets and shelter in the lee of Inhaca Island, forty miles back. As we were anchoring at 4:00 the next morning it was blowing a steady 35.

We were up at 7:30 A.M. after a reasonably peaceful few hours sleep. Now that we were here, why not visit Maputo? In Portuguese colonial days the capital of Mozambique, Maputo, or Lourenço Marques as it was then called, had been a glamorous holiday centre for Rhodesians and

South Africans. Colin, Charlotte's brother, who had helped us with *Bagheera* in Kilifi had encouraged a visit and had told us it was safe to go there. He had been living in Maputo for several years.

"Although after fifteen years of a communist government the town is very run down, it's well worth a visit," he had told us.

Maputo harbour lies in the southwest corner of a huge, shallow bay, with only a few channels deep enough for access. Expecting the entry to be tricky, the charts and pilot book both warning of intermittent navigational aids, it was a surprise to find that the buoyage system was excellent, with even a racon radar beacon.

"I can see eight ships coming in and out," commented Jamie. "That's an awful lot."

"It's incredible, much busier than Mombasa," I agreed.

"Yes, it's hard to understand all this shipping with the poor economic state of the country," said Andy.

"And it's Sunday too." This was yet another country we had managed to arrive at on the Sabbath.

It was still blowing hard as we entered the channel into the harbour and *Bagheera* rocketed through at seven knots, despite only having a 'pocket handkerchief' of sail.

"I can't see anywhere obvious to go," I told Andy, as I scanned the docks with the binoculars.

"Why don't you try raising some officials on the radio?" he replied.

No-one answered. A friendly teenager sailed up in his dinghy and jumped up onto *Bagheera*, offering to guide us into the yacht club. Unfortunately the water by the docks was too shallow. Then we heard *'Bagheera'* on the radio. The yacht *Moonshine* was calling us.

"We're round at the small ships harbour," they said, "by the wall. Come and raft alongside and you can clear-in." The officials were friendly and relaxed, charging us just $5.00 each for visas.

"You're lucky you're here this year," Colin, the South African owner of *Moonshine* told us later. "The government have really eased up on the bureaucracy. Last year you couldn't have entered without having visas in advance."

The officials talked about the political situation, a one party republic, which they hoped would become a two party democratic system. They also told us about the terrible exchange rate at the bank.

"I hope you have cash," they said to us. "Then you can change it at the market. You will get about three times the bank rate."

Unfortunately, having been living mostly on cash across the Indian Ocean, we were down to our last $50. "Let me lend you some South African rand," suggested Colin.

"If we're short, $50 worth would be great."

"Why don't you come over and I'll give it to you now," he replied.

I followed him over to *Moonshine*.

"Here's eight hundred rand," said Colin. "That should tide you over."

"Eight hundred rand, that seems far too much. How much is it worth in U.S. dollars?" I spluttered, overwhelmed.

"Around $400, but just keep it in case you need it," was the nonchalant reply. "You can repay me when you get to South Africa."

This instant bond and trust between yachtsmen, which we came across all over the world, is without doubt one of our most treasured cruising memories.

Although it had obviously seen better days the city appeared to be starting to boom again, and we enjoyed it ashore. It had become a 'sanction busting' port for South Africa we learnt, hence the density of shipping. A super highway had been built to Johannesburg, and the port area was filled with huge South African trucks. With the government's recent relaxed policies on private enterprise and investment, many Portuguese were returning, with businesses reopened and flourishing.

Compared to many of the places we had visited recently, there was an air of prosperity and sophistication. We expressed as much to some South African tourists we met. They had been running the place down, comparing it to South Africa. We were to be reminded frequently during the next six months how one's positive or negative reactions to a place are greatly influenced by comparison to the lifestyle one has come from.

The market was colourful and alive, with a wide variety of appealing fresh produce; there were large, seedless oranges, new potatoes and large onions, crisp fresh lettuce, shiny peppers and firm tomatoes. Several stalls were devoted to native crafts, some with Maconde carvings—"although not nearly as good as ours", commented the boys!—and sandlewood carvings that were not as intricate but were very attractive.

"Not more logs to weigh the boat down," moaned Andy who had just caught up with us. "I need 12,000 metacal to clear out." After all our shopping there were only 3000 left. These large amounts always sound frightening but after I had changed 20 rand we had plenty of money again.

We talked with *Moonshine* about the weather patterns for the passage between Maputo and Richards Bay, the first port on the South African coast. Ideally we wanted a 48 hour good weather window between the depressions and cold fronts that march up the East African coast. These bring strong southwesterly winds which pit against the swift southerly flowing Aghulas current, producing the renowned huge seas that cause many a large ship to founder, let alone a small yacht. This is one of the most dangerous areas in the world for shipping. More 'freak waves' are encountered off the south-west coast of South Africa than in the rest of the world combined.

"There are typically two to three day cycles alternating between the comfortable north-east winds and the uncomfortable and dangerous south-westerlies," Colin told us. "The ideal wind is obviously a north-easterly, but unfortunately, with 200 nautical miles to go to Richards Bay it's unusual to make the whole distance without a front coming through and a wind change."

We listened to weather forecasts from South Africa and analyzed faxes from South Africa and Réunion. Every evening there were spectacular electrical storms inland. After moving out to Inhaca Island a good weather window materialized. Although there had been a moderate coastal low, the weather forecasts stated that it was petering out. Colin, who came from Richards Bay and was an experienced sailor in the area, agreed it seemed a good time to leave.

There was a strong north-easterly wind as the two boats set out at 07:45. At 17:00 the wind clocked around to the east; by 18:00 it was blowing 25 knots, still from the east. Then on the horizon we could see the front. As it hit, the wind changed abruptly to the south-south-west only blowing 20 and we seemed to be through the worst when I went off watch at 1:30 A.M. At 03:00 Andy made a note in the log that there was continuous lightning on the horizon, that the wind was increasing rapidly and a bad storm could be seen on our small 8-mile radar. It was approaching fast.

He called to wake me up, turned off the V.H.F. and H.F. radios, then started the engine to hold the boat steady into wind so that we could reef the mainsail.

The interior of the boat was illuminated by lightning while I was climbing into my life harness. Then came an ear-splitting explosion, followed by deafening thunderclaps. At the helm Andy saw a massive flash at the top of the mast and molten material streaming downwind from the mast head. Simultaneously he experienced a jolt at the wheel, as did twelve year old Colin in an aft cabin.

Then I heard Andy shouting from the deck. "We've been struck by lightning, check the bilge. Are we taking on water?"

It flashed through my mind that we had recently heard of a yacht that had been completely perforated at the water line when struck by lightning, and that it is common to have a hole punched through the hull if there is not a conductor for the lightning to discharge into the sea.

"The bilge is dry," I called back with relief, "but there is a terrible smell of burning from the v.h.f. radio and maybe the engine room, and it seems to be getting worse." He immediately killed the engine.

As Andy went below, I went up on deck. There was a raging storm outside and although Andy had furled the genoa the mainsail badly needed a reef.

"I've checked the engine room and the fire is out but it's in an awful mess and the v.h.f. radio is still smoking. I'm afraid several of the other electronics are shot," he informed me on returning to the deck. "But let's get a reef in the mainsail."

As I headed into wind *Bagheera* slowly climbed the huge waves, then came tumbling down the far side. Andy put in a double reef, just as quickly as he could as he hated touching the metal cleats and mast in the still continuous lightning. At least he had no difficulty seeing what he was doing!

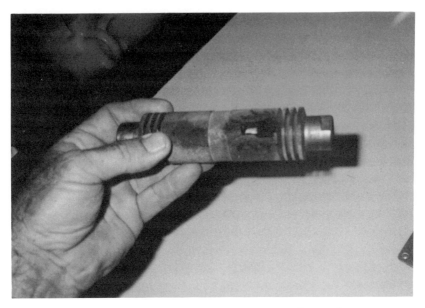

Effects of the lightning strike – hole blown in the top radio insulator

177

We were five miles off Cape Vidal in South African waters, taking advantage of the three knot current when the lightning strike happened. *Moonshine* was several miles astern. Finding our hand-held VHF radio still worked, we made contact to inform them of our damage and warn them about the storm.

"We're okay, but thanks for the warning *Bagheera*; the fishing boat beside us has just been struck too."

It was time to assess the full effects to *Bagheera*. What unbelievable devastation had occurred. Although the factory-installed lightning protection from our port shrouds to the keel had saved our hull, it didn't prevent damage to the instruments. Three radios, radar, wind instruments, depth sounder, log, weather fax, and Satnav were all dead with several emitting the stifling smell of fried circuitboard. The alternator on the engine had melted and the electrical wiring harness burnt up. This was a problem for us later as we had no warning lights or alarms. The bank of batteries in use had completely shorted out. The compass reading was out by several degrees. The autohelm 800, which was attached to the windvane, somehow had survived. It had been switched on at 'standby'. Fortunately our large autohelm 6000 was in England for repair. The electric anchor windlass was also not affected. Two interior fans didn't work but the other five were fine. The bulbs on about half the lights had been blown, as were the fuses in the electrical panel.

It made no difference if equipment was turned on or off. Even our celestial navigation calculator, electronic typewriter and colour T.V. which were totally unconnected to a power source had some parts damaged. For example, half the television screen is now purple!

In a full gale and in huge seas the only safe place to be was inshore, clear of the current. Unfortunately the edge of the current only runs very close to the coast at Cape Vidal and Cape St. Lucia. In driving rain and with no depth sounder or Satnav we were 'blind' whilst it was still dark, as there were no lights on shore. We closed the land with extreme caution, the white surf breaking on the beach looming ahead all too rapidly, then tacked out to sea again. In very little time we were in the current where the seas became so uncomfortable we had to tack in again. It was a nerve-racking couple of hours until daylight when we could see enough to be able to tack away before getting dangerously close.

All day we short-tacked down the coast until *Moonshine*, who was motor sailing, finally caught up with us. Andy managed to start the engine by shorting across the solenoid terminals. Fortunately, the engine sounded all right, and we thankfully tucked in behind *Moonshine*. The

Sri Lanka has beautiful beaches and local craft, and a lot more besides.

Temple of the Tooth, Kandy

Jamie at the Pinnewala elephant orphanage

Greeted by dolphins on arrival in Salomon Atoll

Tanil from Kelebek *with Colin cutting heart of palm*

Idyllic Takamaka Island

Bike riding in the islands

Picturesque La Digue

Seychelles tortoise in Mahé

Not the elephant that charged us but very like it!

Burchell's zebra

Masai village

Pemba midden

A relic of the opulence of Zanzibar

The Mafia Channel with my nephew, Andrew, and local fishermen

Grand Comore

THE COMORES

We generally weren't treated like tourists as we were going about our daily business like everyone else

Home aboard Bagheera—*Colin's 12th birthday*

Tendele, in the Drakensberg

The international dock in Durban

Life wasn't so bad for 14 year old Duncan on New Year's Eve!

The Baths, Virgin Gorda

Mayday rescue of fishermen from the Dominican Republic

Valle de Prehistoria, Cuba

lights of Richards Bay finally loomed on the horizon and by 11:30 P.M. we were tied up at the customs dock.

Shane, Colin's son, and his girlfriend Linda arrived early the next morning with toasted egg and bacon sandwiches; they tasted quite delicious.

"Have you ever been struck by lightning before?" asked Shane. "They say no-one is ever struck twice."

"It's funny you should ask that," replied Andy. "Yes I have, and there's a strange co-incidence. In 1958 I was flying a nightfighter. We had flown off the aircraft carrier H.M.S. Eagle in the Mediterranean and were at about 25,000 feet when we were struck by lightning. With most of the nose missing and a sick engine I was lucky to get the plane down on an airfield in Malta. By strange co-incidence my observer (radar operator/navigator) was a South African!"

"At least you're back to a first world country," said Colin. "You can get everything here, or easily have it flown in, and we're all here to help you."

We had a wonderful visit in South Africa. In all we were there four months, replacing the equipment and doing a considerable amount of sightseeing, but the warm hospitality and assistance we received will always stand out in our memories.

15. South Africa

Richards Bay, Durban, Pilgrims Rest, Blyde River Canyon, Natal Drakensberg, Kruger, Umfolozi and Hluhluwe Gameparks

Richards Bay has always been a favourite resort for fishermen and nature lovers. The largest crocodile ever found in South Africa was found here; it was 6.7 metres long. It is also believed that the hippo, Huberta, who is famous for her long walk to the eastern Cape, started from this area.

Since 1976, with the building of the harbour and the largest coal terminal in the world, the bay has changed, but it was still a very attractive place for us to stay. The Zululand Yacht Club had expanded its docks for international visitors and was most welcoming. With its large grounds, swimming pool, and many children, our boys were very content. There was also a clubhouse in which to relax, great showers, even washing machines.

It was Monday night, the one night of the week the yacht club was closed, and traditionally the yachties have a potluck braai. The South African accent is a clipped one, and like Australia there are many local terms. (Now that we are back home having a barbecue sounds very ordinary!) When we arrived with our food, Americans Muriel and Don immediately came to greet us; they had heard just that morning from Peter and Sandy on *Rai Riva*, who were now in Kilifi, that we were on our way. They had been in Richards Bay for many months building a new boat.

There was a great selection of salads and breads, and we were introduced to boerwors, a delicious sausage that can be quite spicy. It was sold in metre long lengths, coiled around in the package and cooked as such on the braai. We were also given monkey gland sauce, which is sweet and spicy and served with steak.

The company was excellent, although the group was small. As the weeks went by, and more yachts arrived, the Monday evening get-togethers became larger and larger and it was always an excellent party. It was a peak year for boats coming to South Africa and rounding the Cape of Good Hope as it was the year of the Gulf War, which made transitting the Suez Canal a less desirable route. Over seventy foreign yachts visited Richards Bay, and all were made to feel most welcome.

It was a busy first week assessing the damage to *Bagheera* and faxing our insurance broker in London. With communication back and forth so easy, we realized how lucky we had been. Had we been struck any time in the previous year, getting an insurance settlement would have been a nightmare, and it would have been extremely difficult to replace equipment, as some countries had very high import taxes. Mozambique was even charging 100% duty on grain that was a gift from Canada when we were in Maputo; they would have had no mercy with us if the strike had happened there.

Still not adjusted to the time zone, we were waking very early, so I made use of the off-peak time in the laundry room. I had a mere eleven loads! As the morning wore on several people wandered in. The laundry room, and waiting for the telephone, were always great places to catch up on the local deals, gossip and where to go sightseeing.

Keen to get our mail, which had been accumulating in Durban, we hitched a ride there by car with Shane and Linda. Other than going to the local shops it was our first trip ashore. Richards Bay is very spread out; as well as the coal terminal with its specially-built railway that links it to the Transvaal coalfields, there is an oil pipeline to the Witwatersrand. There are also aluminium smelters and a huge pulp mill. Close by, iron, zircon and other minerals are mined from the sands.

Leaving the industrial areas, we entered the far more peaceful and picturesque sugar cane fields. Empangeni started as a sugar town although pulp derived from the huge eucalyptus plantations are now just as important to the economy. Later we were invited to visit the gracious home of friends who owned a sugar plantation.

The roads were heavily used, yet excellent, for the two hour trip to Durban. Shane dropped us off at the attractive Point Yacht Club. Facilities were well organized for international yachtsmen. They quickly produced our mail and graciously offered us the use of the club. A new dock for visiting foreign yachts was just being completed. We returned to Richards Bay by bus after visiting two large marine stores to arrange for replacement electronics and electrics for *Bagheera*. Whilst most of the equipment we needed was available in South Africa, we found it cheaper to order major items directly from West Marine in the States.

The next day another front went through, producing unbelievable contrasts in weather. One moment it was sweltering hot and humid, then 'bang', as the south-westerly hit, it was bitterly cold with torrential rain and gale force winds.

Locals Eric and Anita on *Control C*, (how could you tell they had made their living in the computer business!) suggested we go into Empangeni that afternoon. *Control C* was opposite us on the dock and we thoroughly enjoyed Eric and Anita's blunt sense of humour. We went to the large supermarket Pick and Pay and it was culture shock with a vengeance. When I had got over the size and the choice, I picked out a variety of new products, as well as several bags of the fresh produce we craved. Although we were going to be a few months in South Africa, I was already starting the process I adopt in all new countries when time allows. I try small quantities of different brands to see which are approved by the family, then when I do my final shop before a passage I know exactly which ones to buy. As space is so precious on a boat there is nothing worse than taking up room with thirty cans of baked beans that just aren't acceptable.

The storm was incredible that night, winds gusting up to 50 knots with waves coming right over the docks. Boats were heeled far over, their mooring lines screeching at the strain, competing with the whistling of the wind in the rigging. There was a sudden thunderclap just as we were going to bed.

"Oh no!" said Andy. "I'm starting to twitch!"

Electrical storms were a way of life in this part of the world. The telephone was frequently struck and several boats had sustained similar damage to *Bagheera's* whilst tied up to this dock. The thought of being struck again and having what we had repaired undone was too much!

We had been fortunate in finding Peter, a local electronics wizard, who not only assessed our equipment for the possibility of repair but also told us more about lightning. Furthermore, he was able to give us an explanation for the devastation to all our equipment.

He thought we escaped structural damage and personal injury because Beneteau had built in a lightning conductor which connected the rigging and the keel. This grounding wire included a 'positive gap' connector which was designed to keep an 'open' circuit until the electrical discharge, caused by the difference between the negative charge at the base of the cloud and the positive charge on the ground below, jumped the gap and dissipated into the sea through the metal keel. In fact, the 'positive gap' acts like a spark plug. If the voltage across the plug is sufficient, then the spark will provide a path to ground for the charge produced. As there was no sign of burning at the bottom of the mast, from heat build-up due to resistance to the path of the electrical discharge, the system appeared to have worked satisfactorily. It would also have served to bleed off any static charge from a nearby strike and stop electrolysis between the different metals of the rig and hull.

Incidentally, the total discharge, termed the 'flash', has a time duration of about half a second. The current passing through the boat could have been as high as 200,000 amperes, with a potential of 100 million to a billion volts. To put this in perspective, a toaster carries a current of about 10 amperes and a 100 watt light bulb uses only about 1 ampere. Some of the most dramatic effects of the strike were the removal of the anodizing from the top of the mast, and a huge hole blown in the top radio insulator on our backstay, about three feet down from the mast top. The lightning had apparently travelled down the backstay and then jumped back to the mast.

More pertinent to our equipment loss was the fact that a side-effect of a lightning strike is a simultaneous electromagnetic pulse. This pulse radiates out across the spectrum of wavelengths, through very low to very high frequencies. Little is known about the electromagnetic pulse (EMP); because a lightning strike never happens twice in exactly the same way there can be no comparative analysis. Hence the EMP is often ignored in articles on lightning.

Peter believed that in our case it was the electromagnetic pulse that caused much of the damage to our equipment and it certainly answered the question of why it made no difference whether equipment was turned on or off, or was connected or not. His diagnosis has subsequently been confirmed by the Physics Department at the University of British Columbia. Those who would like to read about the effects of the strike in more detail, and the preventative measures we took subsequently, will find an account in Appendix D.

It took two and a half months to replace everything. Although at the time the whole business was a huge hassle we could have done without, there were some benefits. We were able to upgrade to the Global Positioning System, or G.P.S., the latest in navigation wizardry, which gives one's position within metres at any time of the day. In fact the system was so new at that time it wasn't yet operational twenty-four hours a day. We also replaced most of our standing rigging since the intense heat from the strike at the masthead could have weakened the wire. Where equipment couldn't be repaired we ended up with the latest models.

When we arrived in Richards Bay the local children were on school holidays. I talked to some of their parents and they all thoroughly recommended Richards Bay Primary school for Jamie. The timing was perfect for him to attend the last half-term of their school year. Jamie and I arrived on the first morning of school in torrential rain and the principal and staff could not have been more welcoming. The school had mostly Afrikaans classes but there was room for Jamie in the English one. They insisted on giving him a uniform from their secondhand shop; it was a green safari suit and Jamie was thrilled with it. I showed his teacher the work he would have covered on correspondence and to our surprise it was almost identical to the school programme.

Jamie instantly took to the school and made many friends. School started at 7:30 in the morning and he went with a friend from another boat. It ended at 1:00 so he came home for lunch, then enthusiastically completed his homework. The rest of the day was taken up playing in the pool and in the grounds with many other children. It was a wonderful routine, (except he was tired and needed dinner during our sun-downer time!), and after this experience was quite frustrated when he returned to school in Vancouver.

"I so much preferred school in South Africa," he would complain. "Here school takes all day and by the time I have done my homework it is too dark to play!"

As Colin was in Grade 7 and soon to sit an entrance exam for a Canadian High School I thought he should stay on the Canadian system. He worked away valiantly in the chaos of repairs; by this time he was very independent with his lessons.

Three days later another front came through with more fifty knot winds. In between the fronts a Dutch boat arrived which unbelievably had motored for two days in a flat calm. With no long distance radio the couple, who had sailed from Australia, hadn't been able to listen to weather forecasts but by good fortune their timing had been perfect. Tragically, however, another boat came to grief during this storm. It was a South African sailing school yacht, some 40 feet long, and the skipper had forty years of experience on this coast. They had headed out for Durban, but were dismasted and blown north. Amazingly the boat had ended up going over the reef and landed on the beach with the boat and passengers unharmed. Although miraculously saved from the storm, unbelievably the insurance company put steel straps around the hull and as they dragged it up the beach to a truck, the boat was virtually sawn in half and a write-off.

The days went past quickly with a regular routine. It was back to suburban living again; I even joined Anita from *Control C* for a fitness class twice a week. With all the great food I was putting on weight. A cause of great excitement for the kids on the docks was the Halloween party organized by the yacht club. They spent a whole weekend helping make large spiders, bats and witches to adorn the walls, and working on their costumes. Jamie was an awesome vampire and Colin a horrific Frankenstein. As there was an adult's party too, Andy and I also got dressed up, Andy as a very convincing bandit and I was Medusa with a profusion of snakes coming out of my green hair.

We were looking forward to another visitor. Lyn, Andy's sister, was again coming to stay. Halloween was a chaotic but fun time for her arrival. As she only had three weeks we needed to get some sightseeing organized and between us we managed to pry Andy away from repairing his pride and joy (no mean feat!) to go to some game parks.

Umfolozi and Hluhluwe, two parks that are side by side, are just over an hour's drive from Richards Bay. Hluhluwe, the best known of all the Natal reserves, surrounds the deep valley of the Hluhluwe River and provides varied viewing in forest, dense bush, at stream crossings and in open grassland. Almost immediately we saw some giraffes. What strange creatures they are, waving their long necks around in all sorts of unlikely directions. At first we saw one, then another head popped up and a third; finally there were five serenely peering down at us. There were several of the antelope family to be seen: graceful impala, the large kudu and a glimpse of the beautiful grey striped nyala.

As we drove down a straight part of the road Colin said suddenly, "Isn't that a lion ahead?"

This was a real bonus as lions are not common in this park. It was a male and as we approached slowly we spied a female in the bushes. We were beginning to get used to searching the undergrowth for animals. Looking for game here was very different to viewing it in the wide open spaces of Kenya.

The day passed quickly, watching for and finding the animals. There were the rather eccentric wildebeest, or gnu—who not only look as though they need a hair cut, but who snort, roll in the dust and run around in circles for no apparent reason—noisy monkeys, baboons that came and clung onto the car (one must always be sure to have the windows up when baboons are around), the beautiful wide-stripped Burchell's zebras and a solitary steenbok.

We were about to leave the park, looking down from a spectacular viewing point when a ranger came up. "There's a herd of elephants down the road," he told us. "It's unusual to see elephants here but the herd has recently wandered over from Umfolozi."

The herd was just beside the road, a large group of adolescents. It was wonderful to be able to get such a good look at them. Finally they started wandering off into the bush.

It was getting late and time for us to be heading back. I started the car and eased forward. Andy was still hanging out the window with the video camera, trying to get last pictures of the herd. Then one of the largest males turned round and started coming towards us. Suddenly he was pounding over the hard ground, ears wide and trunk held high—he was charging us!

With my sister-in-law screaming from behind, I gunned the accelerator pedal, hurtling down the dirt road. Ahead was another car. Feeling just a twinge of guilt, I skidded past and ahead of them. Looking back through the mirror I could see the car slithering around; they too were gunning the pedal. The elephant, however, had stopped, then nonchalantly wandered back into the bush. Maybe it was just a game to him, but it had certainly given us some excitement.

Later some friends came over to the boat to ask about our day, so we ran the video through our small TV. As we came to the elephant's charge the camera seemed to have a mind of its own. Sky, grass and bits of elephant flashed on the screen, as Andy had been filming and climbing back through the car window simultaneously, but on the sound track you can hear him quite clearly. "Liza, keep going, **keep going,** KEEP GOING!"

Jamie chose to stay with his friend Jacques, (with whom he still corresponds), so he could go to school while we visited Umfolozi. Slightly larger than Hluhluwe, at 47,000 hectares it is an area of undulating wilderness between the White and Black Umfolozi Rivers. Besides having a variety of animals, Umfolozi is famous for its programme that saved the white rhinoceros. These were dramatically on the decline due to their sought-after horn which is thought to have aphrodisiac qualities in the Far East. Now, one thousand animals are kept in the reserve, its estimated safe capacity, and the surplus is made available to other game parks.

Unlike Kenya, we had no problem in seeing rhinoceros here, but were confused by which was white and which black, as they are a very similar dark grey. Apparently the name white rhino came from the Afrikaans name 'wyd' referring to the white rhinos' distinctive big square lips which are used for grazing. The black rhino, in contrast, has pointed prehensile lips used for plucking leaves. The white rhino is the second largest land mammal and can have a mass over five tons. Needless to stay if they are charging one gets out of their way, once they are moving it's hard to stop! They also have very bad eyesight, and are inclined to go for anything moving in their vicinity so it takes a bold tourist to get within kissing distance to check on their lips.

On a later visit we braved a walking tour with a guide. It was quite eerie suddenly becoming aware of the proximity of an animal, only to realize they were completely aware of us. This happened to us just before a rhino started charging, fortunately not in our direction, but we all instinctively eyed the nearest trees in case we had to make a rapid ascent. We saw several animals close up, definitely an entirely different experience to being shielded by a car. Andy was fascinated to find that the rhinos all defecate in a communal spot, and was particularly interested in the dung beetles who thrive on these huge piles!

The Natal National Parks have a delightful system whereby you supply your own food, but there are cooks to prepare it. This works perfectly for a family as eating out gets expensive, and who wants to cook on holiday? The accommodation was in comfortable huts. Later, when we returned with Duncan, and Bob and Betsy, our Pacific friends on *Belair*, we took a spacious chalet. Our only problem was that the warthogs wanted to share it, and we had a hard time keeping them out!

A trip to Kruger took us through the kingdom of Swaziland; we obtained our visas and started on the long, hot, dusty drive north. As the weather had been so changeable, and frequently quite cold, it didn't seem necessary to spend the extra money on renting a car with air-conditioning. We were to regret it several times, but especially on this long journey.

There was quite a contrast as we went over the border with people living in very poor shanties, but later we learnt this was a Mozambiquan refugee area. Although small, the country is full of contrasts; this eastern half was the scrubby lowveld. On the western side is the highveld where the hills are covered with plantations of eucalyptus and pine. In between is the fertile middleveld where most of the people live.

We were headed for Mbabane, the largest town with about 50,000 people. Situated in the Dlangeni hills, it is one of the cooler places in the country. We arrived at the pretty Ezulwini, or royal (Swaziland has a king) valley, nearly five hours later, having had a long wait at the border, and soon found Smokey Mountain Village where I had booked an A-frame cabin. It was none too soon, as the first part of the journey had been sweltering hot and with five in the car there had been little extra space.

All went well until the receptionist asked me for our passports.

"They're in the car," I started to reply. "Oh, NO!"

"What's the matter?" asked Lyn.

"Darn, I think I locked the keys in the car, in fact I know I did."

"I don't think that will be a problem," said the manager unexpectedly. He smiled at me reassuringly. "I'm sure one of my employees can help you out."

A short while later an employee and I were walking over to the car. It took him two seconds flat to open the door!

As we made a quick tour around picturesque Mbabane the next morning, we were interested to see that all the colonial street names had been maintained. Swaziland had been under British rule for sixty-six years and made an easy transition to self-rule. We enjoyed the market, finding very attractive painted ceramic necklaces, and wooden bowls and carvings of good quality. It was common here to see mixed couples, African and white, many of whom were refugees from the harsh South African laws which forbade liaisons between races.

We then crossed back into South Africa in the Transvaal Drakensberg. I was reading the guide book as we drove along.

"Mt. Sheba Hotel sounds wonderful," I commented. "Not only does it look beautiful but it is set in the last native forest in this area, the rest has been cleared for plantations. Why don't we stop for tea?"

The hotel is situated on a 1,000 metre high plateau in a spectacular setting of the indigenous forest, and a river gorge with waterfalls and pools. The management was very gracious about our dropping-in unexpectedly, and the service was wonderful. The boys were even invited to use the swimming pool with soft, fluffy towels provided.

In 1873 a digger found gold and named the place Pilgrim's Rest as he thought he would now be able to rest after all his searching. For ten years the town buzzed with miners, then in the 1880s, it became a large company town. When there was no more gold it was sold to the government as a historical village. The town is very well kept and the people most friendly. We stayed at the simple but quaint Royal Hotel which prided itself on its old furnishings, antique water jugs and basins. It made Andy, Lyn and I feel very aged as we all remembered those from our youth in England!

The boys were fascinated by a gold panning tour and viewing the old mining equipment. A six kilo nugget was found under the tree beside us, our guide told us, and they were thrilled when he picked up some 'gold' from the ground and handed it to them.

"See this." He showed the boys the sparkling gold pieces of rock. "This used to fool the miners by its gold colour, so they named it fool's gold."

There was very little water now in the streams that had been used for panning. "That's because of the eucalyptus plantations," our guide told us. "The trees take an enormous amount of water out of the soil."

There were dramatic sights the next day as we drove to Graskop and the Blyde River Canyon. Here the highveld drops 1000 metres to the lowveld, at the edge of the Drakensberg escarpment. There are incredible rock formations like the Pinnacle and Three Rondavels and at God's Window we could see right across Kruger Park to Mozambique. The Bourke's Luck Potholes are extraordinary large round holes formed in the rock by the swirling waters of the Treur River, and the Blyde River Canyon was stunning. For more than twenty kilometres the river has cut a winding passage 750 metres deep, which has dense vegetation growing below towering rock buttresses. We also made a detour to the 80 metre high Berlin Falls. Here they were selling beautiful soapstone pots made from the rocks found in the area. They were carved in a zig-zag design around the edge, which accentuates the different colours of the natural striations, making them very attractive gifts.

After stopping in Graskop, to buy groceries for our stay in Kruger Park, we continued on to Numbi Gate. Kruger is one of the most famous, largest and oldest game parks in the world, originally established by Paul Kruger in 1898. Altogether they claim that 137 mammal, over 450 bird and more than 100 reptile species have been found there.

As the summer temperatures average about 30°c. I had booked a hut at Pretoriuskop, this camp being at a higher altitude than the rest of the park. It was beautiful with the rocky outcrops, shady marula, wild fig, and Natal mahogany trees. The bright red grand poinciana and pink bougainvillea were bursts of colour in the otherwise green and brown safari landscape. Our hut, however, was rather cramped for five, so I went to the office to see if we could upgrade. They graciously gave us the luxurious v.i.p. quarters for the night, then a charming cottage became available. It was one of the oldest in the park and built for King George and his family, for their visit in 1947. To the boys delight the park also included a swimming pool; it had been attractively built from the natural rocks, damming a stream, and the water was shared by several terra-pins—fresh water turtles.

On safari that evening Colin noted in his journal that we sighted our first sable antelope. It was ebony coated with white underparts, and had magnificent curved horns. We also saw giraffes, zebra, hyenas, water-buck, and impala.

It is hard to explain the fascination of game parks, how one can be on the road eight to ten hours a day and still wish for more. The slower one drives and the longer one is out the more one sees. Although this might sound obvious, we found one doesn't see just double the animals in double the time, but quadruple the numbers. We were continually learning to attune to the smallest movement, to scrutinise the undergrowth in a more educated way at every stop, and to listen for the slightest sound.

We spent hours on the road in Kruger, always taking a different route and sometimes visiting other camps. The boys found it as fascinating as we did although they did opt out a couple of times to spend the heat of the day in the shady pool. There were baby giraffes, elephants tearing down trees showing us the huge strength in their trunks and their voracious appetite, and glimpses of the rare, but ferocious, honey badger or ratel.

As we drove past a lake full of hippos one was wading to the edge. After he had climbed the bank he started to relieve himself. Simultaneously, to our surprise, his tail started whirling around like a helicopter and there was soon a fine mist of manure behind him. We were in absolute hysterics, in fact I had to stop videoing to make sure that what I was seeing through the viewfinder was actually true in real life! Apparently hippos are very fussy about their waters and don't like them polluted, so they come ashore and spread their dropping over a wide area in this way.

"A lesson to be learnt there," said Andy. "Never stand downwind of a hippopotamus that is out of the water!"

We had yet to see a lion in Kruger but on rounding a bend on our way to Lower Sabi a lone male was lounging right in the middle of the road. Undaunted when we came close to him, he was, in fact, not inclined to move at all. Later we came on a pride of thirteen lions. Two cars were stopped at the side of the road; we recognized one, having talked to the couple the day before at a water hole. They had just witnessed a hyena taking an impala antelope. We had arrived five minutes too late. The couple had been watching the pride for an hour hoping for some action. They finally left and a few minutes later we witnessed the fantastic spectacle of the lions pricking up their ears, rolling over, standing up and listening, and then the entire pride charged an elephant. The elephant let out frantic screams as he burst out of the undergrowth a few yards behind our car, just missing another vehicle that was approaching. This new car, however, made the lions falter and the elephant got away. A lion attack on an elephant is apparently almost unheard of. We were sorry the couple who had waited so long had missed it, but what you see on safari is very much a combination of knowledge and the luck of the draw.

Leaving Kruger by the Crocodile Bridge exit and heading straight south, we were back to the boat in exactly six hours. We were greeted by Tanil and Annette from *Kelebek*, who had completed a slow but uneventful trip down from Mayotte.

We picked Jamie up after school on Friday, two days later, to head down to the Royal Natal National Park in the Drakensberg Mountains.

Our friends Tim and Leisa, whom we had met in Tonga when they were delivering a large yacht to New Zealand, had been enormously helpful in our planning. Leisa, who was Australian, had recommended the schools for the boys there and we had even been able to live in her parents' house while they toured Australia. Tim was South African, and had given me a list of 'musts' to visit. We had been working our way through them very successfully but close to the top of the list was Tendele in the Natal Drakensberg. The roads were excellent and it was a varied drive, through rich undulating farmland, prairie flatness and rocky arid terrain, before reaching the Drakensberg. We just made it through the park gates before they closed at 6:00 P.M.

It was a beautiful camp with thatch-roofed bungalows in the most dramatic of settings, definitely rivalling the Transvaal Drakensberg. 'Our' cook prepared a stylish dinner with the ingredients we had given him; I could easily get used to this life!

At 5:30 the next morning we were wakened by noisy guinea fowl at our window. They definitely had no intention of letting us sleep in, but we were grateful. In the sunrise the mountains were a spectacular golden colour, and the dawn was beautifully fresh. We fed the guinea fowl and went for a long walk trying to identify the famous peaks of Devil's Tooth, Eastern Buttress and the Sentinel. The grandeur of the rock formations was breath-taking with their angular weathered peaks, giant chasms and narrow ravines.

"'Drakensberg' means Dragon mountains," Colin read from the guide book, "and the Zulus named them 'Battlement of Spears'."

"Well, the jagged mountains look like a brigade of spears," Andy commented.

"And the eeriness of the mountains makes them a good home for dragons," I added.

Leaving reluctantly we drove south to Giant's Castle, stopping on the way for a cool drink at a hotel—what a different touristy world. We found Giant's Castle an equally wondrous game reserve. With its lowest point at 1300 metres and highest 'spear' at 3280 metres, the camp again had incredible views.

Tim's parents live in Pietermaritzburg and they had generously invited us for the night. It was lovely to meet them and Pietermaritzburg itself was in its glory with the jacaranda trees in full purple bloom. Arriving in Durban, the Workshop Market looked fun so we went inside for lunch. Suddenly Lyn took off, returning with some-one she obviously knew.

"This is Joan," she introduced. "Joan and I were sitting next to one another on the plane. What an amazing coincidence running into each other here!"

Meeting Joan was most fortuitous for us, too: she was marvellous when we arrived in Durban with Bagheera. Meanwhile, she invited Lyn for the night, as Lyn was leaving for Port Elizabeth by bus the next morning.

During the next month *Bagheera* came back together, although not without some hitches and delays. Some of the equipment took an age to arrive, and we found that some items which we thought were repairable had in the end to be replaced. Frequently new units were a different size and shape to the old, so Andy had a good deal of fibreglassing to do, as well as the installations.

The only way to take out a mast in Richard's Bay, short of using a crane, was by using the very rickety telegraph pole planted by the wharf for that purpose. Many of our friends came to help us and despite the pole bending and creaking dramatically we successfully lowered the mast onto tressels for new rigging. A few days later we reversed the process and heaved a sigh of relief when it was fit to go to sea again.

The surveyors appointed by Lloyds to supervise the repairs were extremely helpful, from arranging for a haul-out and inspection for hull damage on arrival, to final settlement of the claim.

Colin, from *Moonshine*, generously offered me the use of his office computer to do my Christmas newsletter. It was the first time I had used a computer extensively and I have never looked back. Andy drew a cartoon of our route across the ocean with a great rendering of us being struck by lightning for the cover, and fortuitously some French Canadians were leaving for England and Canada just as all 120 overseas letters were finished.

Meanwhile boats continued to arrive, several of whom we had met years before. Bejorn, from Norway, and Ria, from Ireland, on *Orchestern* went back to early 1987 in the Caribbean. *Belair* finally arrived and with them *Kendaric* which had been anchored with us in Pittwater, Australia. We had also made many new friends, in particular the Services on *Jean Marie*, and locals Jenny and Jim Rochford. There was also another Canadian family—the Bogars on *Wind Woman* from Toronto.

Jamie finished school. It was the end of the school year and the prize giving and carol singing, in both Afrikaans and English, was very moving. Jamie came out proudly showing me his certificate for being 'so happy and friendly'.

After Duncan arrived from Vancouver for his Christmas holidays, Shane and Linda took us inland to visit Linda's parents on their farm. It is always interesting staying with people, and getting a feel for the local life. They also took us on a tour to Ulindi, the capital of KwaZulu, which is a new town although many of the Zulu kings are buried in the area, then on to Shakaland, the site for the film Shaka Zulu. The traditional Zulu homes are large dome-shaped dwellings with tiny entrances, which are delightfully cool inside.

Andy's birthday was celebrated in style and we were also invited to the gracious home and sugar plantation of some fellow cruisers. The owners' yacht was one that had been struck by lightening at the yacht club dock.

We had a great party for Jamie, which in the end ran to twenty-seven children. There were about that number, too, for Christmas dinner. It had been a lovely day celebrating with South Pacific friends, Indian Ocean friends and Jenny and Jim Rochford even invited us for Christmas lunch at their water slides. I seem to remember the evening ended with some delicious South African Peach Schnapps.

Then on 27th December *Bagheera* set out to sea again and headed south to Durban. It was an easy overnight passage but the next trip was very much on our minds. It isn't actually the rounding of the Cape of Good Hope that is the treacherous part of going around South Africa, it is the Durban to East London leg, where the current comes close to the coast and where, for over 200 nautical miles there is nowhere to shelter.

Richards Bay had been wonderful for us. As in all our travels there were many new friends we are unlikely to see again. Meanwhile we have some great mementoes, like this entry in our visitor's book from *Control C*.

A bolt of lightning brought you here

Stopped your engine,
Warmed your beer,
Frazzled your radar,
Deafened your ear.

You stayed awhile,
And brought us cheer,
We all had a good time,
'Cos Andy aged a year.

But we are sad to say,
That we know one day,
With high tide and nor'easter,
You will sail away.

Who knows what awaits us,
What our fates will be.
We await the joyous meeting
Of *Bagheera* and *Control C*.

Bon Voyage

It is accompanied by a drawing of us being struck by lightning. All our hair is standing on end, including our budgerigar's feathers!

16. Rounding the Cape of Good Hope

Durban, East London, Port Elizabeth, Mossel Bay, Hout Bay and Cape Town

Although we would have liked to have hurried it took us five weeks to complete the 800 nautical miles around to Cape Town, a trip that would have taken about five days if sailed direct. The trip from Richards Bay to Durban was the only leg where the weather allowed us to follow our planned schedule.

Durban is not only South Africa's principal harbour but with its long sandy beaches and year-round sunshine it is also the country's major holiday resort. There were many other yachts on the international jetty next to the hospitable Point Yacht Club. We rafted up with *Belair* and *Kendaric*, three boats out from the dock.

As mentioned before, the South African coast is justly feared by sailors and the original name for the Cape of Good Hope was the Cape of Storms. Every year lives are lost and during our brief stay two yachts were totally lost, another abandoned but later recovered, and one rolled but saved.

The trip from Durban to East London is the most difficult. Firstly, it is the longest, nearly 220 nautical miles with no anchorages or places of refuge from winds in either direction. Secondly, it is where the strongest part of the infamous Aghulas current (caused by the meeting of the great drift of the South Equatorial current with the strong flowing Mozambique current) flows close to the shore. The fronts down here can be vicious, with winds that are opposite to the current. The conflict of the fast southerly running current and strong winds from the south-west is the reason for the formation of some of the biggest waves found anywhere. Known as Cape rollers they have been recorded at 20 metres and more.

The worst area is close to East London so one wants a long (preferably 48 hour) weather 'window' between the lows or 'busters' coming up the coast. As the current is up to 200 miles wide, there isn't an option of going outside it. If a buster hits, you need to minimize the current by staying within a mile of the shore, at the 40 fathom line, where one can heave-to or beat into the wind in rough but tenable seas. Unfortunately all the other shipping is there too, which can be hair-raising at night.

We attended an excellent, illustrated weather briefing, with all the other 'internationals', given by Chris Bonnet who runs the largest sailing school in South Africa. The theory is that you watch the barometer until it tops 1020 millibars, then on the tail end of the low, whilst the south-westerly winds are fading, you leave to get the maximum good weather gap before the next buster hits. Watching the barometer is all-important in predicting the fronts, as the faster it falls the sooner the front arrives. But leaving was not as easy as it sounded. Firstly, it can take a day to clear Customs, Immigrations, etc., and if you don't leave within 48 hours you have to repeat the procedure again! Secondly, the season was delayed due to the late monsoon up north, so the fronts were still coming fast and furiously and the barometer never reached anywhere near 1020.

Another problem was that although at times the weather fax picture looked great, unexpected lows would form and 'pop' out of the south coast and roar up the east coast. Although many would die out before they reached Durban, by the time it could be established that they were slowing down, one had missed the critical departure time to catch the next 'window'. Also frustrating was the fact that you could phone the marine forecasters in Port Elizabeth, East London, Durban and Pretoria and get conflicting forecasts. In fact, the four day forecast from England generally was the most correct. SO, if you have managed to stay with me, you will realize why the anxiety level escalates on the dock and with it the difficulty in making the decision to leave.

However, there are always chores to be done and fun to be had. Joan, Lyn's travel acquaintance, was marvellous with entertainment and ferrying us around by car. We had to get some reinforcing stitching on the sails, pick up our replacement radar which the Richards Bay Port Control informed us had arrived, and complete a huge shop.

The prices were excellent in the supermarket, and with a top-up in Cape Town, these supplies lasted us through the Caribbean. Joan couldn't get over the quantities initially, but by the time I had filled the third buggy she was catching on fast.

"How about twenty cans of mushroom soup, Liza?"

"Make it twenty-five, mushroom soup is a great base for casseroles."

"Thirty cans of tuna?"

"Sounds great."

In all we filled ten buggies!

"This is really fun," concluded Joan, but I have to admit it wasn't such fun stowing it all!

With a population of 800,000, Durban is a sophisticated city and we enjoyed the shops and restaurants, but being the height of the holiday season with visitors down from Johannesburg, the city was very busy. Parties were frequent around the boats and as there were several teenage girls Duncan was far from bored. The dockside New Year's Eve party was a particular success. Duncan was now very much the teenager himself. He had easily topped me and at 6'2" also condescendingly patted Andy on the head! Shortly after New Year we sadly saw him off on the plane to return to school in Vancouver. It was a relief to know it was a direct flight to London after the Madagascar fiasco, but it distressed us that we would not see him again until we were almost back in North America.

We were then ready to leave, but the weather was not to oblige. Finally, a group of us left on January 13th with good forecasts, but with the barometer reading only 1018 millibars; another group left three days later. As we reached the harbour limits we could see another yacht was tying alongside, to await Customs and Immigration.

"My goodness it's *Archangel*," I cried.

"You mean *Archangel* from the Pacific?" asked Jamie, eyes wide.

"That's right," replied Andy smiling at Jamie's excitement.

We had great memories of our times with *Archangel*. We had first met transitting the Panama Canal and again in the Galapagos. We had talked everyday on our longest passage, 19 days from the Galapagos to the Marquesas and had a great landfall in Hiva Oa on Bastille Day with Michael Davies, *Archangel's* owner from Kingston, Ontario and his three sons that were on board, also with Jerry and Kai, his crew. We had last talked to Michael on the radio when we were in Australia and *Archangel* was in Fiji, and had since heard from him through his letters to Jamie.

It was great to see them, but what bad timing.

"Not to worry," they replied, "we'll soon be with you in Cape Town."

We experienced strong north-easterly winds, up to 30 to 35 knots and a mild south-westerly low, but there were no traumas on our way to East London. We did find, however, that the waves could become huge even with following wind and seas, especially outside the 100 fathom line which was at the edge of a steep bank—we were pooped for the first and only time, a wave breaking over our stern, drenching Andy and filling the cockpit. This was also where the current was strongest, helping us along at 3.9 knots and as we passed over the bank there was a definite change of colour from murky brown-grey to a deep clear ocean blue.

Our back-up auto helm 800 which attaches to the windvane (our 6000 still undergoing repairs) was definitely complaining of stress. We took pity on it and reluctantly did some steering, but then found it was unbelievably exciting at the helm as *Bagheera* surfed down the white, turbulent waves at ten knots or more.

We stayed in East London for a few days beside the Service family on *Jean Marie*, enjoying the hospitality of the local yacht club. High above us trains clanked over a steel bridge; later our deck was a measled mass of rust spots from the iron filings that fluttered down.

The 130 nautical mile trip to Port Elizabeth was uneventful. The winds were from the south-south-east 10-15, and the seas quite bumpy but we made good time. Just before we departed, the Gulf War broke out, so we had the single-sideband radio on almost continuously. We knew some yachts had decided to risk it and were transiting the Suez Canal, but they all went through without incident.

Mary-Rose, a friend from Andy's Royal Navy days, whisked us off from Port Elizabeth to Cape St. Francis, a lovely area of white sandy beaches and dramatic rocks, and the boys had a great time surfing on their boogie boards. The development along the banks of the canal was done in an attractive old English 'black and white' thatched style whilst where we were staying, it was a Mediterranean plan with rounded arches and terracotta roofs.

"Just like the Balearic Islands, in the Mediterranean," I mentioned to the boys. Then looking down we saw the street sign actually said 'Menorca', the island where we had wintered.

It was a relaxing break and we particularly enjoyed visiting Sealpoint lighthouse, which was mentioned in the 'actuals' every day in the coastal weather forecasts. We climbed up to the lens of the light and then inspected the weather recording equipment. Although full of the latest electronics, the lighthouse keeper proudly showed us the old mercury barometer, which he claimed was far more accurate and reliable! Looking out to the west as we left we saw yet another front approaching. In contrast to the previously warm, sunny day, it became cold and wet with visibility drastically reduced.

Set in Algoa Bay, Port Elizabeth is the second largest city in Cape Province with a population of 250,000. The yacht club was most hospitable but we could only live from weather forecast to weather forecast as we were all impatient to leave. Although the next trip was only 160 nautical miles, there were headlands for protection and the current was not so close to the coast, we still wanted to avoid bad weather if possible. Without doubt the lightning strike had not only made us more cautious but Andy had definitely had his fill of fixing the boat. Confidence was not helped by the cautionary talks that we heard from officials and the photographs of shipwrecks and disasters that seemed to adorn every yacht club wall.

Finally, there was a gap between weather fronts, and it was a fast and comfortable run to Mossel Bay. *Belair* and *Kendaric* had wanted to visit Knysna, an attractive inlet that has a tricky pass at the entrance, but the sea conditions weren't suitable so we visited by car. The next morning the group went inland to Oudtshoorn to visit an ostrich farm, in the fertile plain of the Little Karoo. With its invigorating winters and hot humidity-free summers it is the most successful place in the world for raising ostriches and it boomed during the Victorian and Edwardian eras. After a comprehensive tour we were invited to stand on the huge eggs to show how they easily take the weight of a person, and to watch some ostrich racing. There were ostrich hot dogs and hamburgers for lunch and we learnt that ostriches digest their food by swallowing small pebbles—including the occasional diamond!—which churn around in their gizzards and grind up what they have eaten.

It was ostrich riding in the afternoon, the cause of great amusement. One of Andy's most treasured minutes of video is my hanging on for dear life. Ostriches are worse than a camel to ride and a lot faster, is all I can say!

Mossel Bay was the landfall of the Portuguese explorer Bartholomew Diaz, who was the first to round South Africa into the Indian Ocean, and the 500 year anniversary was celebrated in 1988. A replica of his vessel had been built and sailed out by the Portuguese. It is now on display in the interesting Maritime Museum. Going on board we were amazed at how small these craft were for the number of crew and cargo and also interested in the similarity of the design to the dhows on the East African coast. We saw the main museum, enjoyed blustery walks on the cliffs watching the small 'dassies' (Cape Rock Hyrax) scampering over the rocks, and were entertained royally at the yacht club with a group of racers from Cape Town.

Many times a day "40 knots off Cape Agulhus", could be heard on the weather forecast. Finally, on the morning of the return race to Cape Town, despite the forecast, the local yachtsmen assured us the weather would be fine. And so it was. It was fun listening to the race participants along the way, and we even had to motor as the wind died altogether. Jamie and Colin were fascinated to see penguins swimming around the boat.

There were overcast skies as *Bagheera* sailed past the Cape of Good Hope. (In fact, Cape Agulhas, which we had rounded earlier in the day, is actually the most southerly point of South Africa). But, as we neared Hout Bay, south of Cape Town, the sun burst out, highlighting the spectacular rock formations on the shore.

It was already February 2nd but we could finally relax and enjoy; we had made it around. As we glided through the calm water some local fishermen came by.

"Got any beer for some lobsters?" they called.

We had just a six pack left. "This any good?" said Andy, and we were passed a bag of eight lobsters. This is the life!

Cape Town is the only city that we visited during our travels that can physically rival the beauty of our home town, Vancouver. The rock formations are utterly stunning, with the backcloth of the 1000 metre high, flat Table Mountain. To our surprise we were invited to climb Table Mountain. We were convinced it was a joke, as the sheer cliffs looked formidable. Access is normally by cable car which from the bottom of the mountain dwindles to a tiny speck as it disappears over the top. However, we were assured it was an easy hike. We set off early in the morning and were very proud to get to the top in 1 hour and 50 minutes—although we didn't start quite at the bottom! Most of the climbing consisted of stepping up high boulders, fine for us but each one was a hike in itself for Jamie. We were all hot when we finally made it to the top, the last deep ravine had continued forever, and we were down to shorts and t-shirts. As the mountain was in cloud and quite cool everyone who had come up on the gondola was clad in long pants and thick sweaters. They looked at us as though we had come from Mars! There is an incredible view from the top, overlooking the sprawling city of Cape Town flanked by Lion's Head and Devil's Peak across to Table Bay and the South Atlantic Ocean. Then on the south side we could peer through the hills to Hout Bay and down the peninsula, the tip of which is the Cape of Good Hope.

One of the special pleasures of South Africa is the wine; not only is the quality superb but the price is remarkable. A five litre carton of extremely drinkable white, for example, cost us about $4.00! A 'must' on the agenda whilst in Cape Town was a visit to the Stellenbosch and Paarl Valleys. With deep blue skies, undulating hills, white Cape Dutch manor houses and vineyards, and colourful, landscaped gardens, the valleys are quite beautiful. Names such as Ruste en Vrede, Blaauwklippen, Neethlingshof all add to the atmosphere and with the added bonus of the wine tasting, it makes a perfect day. As you can imagine we did a good stocking-up job, anticipating those happy 'sundowners' in the Caribbean and remembering the high prices there.

A group of yachts moved around to the Cape Yacht Club, in the centre of Cape Town, before leaving for the South Atlantic crossing. We could tell by the air that the water temperature had dropped now that we were in the north-flowing Benguella current which comes up from the Antarctic. Great numbers of enormous sea lions and quantities of sea birds are attracted to the richness of the sea life here.

Neethlingshof in the Stellenbosch valley

We again had delays, this time due to our autohelm 6000. Although technicians in both Durban and Cape Town had done their best and the computer had been back to England twice, 'Otto' was still overturning, if indeed it worked at all. Finally, Autohelm in Britain generously offered to give us new electronics (except for the drive) with no more cost. We excitedly left on a test sail—but no joy. Andy was in despair. As the bimini over the cockpit (which we had bought after my scare of skin cancer in Panama) interfered with the airflow over the Aries windvane we had got into the habit of relying on the electric Autohelm.

Suddenly the technician called up from below, "There appears to be a switch on this new unit I haven't seen before. Lets try it."

Magically all was fine and 'Otto Van Hellum' has since done a sterling job of steering an accurate course, as indeed he had for the previous five and a half years.

In the Galapagos Islands we had enjoyed the company of single-hander Julia on *Jeshan* who was originally from Cape Town, and her mother very kindly took me for a last shop. Julia was now shore-based in Australia. Cape Town is an old town with a 350 year history; its narrow streets, cobblestone squares and a profusion of flowers making it very attractive. It has a different personality to the rest of South Africa, being more European and cosmopolitan, particularly due to the exuberance of the Cape Coloureds, descendants of blacks and whites from centuries ago. Here we felt more insulated from the aggressive racial problems that were evident in Durban and even in Richards Bay.

Although superficially it appeared that blacks and whites were living amicably together, with many well dressed and prosperous blacks in the line-up in banks or stores, we had sensed an undercurrent of hostility from the day we arrived in South Africa, that we had not experienced in Africa before. In Arboretum, Richards Bay, for example, there were two parallel shopping malls and on the side where there had mostly been black shopkeepers both Andy and I independently had felt very uncomfortable. In Empangeni when I had driven unwittingly into the blacks' bus station, two buses started up and cut me off. Lyn and I both involuntarily locked our doors and wound-up the windows, hostility pervading the car, quite frightening with large numbers of people around. Our friends with farms were also concerned about their isolation should the situation erupt and become violent. In Durban the blacks were very aggressive in the streets, particularly the women, purposely getting in one's way. In both Durban and Hout Bay there had been demonstrations. However, on the rare occasions when we had glimpsed the barren, litter ridden townships, with masses of small wooden and tin-can shacks which contrasted so much with the comfort and affluence of the white areas, we could hardly blame them.

Without doubt the situation was coming to a head, and even with our limited exposure we could see tremendous potential problems. In particular we had been with four very different 'tribes', two black and two white. The two white, the Afrikaner and the British, had previously controlled the country. The Afrikaner traditionally worked the land and subsequently had been in power in the government due to their greater numbers, while the British dominated mining, manufacturing and finance, and they had very different outlooks regarding their future. The Dutch 'Boer' Afrikaners had struggled long and hard for their status in the country, South Africa was their homeland and they had no-where else to go, whereas the British have a tradition of having one foot in Africa and one still in Britain, with Australia and Canada also very attractive options. Of the black South African races we had been mainly with the Zulus and Xhosas, the latter having formed the African National Congress. The two tribes are traditional enemies and again they had very different ideals for the country and their separate futures.

The 'New South Africa' was on everyone's tongue, a regime that gave an equal vote to all and the opportunity for an equal lifestyle. Having seen the abysmal standard of living in East Africa, which in all of the countries had declined dramatically after independence, we could only pray that this magnificent country, which was first world in so many ways, would be the exception, and that it could adjust both socially and economically so that true democracy could be introduced without violence and economic decline.

Without doubt Table Mountain is most dramatic when viewed from the ocean; we left Cape Town with regret watching the famous mountain with its feathery cap disappear over the horizon. Like so many who spend time in Africa, the continent's raw vibrancy was now in our blood.

As we rounded the Cape it felt as though we were on the final leg home. In fact, we still had over 8000 nautical miles to sail before reaching North America, the equivalent of forty percent of the way around the Equator.

The South
Atlantic
and
West Indies

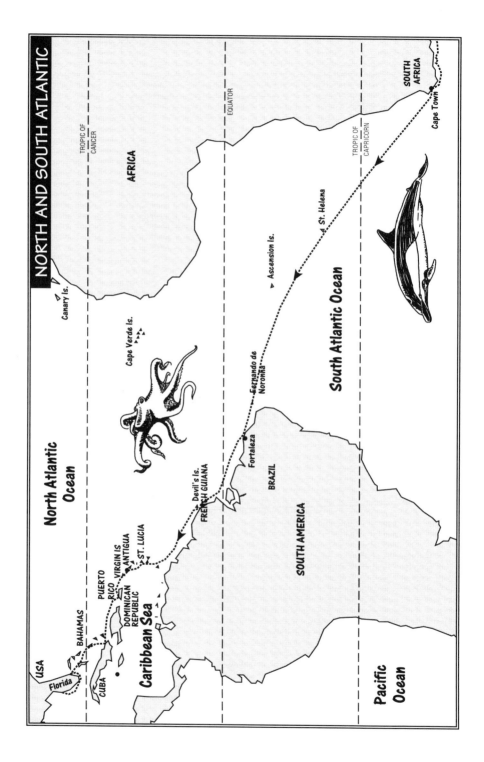

NORTH AND SOUTH ATLANTIC

North Atlantic Ocean

South Atlantic Ocean

Pacific Ocean

Caribbean Sea

AFRICA

SOUTH AMERICA

BRAZIL

FRENCH GUIANA

Devil's Is.

Fortaleza

Fernando de Noronha

Ascension Is.

St. Helena

Cape Town

SOUTH AFRICA

TROPIC OF CANCER

EQUATOR

TROPIC OF CAPRICORN

Canary Is.

Cape Verde Is.

USA

Florida

BAHAMAS

CUBA

PUERTO RICO

VIRGIN IS

DOMINICAN REPUBLIC

ANTIGUA

ST. LUCIA

17. St. Helena – South Atlantic

Fernando de Noronha and Fortaleza – Brazil, Devil's Island and Kourou – French Guiana, St. Lucia and Antigua – West Indies

The South Atlantic doesn't have hurricanes and is renowned as a benign ocean. What a pleasure it was after the anxieties of the Cape trip and the uncomfortable sloppy Indian Ocean. As we left Cape Town the winds were light, the motion was gentle and school in the cockpit was so pleasant after our previous labours battened below in the heat and humidity. *Bagheera* sailed 6000 nautical miles between late February and mid-April and it was remarkably relaxing. We particularly enjoyed listening to tapes through our cockpit speakers. Now, how those tunes take us back!

The one annoyance was that three days out of Cape Town our refrigeration packed up. Of course it had worked perfectly for the four months we were in South Africa where repair would have been easy. Andy tried topping up with Freon without success. It was especially irritating as the day before leaving a salesman had talked me into buying extra meat that was vacuum packed. This method of sealing is becoming very popular on boats but goods do have to be kept cool. We cooked as much meat as we could, but as the days went by packets inflated and the contents had to be thrown overboard. Cheeses and margarine were stowed under the floorboards, now the coolest place on the boat, and they kept well. Beer and wine kept well for another reason: not being cold they weren't so appealing!

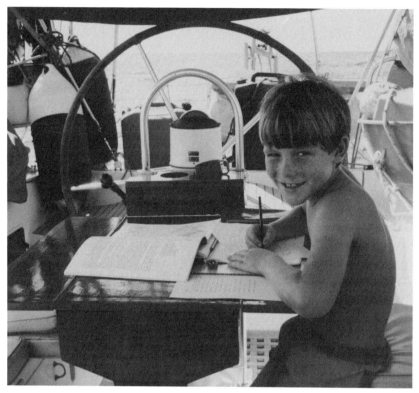

School in the cockpit

Not knowing of the delays we would experience in Cape Town due to our autohelm, I had arranged that Colin and Jamie take the entrance exam to St. Georges (Duncan's school in Vancouver) in St. Helena, our first stop in the Atlantic. This tiny speck of an island, which arises from the South Atlantic, had just come on the telephone via satellite and St. George's agreed to fax the exams to the accommodating British headmaster with whom I had spoken.

We were all keyed up on arrival, having worked many extra school hours on the trip, with some help from other yachts. I was concerned that we knew very little about Canadian history, but I need not have worried, Tanis on *Wind Woman* was very well informed. After an hour on the single side-band radio we had the basics written out.

The anchorage by the quaint, very English Jamestown, is unprotected. It was fortunately calm for us but friends had told us that it was extremely rolly during their visit. Psychologically it is more irritating rolling at anchor than at sea; you feel you have earned the respite, especially after a long passage, and should not have to stow every little thing away. We found getting ashore was tricky, requiring careful timing and leaping out of the dinghy as the waves surged up onto the wharf. Fortunately there were generally several helping hands from the shore. The alternative was trusting your fate to the local ferry which also relied on the same technique!

I phoned the school on arrival, and was aghast to find that the exam hadn't been sent. I finally got through to St. Georges in Vancouver and was informed by the secretary that the test would have taken some time to fax so she had decided to send it by express mail.

"But there isn't an airport here," I told her, "and the next ship isn't due for six weeks."

"That can't be so! Canada Post guaranteed me a two day delivery," was the unwavering reply.

We were devastated; it was such a let-down. On the way back to *Bagheera* we stopped aboard *Lion Wing*; we had enjoyed being with Beau and Annie, the owners, in Hout Bay.

"The boys will have to take the exam in Fortaleza now," I told them, "and I'm kicking myself because I met someone by the phone in Richards Bay who was going to give me the name of a great friend of his in Fortaleza, but I never saw him again."

"That's not a problem," said Beau unexpectedly, "I know who you are talking about, he was opposite us on the dock. I think it is Tom you want to contact and we have his address and phone number right here."

I couldn't believe it, and immediately went ashore to phone. Luck was with us, not only was Tom home but he was also an English teacher at the U.S./Brazilian school. As the boys had to take the exam at a regular school this was perfect. The headmaster at St. George's was very understanding and another set of exams was sent to Fortaleza—it sounded so foolproof . . .

Now we could enjoy the island and what a fascinating place it is. A barren rock as you approach from the sea, it is hard to believe that it has a population of about 5500 people. We arranged a tour with *Lionwing* and *Just Cruising*, who had also just arrived. There are only 85 kilometres of road on St. Helena but it took us most of the day to get around. The island is volcanic in origin, its surface rugged and mountainous and the contrasts are stunning, from the fertile interior valleys to the almost lunar landscape of the coast. We visited the palatial governor's residence, the boys enjoying the pet Seychelles giant tortoise which had reputedly been alive when Napoleon was incarcerated on the island, and also went to the new, attractive Prince Andrew school where the boys had been scheduled to take their exam.

Lunch was in the grounds of Longwood farmhouse, where Napoleon spent the last six years of his life (1815-1821) in exile as a prisoner of the British after his defeat at the Battle of Waterloo. The property is well maintained as a museum by the French and the memorabilia was interesting to view. I hadn't realized that besides being a great general Napoleon was also an enlightened, if dictatorial, emperor. He not only reformed French law to his Code Napoleon, the basic structure of which is still used today, but he also tried to give the continent of Europe a common Law. That he obviously gloried in the pomp and notoriety of being both a general and emperor was shown in the many paintings on display. Undoubtedly this was a devastating end to his life.

On our return we looked down on small, picturesque Jamestown with its smartly painted houses, set in a gully at sea level between high barren hills. Our guide suggested we descend by Jacob's ladder, 699 steps to the bottom, but he didn't get any takers. We all agreed we would rather climb up than down; it was a long way to fall.

St. Helena is supported by Britain and the people are a mix of European, South American Indian and African. They were very friendly and extremely up to date, despite the limited shipping from either South Africa or Britain. When we were there the last two ships had broken down but supplies were still abundant in the stores and a local personality 'Annie' served great meals every night. We ate there a couple of times and when we were leaving she presented me with a birthday cake to have underway.

It was another twelve day passage to the Brazilian island of Fernando de Noronha, and we flew the spinnaker much of the way. My birthday was celebrated two days out. Andy and the boys put up decorations and they had taken great trouble with my presents and cards. Colin's seahorse picture in particular had taken a lot of work and time, whilst I was off watch and sleeping.

The voyage was slow but comfortable, the waves wide apart lulling one into a false sense of safety, but every so often the boat could take a roll despite the seas looking so calm. Later we heard of one girl on another yacht who was flipped overboard as she leaned over the lifelines to attach a block. Fortunately she was easily recovered but it was a huge shock for everyone on board.

Our last day alternated between calms and squalls, but we were able to fill our water tanks with rain. *Journey* and *Pendragon*, with whom we had been talking on the radio, greeted us on our arrival at Fernando de Noronha. A French yacht also welcomed us. They had just sailed from the Cape Verde Islands and were on their way to Argentina.

After pumping up the dinghy we headed ashore. It was reminiscent of Venezuela with the blue painted fishing boats and sea wall covered with noisy boobies and pelicans. Further along the beach the fishermen were holding up fish for the frigate birds. Although most birds hovered overhead then swooped down, others were very bold and came in confidently at a low level, grabbing a fish and continuing on their way.

Lionwing arrived just before midnight and the next morning everyone came over for a belated birthday champagne breakfast. *Journey* then left for the States, *Pendragon* for Europe and in the afternoon *Just Cruising* arrived. We all went ashore to explore; it was very hot and humid and a ride to the hotel in the back of a truck was most welcome. The hotel was made up of renovated U.S. Nissen huts dating back to World War II but we were able to get ice cold beer and I finally got through to Canada on

Fernando de Noronha

the phone. The exams had been sent off to Fortaleza, I was told. We walked back across the pretty island in the cool of dusk, the volcanic core Pico with an old fort below being particularly picturesque. En route Jamie found a small pool full of tadpoles and insisted we had to take some back to *Bagheera*. They developed into very active large toads which were subsequently released back into the wild.

The two day trip to Fortaleza was squally with several heavy rainshowers. We had been given mixed reports about this city on the North Brazilian coast. On the one hand we had been told it was a fascinating town, full of South American vibrancy. The other report was via a frantic radio conversation from a single-hander. He told us that he was tied up to a yacht whose captain had to keep watch in the cockpit all night with a gun in his hand, because of the extreme risk of theft and violence. Several people decided to give Fortaleza a miss on hearing this transmission but of course we had arranged for the exam to be taken there. Moreover, we'd had some experience with these situations.

On arrival we were pleased to find two other yachts in the rather exposed bay and we anchored close to one with a noisy dog, hoping it would 'guard' us too! A German contact, who spoke Portuguese, graciously offered to give up his day to clear us in. We were fortunate to have him as we hadn't realized that with the delays and slow passages Jamie's visa had expired two days before. The rest of us were fine, not requiring visas on our British passports. It had taken considerable organization to get Jamie's visa in South Africa as I first had to get new pages put in his Canadian passport and everything had to be done long distance whilst we were on the move. I thought this more than showed our good intent.

"Tell him we had very light winds and were stuck out at sea," I suggested.

After much voluble interchange in Portuguese, several phone calls and considerable name dropping of people in high places by our new friend, Immigration finally, but still somewhat reluctantly, decided that eight year old Jamie was not a threatening alien and could be allowed ashore.

I then went off confidently to arrange for a time for the children to sit the exam only to find to my horror that yet again it hadn't arrived. The school where it had been sent did a search, the post office did a search but despite the fact several regular letters had arrived for us in record time, nothing arrived by the guaranteed two day special delivery. It was a tense time, aggravated by delays due to the Easter holiday.

However there were some compensations. Fortaleza was a marvellously vibrant city with superb and very inexpensive restaurants. After completeing school on board we had wonderful lunches ashore before sightseeing, particularly enjoying the tender beef. The individual dishes were big enough for two, and there was extra rice and vegetables besides. After we had our fill there was always food left over. This went to the local children waiting outside and we were always impressed how fairly these urchins divided their spoils.

Tom and his girlfriend took us on a tour into the green, lush interior. The villages were very attractive with the houses covered in terracotta tiles. We stopped at a market and gorged on local fruit and vegetables, climbed up to a monastery for a spectacular view and stopped for lunch at a restaurant by a waterfall that had great Portuguese cooking aromas. The local music was loud but it was delightful to see a granny get up amidst much applause and sing a song in typical lusty South American strains.

Other days we explored the town which is renowned for its lace work. Blouses, tablecloths, embroidered shirts and hammocks hung outside the shops everywhere and there were plenty of gem shops for Colin. We chose some presents for friends and bought a hammock to relax in at home. I have yet to use it! One evening, leaving friends in charge of *Bagheera*, we visited the beach market, and found perfect, two-foot long, fossilized fish millions of years old being sold for a mere $10 each.

A real bonus was the hospitable yacht club. A refreshing swim followed by relaxing sundowners with Jan and Anthony from *Just Cruising* became the pleasant routine at the end of the hot humid days. We were puzzled as to why the club was always empty. Finally we asked the barman.

"The club is closed to members over the Easter holiday," he told us, "but we are keeping it open for you."

So we had the club and pool completely to ourselves, and our own private bar and waiter!

We always returned to the boat at dusk and had no problems with theft. However, another yacht was boarded one night. The owners were out late, and hadn't left any deterrents—lights, music or the radio on—or told anyone on the other boats they would be away. The couple arrived back to find two men with knives on board, but surprised them and the thieves jumped overboard. They were later identified by their dinghy and caught.

Every morning while we practised times tables, and chanted Canadian history and scientific facts, we watched the fishing boats heading out. These craft were sailing rafts and originally were made of balsa logs lashed together. Because of the scarcity of this wood, plywood is now used. With a centreboard, huge sails made from flour sacking and primitive anchors made from wood and rock, just like those used in ancient Roman galleys, these rafts are surprisingly efficient.

Time was passing and Andy wanted to leave. I called Vancouver again to ask the headmaster if he would send another exam to Antigua, shopped, loaded the boat and went to pick up the children from their last swim. But they had news—the exam had just arrived . . it had taken 18 days. On the radio the next morning the boys received a terrific confidence boost as they were wished 'good luck' from boats who were in St. Helena, the North Atlantic and all the way up the Caribbean chain to the Virgin Islands. The exam was written in the noisy school office, but it was air-conditioned, and both boys thought they had done well; there were no questions on Canadian history!

Fortaleza fishing boat

The Guianas were developed due to British, French and Dutch attempts to be part of the colonial action in South America, much to the annoyance of the Spanish and Portuguese who believed South America was theirs to divide. There have been several disputes over the borders. Originally populated by Carib and Arawak Indians and other tribes, French Guiana has been French, Dutch, English and then French again. As the colony was never profitable, from the 1850s the French used it for penal settlements and established several around the country. One, Ile du Diable (Devil's Island), has become famous due to Henri Charriérre's book Papillon; as it was on our way we decided to visit it. There are in fact three main islands with Ile St. Joseph having the ruins of the prison. We wandered around Ile Royale, a charming island with delightful paths made by the prisoners and the ruins of a church. The old warders' mess hall has been turned into a hotel and while we were having a drink the operator of the tourist boat said we would have no trouble going into Kourou. The coast along this shore is mostly very shallow so we hadn't previously planned to stop on the mainland.

Heading over to Kourou I chatted on the radio to *Just Cruising*. Then another voice came over the air.

"*Bagheera, Bagheera* this is *Jean Marie*."

"*Jean Marie*? I can't believe it. How great to hear you, Tom. Where are you?"

We hadn't seen or heard of the Services since leaving Cape Town as they didn't have a long range radio transmitter. However they did have a receiver and had been listening to all the boat schedules so knew where we were. In fact they had never been far from us, but greater than the thirty mile range of the v.h.f. radio.

They invited us on board for dinner; but first we had to find somewhere to anchor. What we hadn't been told about was the unbelievably strong tidal current in the river, which not only flowed at four knots but also changed abruptly with every tide. There were vicious squalls that evening and *Bagheera* managed to sail over the anchor chain during slack water and wrap it around her keel. As the ebb strengthened the anchor was lifted. In seconds *Bagheera* was charging down river past *Jean Marie*. Luckily Tom was on deck and saw it happen, and *Bagheera* had turned into the middle of the channel rather than into the mass of boats on buoys, where she could have caused considerable damaged.

Up to the early 1960s Kourou was a small village with under a thousand inhabitants, then a new town was built for the staff of France's Space Exploration Centre and the population increased to over 7000.

We had just a quick trip ashore; it teemed with rain as another squall went through and not surprisingly we left later that morning, but not before we released the toads from Fernando which had not only grown huge but very noisy.

On our way up to the West Indies *Bagheera* had her fastest passage ever. At the confluence of the North and South Equatorial Currents which pour from the Atlantic into the Caribbean we achieved 219 nautical miles (405 km) in a 24 hour period. For all you non-sailors that is FAST! There was also incredible phosphorescence, a phenomena that we had enjoyed all around the world. Produced by plankton this chemo luminescence is common to marine animals and it is believed to be a protective reaction to danger. As the spray bounced off the hull it sparkled a brilliant white/blue and astern *Bagheera* had a solid metallic blue wake.

We had just a quick stop in St. Lucia's Rodney Bay, where a modern, full service marina has been built, to wash the ingrained salt both off ourselves and the boat. Meanwhile I made use of the laundry service and Andy checked out some boating equipment and looked for parts for our refrigerator. Later an old friend came over. Andy had got to know Jay when they were both outfitting boats in Lymington, on the south coast of England, six years before and we had sailed with him down the Atlantic European coast.

As we sat chatting in the cockpit Jay commented "You have no idea how hard it is to run a charter boat in a third world country."

We both looked askance. A third world country with every technical help right at hand, instant fax machines and two-day delivery guaranteed from the States? We knew what third world countries were like and besides we had run charter boats in the Caribbean twenty years before when facilities were very different. It was hard to be sympathetic, but again it was the comparison to one's frame of reference that we would have to get used to.

There is always a special magic approaching Nelson's Dockyard in Antigua, sailing past the rock formations called the Pillars of Hercules into Freemans Bay, then round the corner into English Harbour and the dockyard itself. With its old buildings renovated and trailing pink and purple bougainvillea, it is a very attractive setting. After clearing in, we sailed around to Falmouth Harbour, which is separated from English Harbour by a narrow strip of land, and anchored in the cool breeze off the Yacht Club.

At the club that night we ran into several old friends.

"I thought I heard *Ticonderoga* on the radio earlier. Is she here?" I asked.

"Yes, she's been here for a few days and is tied up in English Harbour," was the reply.

Andy and I were married aboard 'Big Ty', sailing across the bay in Martinique and it would be lovely to see her again.

"Isn't your wedding anniversary soon?" someone else asked.

"Actually, its tomorrow," Andy replied.

Word soon got around and the crew of *Ticonderoga* invited us on board to celebrate our eighteenth anniversary with French champagne the next day. We were also pleased to see that this magnificent old 70 foot Hereshoff-designed yacht was still kept in such fine condition, particularly all its beautifully varnished wood.

Andy was involved in the founding of Antigua Race Week; this year it was the twenty-fourth event. We had arrived in Antigua just in time for the Classic Yacht races, before the big week itself. The classic yachts were magnificent but outstanding was 130 foot, deep blue, *Endeavour*, a sloop-rigged J-boat built in the 1934 by Camper and Nicholson in England, to challenge for the Americas Cup. With her unbelievable overhanging bow and stern, she has been beautifully restored. While watching the start from *Bagheera* I was using the video camera. Suddenly *Endeavour* headed up and looking through the camera I seemed very close, in fact felt right in the cockpit. Within seconds she was away, gliding swiftly through the waves.

Antigua lived up to all our memories and Andy was particularly touched by the welcome he received from his old employees at Antigua Slipway. This time with the far more relaxed interaction between whites and locals many of them joked about the number of times Andy had hired and fired them. What a huge number of yachts there were, from the beautiful 'oldies' to the highly equipped stripped-out racing machines. The biggest Race Week yet, there were 141 entries and as many 'hangers-on' like ourselves.

For the first time during Race Week, instead of being a competitor I volunteered to help out, and was amazed by the extensive organization and the number of volunteer hours that are put in by the same people year after year.

We cruised around the island with the fleet, listening to many a steel band, and made a few detours with our cruising friends, including old favourites such as Great Bird Island and Green Island. It was an exhilarating time with far too many rum punches!

130' Endeavour

There was also another very special celebration. Sailing up from South America we had crossed our 1986 outbound route between Barbados and Grenada. To our delight we could share our celebration in the Admirals Inn with two other families that we had got to know well, who had also just completed their circumnavigations—American *Jean Marie* with Jean, Tom, Dawn and Jennifer Service and Canadian *Wind Woman* with Tanis, Peter, Jennifer and Alex Boger.

For just one day several of us, who had talked on the radio every day since South Africa, were in Antigua together—*Wind Woman, Just Cruising, Orkestern, Lone Rival, Counterpoint,* and *Lionwing. Jean Marie* put on a party in the huge centre cockpit of their CSY 44. Also in Antigua were Stuart previously from *Asteroid* (last seen in Thailand), *Cool Change* and *Noa Noa* (last seen in Bali, Indonesia), *Yarandoo II* (last seen in Australia). *Archangel* was up in the Virgin Islands and *Belair* and *Kendaric* were further down the Caribbean chain. *Journey* was close to Texas and *Pendragon* was almost at the Azores. We were particularly pleased to see Dusty on *Magnum.* Well into his late 70s now, Dusty had sailed single-handed through the Red Sea and Mediterranean then crossed the Atlantic, since leaving us in Thailand.

It was a time for catching up with our visitors book, including a rendering from *Jean Marie.* Tom made me promise not to edit it!

SHIPMATES

Bagheera is a vessel with class we agree, equipped as a cruiser
    sporting a racer's pedigree
Andy's her intrepid skipper—a mariner unmatched, his judgement
    is sound though he's only partially thatched.
The Admiral's a redhead with freckles galore, Liza's never without
    words . . . and she's never a bore.
Colin's a rock hound, he selects them by weight, the captain wants
    to deballast, and let the boy pay the freight.
Jamie's a boat kid that much is quite clear, he's ready and able to
    hand, reef or steer.
Duncan's 'Joe college' he matriculates ashore with studies and
    rugby and coeds amour.
They're world class sailors, they've been all the way round with
    friendship and strange sights their memories abound.
God bless you each one, as you sail this grand sea, we'll think of you
    often aboard the cutter *Jean Marie*

—T. Buchanan Service

The circumnavigator's celebrate . Andy, Tanis and Peter from Wind
Woman, *Tom and Jean from* Jean Marie, *Liza*
(the kids were having their own party!)

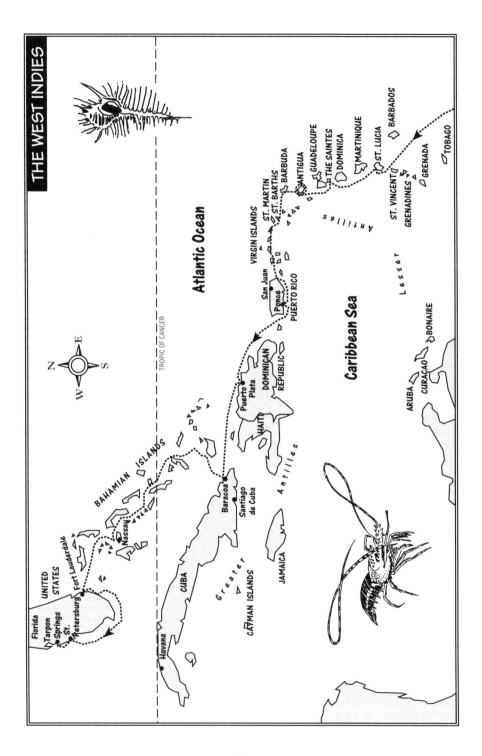

THE WEST INDIES

Atlantic Ocean

TROPIC OF CANCER

N
W — E
S

UNITED
STATES

Florida
Tarpon
Springs
St.
Petersburg
Fort Lauderdale

Havana

CUBA

Baracoa

Santiago
de Cuba

Nassau

BAHAMIAN ISLANDS

CAYMAN ISLANDS

JAMAICA

Greater

Antilles

Caribbean Sea

Puerto
Plata

HAITI

DOMINICAN
REPUBLIC

Ponce

San Juan

PUERTO RICO

VIRGIN ISLANDS

ST. MARTIN
ST. BARTHS

BARBUDA

ANTIGUA

GUADELOUPE

THE SAINTES

DOMINICA

MARTINIQUE

ST. LUCIA

BARBADOS

ST. VINCENT

GRENADINES

GRENADA

TOBAGO

Lesser

Antilles

ARUBA

CURAÇAO

BONAIRE

220

18. Barbuda, St. Barts, St. Martin

British and U.S. Virgin Islands, Culebra, Vieques, Puerto Rico and the Dominican Republic

Antigua is a second home to us. Andy worked and had a home there for several years, and we had spent considerable time in the harbour whilst running charter boats in the early 1970s. It was hard to leave, but we now had to think seriously of the hurricane season and getting home to Vancouver on schedule.

After several farewells we left Antigua at 2:00 A.M. on May 14th for Barbuda, an island that is governed by Antigua, 25 nautical miles to the north. In the past Barbuda has claimed many a wreck as most of its scrubland barely clears the water and the approaches are shallow and reef strewn. Cruisers are inclined to give it a miss, but it has long been a favourite diving destination of Andy's. We anchored on the west side, by a long sand beach, and immediately donned our diving gear. The reef was teeming with squirrelfish, tangs, damselfish and parrotfish, which gave brilliant flashes of colour as they darted through the huge arms of staghorn and elkhorn coral. Unfortunately, due to the swell, Andy was unable to dive deep for lobster but there were queen conchs for the taking. We had an excellent communal dinner with Anthony and Jan on *Just Cruising* sharing our conch chowder and the fine cero mackerel they had landed along the way.

The dawn air was fresh when we headed out at 6:00 the next morning. It was a glorious day with brisk twenty knot tradewinds, deep blue sea and sky, and white fluffy clouds dancing along the horizon. St. Barts has always been one of our favourite spots with its sleepy town, Gustavia, circling the harbour. From the late 1600s the island prospered under the French and most of the population is descended from the original Breton fishermen who settled there. In 1784 the French sold it to the Swedes, the buildings from this era adding to the charm of the harbour. In 1878 the French bought it back again. Until recently St. Barts was one of the centres of smuggling for the Caribbean and, on our first visits, there were generally battered old local sloops loading at the dock, with just the occasional yacht swinging at anchor. Now the town, Gustavia, has become much more developed and upbeat, and the harbour was packed with yachts, many stern-to the quay.

"What an incredible change," commented Andy.

"I know but it's been ten years since we've been here," I replied.

Jamie had sailed with Jan and Anthony for the trip and they had hooked a couple of mackerel and a tuna. For fun we took them around to the restaurants to sell. The best offer we could get was a free round of drinks for the tuna. Andy went right into French mode ordering a round of the aniseed based pastis and we were all soon buying French paté, cheeses and baguettes. After a whirl around town the next morning, to find my favourite Caribbean-batik fabric and a visit to 'shell' beach for a swim and shell hunt with the boys, we headed north on the short fourteen mile trip to the island of St. Martin. Sadly it would be our last sail with Jan and Anthony on *Just Cruising* as this was their final destination.

Although small, St. Martin is half French and half Dutch, the Dutch calling their side Sint Maarten. Entering Philipsburg, the Dutch free-port, we were again struck by the numbers of yachts. With several charter fleets now operating in the area the bays and beaches around the island were no longer empty. The hotels were also booming and the many developments had enticed several cruisers to look for work. In particular it appealed to South Africans, who were limited in the countries they were welcomed in. Jan and Anthony had several friends who had been to St. Martin which is why they had decided to stay here.

As usual we found bargains in the two rows of duty free shops in Philipsburg—a watch for Andy, and waterproof walkman radio-tape machines for the boys. Colin and Jamie deserved them after so many miles at sea and now they could relax in their own cabins with their individual tastes in music, which we didn't have to listen to! We had a final ice cream with Jan and Anthony ashore, all of us yawning after the previous night's partying with many an excellent rum punch. We would really miss these lads. Jamie was in tears, but was cheered up by the wonderful farewell mementoes that Jan and Anthony had brought for us.

There was a good breeze for the seventy mile trip north-west to Virgin Gorda, in the British Virgin Islands. When coming south-east into wind this trip across the Anegarda passage can be a hard grind in confused seas, often the most uncomfortable passage between Florida and South America. Heading north it is all downwind but the boat can still be tossed around.

Virgin Gorda was almost obliterated by squalls and heavy rain as we approached but we were anchored in time for the 7:00 A.M. radio schedule. *Lionwing* and *Counterpoint* were now north, on their way to the U.S. east coast and out of the tropics, and had very light winds. *Journey* was half way to the Dutch ABC islands off Columbia and was making a fast passage, *Orkestern* was leaving for the Azores, and *Lone Rival* was just off to Bermuda. *Just Cruising* had met friends in St. Martin and was moving round to Simson Lake, a protected shallow lagoon, to lie at anchor for a few months.

The Virgin Islands have long been a popular destination for sailing holidays. Stretching 45 miles from east to west the big islands are mostly mountainous while the many small islands provide perfect gunkholing opportunities in protected waters. The U.S. Virgin Islands to the west include the islands of St. Thomas, St. John and St. Croix, the latter to the south and separated from the rest of the group by a 40 mile stretch of open water. St. Thomas and St. Croix are duty-free ports full of tourist shops, supermarkets and air-conditioned homes, and have a constant parade of cruise ships. The quaint old-fashioned British Virgins to the east have always been our favourites. The islands run in two lines about three miles apart, enclosing the Sir Francis Drake passage. Tortola and Virgin Gorda are the largest. The many bays make the magnificent anchorages that have been enjoyed by the Arawak and Carib Indians, Columbus, Sir Francis Drake, pirates and modern cruisers alike.

Although times have changed in the British Virgin Islands in the last twenty years, with Road Town, the commercial centre, a boom town from increased tourism, they are still delightful to visit. Tortola was becoming the centre of yachting, we noticed, instead of St. Thomas, and now had several marinas. These cater particularly to the bareboat fleets, whose charterers take the yachts out themselves rather than having a skipper and crew, the norm twenty years ago. With distances short, exhilarating sailing in calm seas, beautiful scenery and excellent diving, this is a wonderful area to cruise, and a great place to charter as a first 'offshore' destination.

Although busy in season (December–April) we found the islands uncrowded at the end of May with many cruisers being old friends who were also heading up to the States. In particular we had time to visit with Jerry and Kai, who ran *Archangel*, and were cruising with their two year old daughter, Kailou, and reminisce about our cruising since first meeting them four years before when transiting the Suez Canal. After eight years on board they too were leaving the life of the sea. There was also great interchange between the children on *Jean Marie*, *Cool Change* and *Bagheera*, all of whom had at least 35,000 miles at sea under their belts, but who were now all excited, and a little fearful, of returning to the world of school and their regular peers.

After cruising up Gorda Sound, we anchored off the Bitter End in a deep turquoise sea and had excellent diving off Prickly Pear Island. The water was remarkably clear and again there were many fish around the reefs. Jamie enjoyed watching the long pipe fish which barely seem to move and the distinctive black, yellow striped, triangular shaped French angel fish. The tiny damsel fish were very cheeky charging headlong at us as though we were another fish.

At the southern end of Virgin Gorda are the Baths. Amidst sparkling white sands these phenomenal rock formations are like giant smooth boulders and the enclosed pools of crystal clear green water are illuminated by shafts of sunlight. Wading through them we were frequently drenched by the ocean waves that crash through the high, cathedral-like caves. The boys could have stayed all day.

Gradually we made our way to St. Thomas, but we were all suffering from colds, unpleasant at any time but especially debilitating in the tropics. As the weather cleared there were some incredible night skies. Not only were the individual star constellations dazzling but the milky way was a brilliant blanket across the sky. It was beautiful out in the cockpit and with books at our side we tried to identify the blaze of light.

"There are the seven stars of the Plough," Jamie would cry out.

"And there's the Little Bear, or Ursa Minor with Polaris," added Colin.

They searched for Orion, a constellation they knew well, but it wasn't visible at this time of year; but they did identify Libra, Hercules and Virgo.

The U.S Virgin Islands were purchased by the U.S.A. in 1917, having been Denmark's only colony in the Caribbean for the previous two hundred and fifty years. St. Thomas attracted shipping, particularly pirates, from the earliest days because of its magnificent sheltered harbour and it now teems with yachts, motor boats, and cruise ships.

Although attractive, we had always found the main town Charlotte Amalie too touristy for us, besides being ridden with crime in the sixties and seventies. After stocking up at the supermarket we would leave St. Thomas as quickly as possible. On this visit, however, we were given a tour of the island. Tony Garton, a great raconteur, accomplished chef and bon vivant, was an old friend from our early days in Antigua when he day-chartered his *Warrior Geraint*, a converted World War II fairmile naval-patrol boat, and he insisted on showing us around. We were impressed at the pretty hilly interior and lovely bays, and delighted that in spite of the scramble for the tourist dollar there was still much unspoilt.

He also took us to the Tutu 'dig'. We knew about the Arawaks, the original inhabitants of many of the Caribbean islands, from Desmond Nicholson in Antigua who has put together an interesting museum in St. Johns. The Arawaks lived a peaceful existence and, judging by the numbers of pieces that have been found, were skilled potters. Then came the warlike Caribs who, dressed in red paint and feathers, made their way up the islands from South America in their swift canoes. When Columbus arrived in the Virgin Islands in 1492 the Caribs were making frequent raids, stopping before they moved on to what is now Puerto Rico, looking for a tasty Arawak for dinner. Although the Spaniards were more of a match for the Caribs it wasn't until 1555 that the Caribs were wiped out of the Virgins altogether. As soon as they were gone the pirates arrived!

Having heard that Vieques Sound was attractive for cruising we headed for Culebra, about 20 nautical miles west of St. Thomas. Before July 1975 this area was designated as a 'danger zone' for U.S. military exercises so didn't develop for cruising like the Virgin Islands. Culebra has a wonderful natural harbour and lovely small bays. But here disaster struck; our small bird Aussie Boo passed away. He had been ailing for the previous week. Colin had nursed him devotedly, often not leaving the boat when our little bird lay down pitifully. This final day Aussie just wanted to be held. He died in Colin's hands. We buried him ashore, making a conch shell grave. Everyone was heartbroken, especially Colin. For so long, when there were no others around, he had been the boys' friend and entertainment with his endearing personality.

We soon left for Vieques Island. Approaching the coast we called the coastguard as there were still some military artillery and bombing ranges active along the coast. Getting no response we then tried the Atlantic Fleet Weapons Training Facility Radio Advisory Service— quite a mouthful on the radio!—to ask if we could stop at Chiva. We were given permission but were told to keep two miles off the shore until we got there.

"Are you sure that's what they said?" questioned Andy surprised.

I'd barely replied in the affirmative when a huge explosion went off on the south-eastern shore, right beside us!

We anchored further along in the Bay of Chiva where we had been assured there wouldn't be any military activity, and found it very pretty with excellent diving. The reef was close to the surface and we swam through pillars of coral. Andy caught a lobster and the boys found some large helmet shells, delighted with their large shiny triangular mouths.

The crescent-shaped beach at Ensenada Sun Bay is beautiful, our cruising guide likening it to a 'Bali Hai' landscape. We ate ashore that night in Isabel Segunda, the largest town on the island, enjoying the Spanish atmosphere. Everywhere was so peaceful it was hard to believe that Vieques Island is actually larger than any of the Virgin Islands, except for St. Croix. With its rolling hills and pasture it is the main cattle producing area for Puerto Rico.

Our friends the Services on *Jean Marie* had meanwhile pulled into the U.S. Naval base on Puerto Rico.

"You'll probably be boarded by the U.S. Coast Guard," Tom warned us on the radio. "It seems to be pretty routine at the moment with overseas yachts."

We had heard horrendous stories of boats being boarded by coast-guards in hobnailed boots in the middle of the night, waving guns and spending hours searching the boat, and repeating the procedure a few days later.

Andy called me at 7:00 the next morning as we were sailing west along the southern coast of Puerto Rico.

"The Coast Guard have been tailing us since 5:00," he told me, "and they have just called on the radio to say they are coming over for an inspection."

I woke the boys and we were all ready for the arrival of their huge inflatable. The search was quick, the questions polite and brief, there were no weapons in evidence, and they were soon on their way. To Andy's relief they hadn't asked us if we had a bell for anchoring in fog. Very few yachts had room but it was apparently a favourite question. The inspection had been very professional with a minimum of inconvenience to us.

"Did you notice their shoes?" said Jamie. After all the criticism the men had been wearing brand new yachting shoes!

Ponce is an attractive stop on the south coast of Puerto Rico, with its enclosed harbour, and a yacht club that is reputedly very friendly—although we were told we couldn't use either the showers or the pool. It was a spectacular drive over to the capital, San Juan, on the north coast with the bright red flamboyant trees in full bloom. We again enjoyed the Spanish atmosphere indulging in the Hispanic cuisine and wonderful fresh produce.

Just before we left, *Jean Marie* pulled in.

"How was the Base?" we asked them.

"We met some other kids on boats," replied Jennifer, "but one girl was awfully snooty. You know she even had a regular refrigerator, air-conditioning, a computer and videos on board."

"I know," replied Colin, "the newly 'outs' are a bit of a pain aren't they; they just don't know what it's all about!"

We decided to stay another night and had a great evening with the Services. We were going to sorely miss them, as they were now headed for St. Petersburg in Florida. Jennifer and Dawn came aboard *Bagheera* at 7:00 the next morning, to talk on the radio to *Windwoman*, as *Jean Marie* didn't carry an H.F. transmitter. Jennifer was elated that she had finished her school year; Dawn had two more days to go. Later Jennifer came over again offering to teach Jamie. It gave me extra time for laundry and shopping and gave Jamie a welcome break from me!

Bagheera was finally underway by 4:00 P.M. after we had gone aground 25 metres from the fuel dock and, after barrelling our way through the mud, found the pumps were not working.

"They are fixing," the friendly attendant told us.

"How long will it take?" asked Andy.

There was a typical Latin shrug. "Five, maybe ten minutes."

Andy and I looked at each other.

"Shall we risk it and leave?" suggested Andy.

"But we don't know how easy it is to get fuel in the Dominican Republic," I replied, remembering all too vividly the many hours of organization it had required to get fuel in the past and lugging cans on board from the dinghy.

There was a terrible surge grinding us onto the dock but the pumps were repaired fifteen minutes later. As it was very calm all night it was fortunate we had waited. At dawn the wind filled in from the south-east, gusting up to 30 knots. The waves built surprisingly quickly and *Bagheera* was soon surfing down the foaming crests at speeds of eight and nine knots.

We had seen some regular shipping but were amazed to see a big tug towing three huge barges. We talked to them on the radio.

"We're taking heavy equipment from New Orleans to Venezuela," they told us.

"Isn't that a long way to tow that kind of load at sea?" I enquired.

"No, it's quite common, but we do have to fuel on the way and that can cause some excitement." With such unwieldly barges we could well imagine the dynamics.

Hispaniola is the second largest island in the Caribbean, after Cuba, and it is shared by two countries, Haiti to the west and the Dominican Republic in the east. The countries are remarkably different and no love is lost between them. Haiti, although echoing its French colonial past, still reverberates of Africa, while the Dominican Republic has a Spanish speaking, Latin American culture.

The island was discovered by Columbus on December 5, 1492, and he established a settlement on the north coast not far from our destination of Puerto Plata. Hearing some other yachts on the radio that were in the harbour, we made contact.

"Everyone dragged anchor today," they told us. Just what we wanted to hear!

It was easy to identify the harbour with the old fort at the entrance and 8,500 metre Mount Isabel de Torres rising behind. We arrived in the town in the early evening.

"You've half an hour left to clear in," another boat told us. "We can take you ashore and show you the way."

After anchoring Andy leapt into the dinghy with all the documents. On his return he invited our helpers on board, and the owners of the two other boats with whom they were cruising.

It soon became apparent that they were very worried. All newcomers to the cruising life they had spent the last three months cruising the Bahamas, in boats they had bought in Florida.

"But what do we do now?" they asked. "We're really worried about the hurricane season. Where should we go?"

"There's no problem," we assured them. "Just dead-head for Venezuela which is out of the hurricane belt. It will only take you three or four days."

There was a deathly silence.

"Three or four days," someone finally dared to say, "but that's such a long trip."

It was hard for us to relate to, particularly our children, but was the shock treatment needed before returning to the 'real world'. In the last few months our main contact had been with experienced long-distance cruisers. This situation jogged us into talking to the boys about some of the differences in interests and attitudes that they would experience when going home. In particular, that some people probably wouldn't even be interested in our trip, or wouldn't see it in the same light as they did, particularly their peers. Also how careful one has to be about not sounding like a 'know it all'.

With local music on the radio the next morning, and Jamie doing a great rendering of Spanish dancing, we were in just the right mood for visiting the town, and we loved it. With old wooden buildings lining the narrow streets, Puerto Plata has an old-fashioned, colonial windblown charm. Close to beautiful beaches that have been developed for tourism it had some facilities but still maintained a quiet sleepiness.

Colin was delighted by the amber for sale. The Dominican Republic has one of the largest reserves of amber in the world, after the Baltic, and its main mining area is just south of Puerto Plata. Amber is the fossilized sap, or resin, from trees that grew millions of years ago. It varies from yellow to amber to deep red, the deepest colour demanding the highest price. Also prized are the wisps of blue smoke that was sometimes caught inside (blue amber) and the insects that were trapped, some of which are beautifully preserved. The Amber Museum had some exquisite examples. We visited twice with Colin finally deciding on some special pieces, including an amber turtle, to add to his collection of gems and fossils.

Another stone on display in the shops and market was the turquoise coloured larimar which is unique to the Dominican Republic. Set in silver it was very attractive for earrings, pendants and bracelets. Having been told by our fellow cruisers that bargaining was the norm I selected several pieces of both amber and larimar and suggested a price. Colin, who had got to know several of the lively market ladies, insisted I should pay full price or I would make them bankrupt. Meanwhile he ended up with several gifts from them!

Before arriving we had noticed a tear in the genoa, our large foresail, so we got up early the next morning to repair it. Finding it wasn't on a seam but a rip at the edge where there were several layers of cloth we contacted another boat, that made a living doing canvas work and sail repairs. We didn't have room for a sewing machine on board, although at times I had borrowed one to make cushion covers. In our six years we had needed only a handful of sail repairs, particularly because we had taken care to avoid chafe, putting on extra cloth in the greatest areas of wear—such as on the mainsail by the shrouds. Chafe is one of the hazards of long distance cruising and we made other modifications where necessary, such as putting plastic tubing over the genoa sheets where they went through the jaws of the spinnaker pole, and carpeting on the back edges of the spreaders on the mast, again to prevent chafe on the mainsail. We also had triple stitching on the seams of all sails.

Before leaving for another day of sightseeing we checked in on the radio schedule. *Wind Woman* was heading for Canada, *Archangel* was just approaching Bermuda.

Having been told that clouds form around the mountain later in the day we were up Mount Isabela de Torres before 8:00, getting rides on the backs of motor bikes to the cable car. The views were amazing; on the one side we soared above fertile, well-cultivated land with the many dwellings stacked up the hillside. Several people were riding donkeys for their transportation, winding their way through the banana trees and royal palms. On the other side a spectacular, panoramic view of the coast emerged, with mile upon mile of white sand beach.

Away from the buildings and the huge floodlit statue of Christ it was very peaceful and cool on the mountaintop, especially in the botanical gardens. Here huge tree ferns intermingled with pines and there was a profusion of flowers—colourful red ginger, spectacular lilies and large bell flowers.

The previous evening, while visiting the noisy No-Name bar with other cruisers, we met Mike, a Canadian, who bred budgerigars. We had been looking for a replacement for Aussie and on hearing the boys' sad tale Mike immediately invited us around to give us one of his. We stopped by when returning from the cable car and the boys chose one that was a month old, again green and yellow but with handsome purple chops with black spots. Several names were suggested; previously the country or place of purchase was incorporated in our birds' names. Finally Jamie had an idea.

"Why don't we call him Dominic," he suggested. "Like Andrew's friend in Kenya and it fits in with the Dominican Republic." So Dominic was welcomed on board.

When clearing out with the Commandante, Andy got permission for us to stop at Luperon, fifteen miles further along the coast, close to Cape

Isabela. There were strong winds but we had a peaceful stop in Puerto Blanca where the boys were excited to find black coral on the beach. It was an attractive setting with the actual fishing village of Luperon hidden behind a lush hillside covered by a banana plantation and coconut palms.

Our brief visit to the Dominican Republic had impressed us; it was a fascinating country not yet overwhelmed with tourism. The second largest country in the Caribbean (about the size of Scotland) it is full of contrasts. Cut by three mountain ranges with both fertile valley and arid, desert-like plains, it has vast lush, dripping rainforest and areas in which vegetation is stunted, where there are dwarf forest of ferns and grasses. Birds are in abundance with those of the forests and plains such as the Hispaniola parrots, rufus-throated solitaires, hummingbirds and wood-peckers, and those of the coast. These include the ibises, flamingos, frigate birds, noddies and terns that we had seen throughout the Carib-bean. The country has spectacular beaches and diving, and we enjoyed its people with their mixed Latin and Caribbean heritage.

Leaving that night so we would arrive in Cuba during daylight hours two days later (although on a Sunday!), we had a perfect 15 knots of wind from astern. Little did we know what a busy trip lay ahead.

19. Cuba, the Bahamas, the United States, and home to Canada

Baracoa and Santiago de Cuba
Georgetown, Nassau and the Islands
Florida to Vancouver

Liza, can you come on deck and keep watch? I think there's a Mayday call on the radio in Spanish," Andy called down to me from the cockpit.

A Mayday is a distress call. Jamie and I immediately went up on deck with the school books while Andy tried calling on the v.h.f. radio. He finally made contact. The call came from some fishermen, who were from the Dominican Republic. Their engine had broken down; they had been drifting for five days and were out of food. We were now off the west end of the Ile de la Tortue, Haiti.

Unfortunately, although we knew they must be within about thirty miles, the radio's range, we had no idea in which direction to find them. They also had no idea of their own position. We tried calling the U.S. Coastguard cutter that we had seen enter Puerto Plata as we were leaving, without success, so contacted the Miami Marine Operator, w.o.m., on the single side-band long distance radio. They immediately patched us in to the Coastguard in the States. Impressively, within forty-five minutes, a U.S. Coastguard plane was overhead and starting a circular search about 10 miles radius from us. Within no time they had called to say they had sighted the fishermen and would drop a container of food. Having been given the fishing boat's position we headed in its direction.

The coastguard then called us again. "*Bagheera* the fishermen now have supplies, but be careful as you approach as the parachute we used is floating in the water near them."

"Thank you for letting us know," I replied. "My eight year old son was very impressed watching the parachute come down."

"Tell your son that he is most welcome to have it as a gift from the U.S. Coastguard," was the gracious reply. Jamie was thrilled and soon became the proud owner of a huge, salty but beautifully-made red and white parachute.

The fishermen were delighted to see us, and particularly with the cold beer we gave them. They were obviously most relieved to finally have had a response to their many calls, not least because they knew they must be off inhospitable Haiti. With the engine out of order their battery was very low, and they could have only called a few more times.

We were asked to obtain the crews' names so that the news that they had been found could be relayed to their families. Then the aircraft left in search of a vessel that would divert to our position and tow the boat back to Puerto Plata. A huge tug with two barges, on passage from New Orleans to Venezuela, agreed but the tug captain did not want to stop for fear of losing control of his tow. Instead he asked us to tow the fishing boat alongside the last barge so that they could attach themselves. There was a tremendous undertow sucking us into the barges and it was tricky getting the fishermen close without crashing into the side of the barge ourselves. Finally we had them in the perfect position. We all held our breath as one of the fishermen leapt onto the back of the barge and slipped. It was agonizing watching him gradually haul himself onto the platform. Then the line he tied came undone and we had to go through the whole procedure again. Finally the fishing boat was attached securely and as we waved our goodbyes the five men couldn't have thanked us more profusely.

As we set sail for the west we discussed the quick response and efficiency of the U.S. Coastguard. We were further impressed when we arrived back home and found a letter from them thanking us for our help. They had only known the name of our boat but had traced our address in Vancouver.

Andy particularly wanted to visit communist (although they call it socialist) Cuba, especially as it was after the collapse of communism in the U.S.S.R. We chose Baracoa as our landfall, at the east end of the island, as it was on our route to the Bahamas. We stayed over twelve miles offshore as required and called the Port Control on the radio to get permission to proceed into the harbour. There was no reply but finally a local radio station contacted us and relayed us permission.

Baracoa is Cuba's earliest settlement (1512) and for the first three years was its capital. Columbus marvelled at its physical qualities of rivers and bays, terraces that rose steeply from the shore and high, square-shaped mountain. However, when three hundred Spanish adventurers went ashore, and planted a cross in the name of the Spanish crown, they were surprised by a very strong force of Indians and it took three months to defeat them. During the 18th Century, as the European powers battled to control the Caribbean, three major forts were built to protect the city. Baracoa, however, always stayed remote, isolated by rugged terrain and it was only after Fidel Castro's revolution in 1959 that a road was built linking it with the rest of the country.

With a population of about 60,000 the city looked modern as we approached, with several multi-storied buildings; it was only when we got closer we realized how run down they all were. The harbour is protected, particularly due to a sunken ship at the entrance. Immediately we were anchored Health officials came out in a rowing dinghy, its high canopy shielding them from the sun. They were all very pleasant, and leapt into action with bandages when Andy bumped his head and blood started pouring down all over the documents! After Andy was patched up, and the officialdom completed, they went ashore with our passports. After lunch Customs arrived and did the most in depth inspection we have ever had. It was hard to know what they were searching for but they spent a considerable amount of time looking through our photo albums, medical kit and Colin's gems. As the boys remarked, they missed several lockers altogether.

The boys and I got on with more school work. We were just beginning to wonder if we would get ashore that day when Immigration came alongside. They were extremely efficient and brought along an apprentice to translate. Soon they sent the security guard ashore to collect our passports and granted us permission to go where we asked. We were given the impression we could stay as long as we wanted and go anywhere we liked. All in all clearing-in had been very relaxed, if somewhat protracted, and we were now free to go ashore.

Wanting to rent a car to see some of the country, we went to the Hotel el Castillo as instructed. Built in the old fort battlements on a sheer cliff up from the shore, it was reached by a winding driveway or steps. We chose the steps, all ninety-seven of them, but at the top there was a panoramic view of the bay, port and city. The guests at the hotel were all high-ranking government officials. We had been told we could rent a car through the hotel's gift shop and between the assistant's English and Andy's Spanish the arrangements were easily made; we could even use credit cards. In the bar we found the Immigration interpreter so we bought him a beer. Andy, a connoisseur of beer, determined that the local beer tasted like Indian beer and was good, although surprisingly the German imported beer was cheaper. The interpreter taught English he told us but it was hard for him to practise speaking, with the restrictions on leaving the country and the lack of overseas visitors.

Before exploring in our rental car we thought we should get some local money so we could buy coffee and snacks along the way. In the tourist hotels everything had to be paid for in U.S. dollars. It took over a hour to change $20 and seemed a very complicated affair. In the end we were only able to spend 30¢ of it! There were regular shops, although goods were sparse and very old fashioned, but items were mainly bought by government coupon we learned, and were rationed. It was the same in the restaurants so we could not use cash for a meal or even a coffee.

There were no concerns leaving *Bagheera* unattended, as the harbour was constantly patrolled. Our car was waiting promptly at 8:00 the next morning, and we were given fuel coupons that we had to pay for in advance. We had to drive to the museum, in one of the other forts, to get a road map.

Stretching 750 miles from east to west and averaging about 60 miles in width, Cuba looks rather like an alligator in shape. It is the Caribbean's largest island, about the size of England, and is divided by three mountain ranges. In between there extremely fertile plains, which is where Cuba's well-known sugar cane and tobacco is grown.

The trip to Santiago de Cuba, Cuba's second largest city, took us through the Sierra Maestra mountain range in the south-east. The hills were spectacularly beautiful with a great variety of trees (even teak trees), and colourful flora. The fertile valleys were covered with banana, citrus, mango, cocoa and sugar plantations. It appeared anything would grow in the rich red-brown soil. There was an abrupt change in scenery as we approached the south coast, from the lush to the infertile, with double escarpments running along the shore and a coral drop-off into crystal clear water. The roads were surprisingly good, in fact better than in Puerto Rico.

We tried to find a restaurant in Guantanamo, the city where most of Cuba's salt is produced, but they all had huge crowds outside, waiting with their coupons. Noticing a hotel on our map we made our way there; again it was a tourist hotel filled with wealthy white Cubans. The meal was adequate but flavourless and plainly presented, as we had found in the hotel in Baracoa; Jamie and Colin had thick fruit drinks made from the persimmon fruit that smelt terrible but tasted surprisingly delicious.

"How amazing," I remarked as we drove off, "there's a U.S. Naval Base close to here. How can that be?"

It is a surprising anomaly, and not one the communists of Cuba have been happy about, but the agreement was made in 1903 after Cuba had won her independence from Spain. The United States had given her considerable assistance and refused to move out when Castro took power.

There was a fine autopista into Santiago de Cuba and our hotel Las Americas was well signposted. With a population of 350,000, Santiago is the spiritual home of both the Independence Movement and of the Revolution, and Cuba's designated Hero City. It was in the mountains that we had just crossed that the revolutionaries gathered their strength and there are several museums dedicated to the armed struggle in the 1950s against the corrupt dictatorship and monopoly of wealth.

Sitting on the edge of a massive harbour Santiago was founded by the Spanish in 1513; there is also a strong French influence dating back to the influx of 30,000 planters who fled the Haitian Revolution in 1791. With its steep streets and stepped alleyways, lined with 19th Century shuttered houses with wrought iron balconies, the city has a charming, if run down, cosmopolitan air.

As in Baracoa and during our drive we were saddened by the people, however. They seemed so listless with none of the animation usual in Latin and African temperaments. Large numbers wandered the streets aimlessly whatever time of day or night; even the students who sat outside the university were not talking, they just stared straight ahead. There were queues everywhere; lining-up seemed to be a way of life. Although the people were obviously interested in us there was a complete lack of response. Everywhere in the world I had found the bond of motherhood prevails. If I was walking down the street with my children, other mothers would always answer to my greeting or smile. Not so in Cuba. No-one wanted to be seen talking to a tourist.

Leaving the boys watching television, Andy and I went for a drive early the next morning. In most cities it would have been rush hour but here it was hardly busy. Noticing some girls trying to cross the road ahead I stopped and beckoned to them to pass. As first they seem stunned, then realized I meant it. With their faces alight they did a thumbs up and ran across the road. I wasn't sure if their reaction was because I stopped or that a woman was driving, but it was a relief to see some smiles. It was also interesting and positive that despite the communist uniformity, and rationing, the people took considerable trouble over their appearance, with their bright coloured outfits usually in 'sixties' fashions.

Before leaving the south coast we took a side trip to the Valle de Prehistoria, or Dinosaur Park, where early mammals, pre-humans and dinosaurs that are fashioned out of concrete roam the countryside. It was a remarkable sight, with pterodactyls and brontosauri standing on hill-tops silhouetted against the blue sky. Not only had the sculptors had flair in using the natural terrain but all the statues were in action poses.

"Come over here, these dinosaurs are huge," called Colin.

"Yes, they're life size, "said Andy. "Aren't they impressive."

"Those ones are attacking each other," remarked Jamie, "and look at the men with their spears. They look so real."

In many places in the world a display like this would cost a fortune to visit and would always be crowded. Here we just roamed around, having the displays to ourselves.

The car was missing on several cylinders as we headed back towards Santiago. We had already changed our first rental car, a Nissan, which had broken down in the mountains and now had one of the Russian Ladas that looked on its last legs. Sadly, 'run down and not working' is the way to describe most things in Cuba. Wherever we drove there were abandoned trucks and machinery. Many of the buildings were falling down or only half built and most of the sugar plantations had seen better days. Obviously the U.S.S.R. had poured huge sums of money into the country. In many ways it is far more sophisticated and industrial than any other Caribbean country, as we saw when driving through the nickel smelting town of Moa, but everywhere there were signs of economic collapse.

The officials gave us a great welcome when we returned to Baracoa and the boys were delighted to see an ice-cream van by the port. The three of us joined the long line. I was happy to wait there like one of the locals and interact with them, even if in a limited way. It was not to last long, the port officials seeing us at the end of the line rather embarrassingly insisted we went right to the front. The ice-creams cost 15¢ each, the only Cuban money we were able to spend, they wouldn't even let us use it on fuel or on the rental car. Returning the car was a nightmare. Because we had changed it, the mileage on the speedometer didn't synchronize with the initial paperwork and the document that had to be completed and sent off to the government department didn't allow for such anomalies.

One of my lasting memories of how a rigid system that allows no private enterprise is non-functional is trying to buy some produce. I asked the lady who ran the tourist shop in the hotel where to go. She informed me you couldn't get any, and she couldn't remember when she had last had a piece of fruit. Just on the outskirts of the town we had seen laden mango trees, with fruit rotting on the ground, and bananas galore, but the townspeople were not allowed to go to the countryside to collect the fruit and there was no system for getting the produce into town and selling it.

All the officials came together to clear us out. Again they completed a long search of the boat. When they were finished Andy asked them what they were looking for, as they had searched us so thoroughly on arrival.

"We are looking for stowaways," they told us. (They had even looked in the oven!) We also found out that the twenty-four hour a day patrol of the harbour was to catch anyone trying to leave. As the Bahamas are only twenty miles away we could imagine it was a real temptation.

With its seven hundred islands and cays scattered over 100,000 square miles of water, the Bahamas is a diver's paradise. I will never forget my first trip in 1971 through the Exuma group when I was just becoming interested in shell collecting. As we were travelling in only ten feet of crystal clear water I saw hundreds of perfect specimens, looking even grander with the magnification of the water, and I continuously wanted to stop and explore!

It was in the Bahamas that Christopher Columbus first arrived in the New World. The islands were named by the Spaniards after the shallow sea in which they lie, the 'baja-mar'. Stretching from Haiti to within fifty miles of the Florida coast, these low coral outcrops in the Atlantic Ocean are bisected by the Tropic of Cancer. The nation's population of nearly 225,000 live mostly in the tourist centres of Nassau and Freeport. In the other islands, known as the Family Islands, the communities are small and the people have a gentler, subsistence way of life.

Entering at Matthew Town, on Great Inagua, at the southern end of the chain, we made our way north, stopping at Acklins, Crooked Island and Rum Cay before arriving at the more sophisticated George Town. The islands are mostly covered with scrub and wispy casurina trees and there are many salt lakes with old salt pans full of ospreys and the occasional flamingo. Most of our time was spent in the water and from the first day Andy caught spiny lobster and grouper, and the boys were finding shells in abundance—king helmets, queen conchs, huge sand dollars or sea biscuits, and a myriad of smaller shells. With the waters so shallow over the sandbars the sea is a spectacular hue, always brilliant in the heat of the day and varying from aqua to a deep sapphire.

We particularly enjoyed Rum Cay, a former pirate haunt that was named after a shipload of rum had foundered on the reef. Port Nelson's wooden and stone buildings were hidden behind palms, a sleepy settlement with the pickings meagre in the small grocery store; but the lady who ran the wharfside bar and restaurant was a lively personality, and made us most welcome.

"What are those containers doing on the beach?" asked Colin.

We had looked at them earlier wondering whether they had been for a project, then abandoned. They appeared brand new and were huge, looking totally incongruous on the sand.

"They're refrigerated shipping containers and they fell off a ship and washed ashore," she told us.

One of the greatest fears of sailors is running into a container at sea; impact with such a solid object can sink a ship. We had heard that increasing numbers of containers are being lost off the decks of ships, and here was living proof.

Starting fifty miles south of Nassau the 365 Exuma Cays stretch over 100 nautical miles down the centre of the Bahamian Group. Most are uninhabited, others just sandbars that disappear with the smallest rise of tide. We called in at George Town on Great Exuma, the largest island, to do some provisioning. Anchoring off the Peace and Plenty Hotel, the hub of George Town's social life it seemed, we soon found where to shop, do our laundry and post our mail. The post office was in a huge pink, white columned Government Administration Building. There were several other buildings from the colonial past including the handsome St. Andrew's Anglican Church.

We enjoyed the diving off the Bahamas—hardly rivalled by any other during our travels—and then went to busy Nassau to await the arrival of Andy's daughters Alison and Vicky with Steve and Rob. Duncan also arrived at this time. Colin, Jamie and I had worked non-stop so the school year was finished. As it was the finale of Correspondence education the boys tore up their school work books and tossed them overboard with particular relish.

"Aren't there any more papers left?" asked Jamie, disappointed I couldn't find any more.

"I'm going to miss this with regular school," added Colin. "It's so satisfying!"

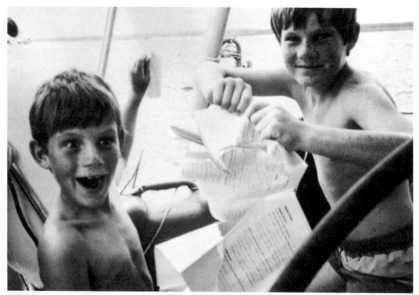

The end of the school year!

Nassau is another world; although New Providence is only 11 by 33 kilometres it houses 170,000 people, two thirds of the Bahamian population, and has always been the hub of Bahamian life. Its pastel gambling 'palaces' with their acres of slot machines attract over a million tourists a year. It was a good place to stock up, meet the family and leave again quickly. So used to covering many miles we had planned an ambitious sightseeing itinerary.

"What's wrong with the next anchorage?" asked Steve, an avid sailor, after we had reached the northern Exumas. "After all, we are here to relax."

It was a great idea and relax we did, diving, wandering ashore and enjoying the iguanas on the beach. *Bagheera* easily accommodated nine on board, although Vicky and Rob did have to rush below on couple of occasions due to the common, but inhospitable, 6:00 A.M. showers!

Our arrival in Fort Lauderdale was on July 2nd and it was back to North American reality with a bang, although we had had some conditioning coming up through the islands. I think our first impressions were how difficult it was to do routine tasks as a visitor in the States. For example, it was irksome trying to make long distance phone calls without an AT & T or similar phone card. The banks wanted nothing to do with our need to transfer some U.S. dollars from an Australian account, and

The Copeland family celebrating Duncan's birthday in Allans's Cay, Bahamas

getting car insurance without a Florida driving license (and if you get one they destroy your Canadian one) was well nigh impossible. The choice in the supermarkets and the different labelling, such as a huge variety of spreads but where was the margarine, was frustrating and time consuming. We were used to a simpler life.

It was one of our American friends who put it in a nutshell. "I would never have thought I would be saying this," she said to some friends, "but let me tell you if you want to get things done give me a third world country any time. Everything is so much more straightforward."

However, some old friends Carl and Elaine Schumacher, who had visited us in the San Blas Islands four years before, lived close by and they soon sorted us out. They also arranged a berth for *Bagheera* on the waterway in Hollywood, close to their motel room on the ocean front and we celebrated our first July 4th in the States. Beside the excellent food and company provided by Carl and Elaine, the day was filled with spectacular bike riding, enjoying the many bands and watching the fireworks.

Then it was down to business. We purchased a Plymouth Voyager van which, with its seven seats and air-conditioning it gave us a most comfortable trip across the States. There was still the problem of where to leave the boat but Beneteau suggested Tarpon Springs on the west coast of Florida and all was arranged. A bonus was a visit to St. Petersburg which was on the way as the Services aboard *Jean Marie* had just settled there on their return. On our arrival Tom was walking down the dock wearing a tie, Jean was decked out in smart working clothes! They were three weeks ahead of us into the job market. They had found us a berth in the marina and it was a great spot for packing up. With temperatures and humidity well in the 90s, the air conditioned rooms of the marina building were more than welcome.

My nephew Jamie, Andrew's youngest brother came to stay and between packing up we visited some of the sights such as Cape Canaveral, Kennedy Space Center and Disney World; we also bought a tent, 'the mansion' the boys named it, and learnt how to put it up. It took us three quarters of an hour the first time, but by the end of the trip it was up in a couple of minutes. After filling six huge boxes and sending them home, the boat looked bare for its last short trip to Tarpon Springs.

Bagheera spent one last night at anchor then went into the dock. She was hauled out right away and snugged down in a cradle in the yard. We drove off early next morning with lumps in our throats.

"I feel as though we are deserting her," said Andy. "She has been such a good home for six years." She did look very forlorn.

It was a quick journey across the country with two significant stops. The first was New Orleans, a fascinating city that was full of music, dancers and colourful vendors when we arrived on a Sunday morning. We had an experience of a different nature the next day as we toured U.S.S. 'Willamette'. This American Naval supply ship had been in dock for some months, having a massive extension completed. Steve Womack, the Captain, a close friend of the Services, gave us a comprehensive tour decked out in hard hats. Coming home late that night we found ourselves locked out of the camp site so had to leave our car outside and walk back to our tent.

"What's that," I pointed. Fleetingly as the moon came out I was sure I'd seen an animal. We stared into the gloom and to our surprise two armadillos appeared.

Further on there was more movement. "Look at these crayfish," called Andy. "I can hardly believe it". Large numbers were crawling across the road between the ditches.

Two days later we were off again, driving through five states a day. One word of advice here, if you need to strike camp rapidly, don't buy an air-mattress that takes 30 minutes to deflate! After a quick look at the curiously patterned, multi-coloured rocks of the 'Badlands' and the four carved heads of U.S. presidents in Mount Rushmore National Memorial, South Dakota, we stayed for two days in Yellowstone Park. We were fortunate to find a campsite and loved the area for its beauty and wildlife. The oldest and largest national park in the United States that stretches across Wyoming, Montana and Idaho, it is known for its spectacular geysers, hot springs, waterfalls and canyons. Like thousands before us we waited for 'Old Faithful' to perform; the geyser blew out steam and hot water as reliably as ever, an estimated forty-five metres high. We were also impressed with the information stations. Each presenting a different aspect of the park, they had some wonderful displays and dramatic films. Several focussed on the raging fire of 1988, a reminder of the vulnerability of the forest but also showed 'watch the world remake', demonstrating how quickly the forest can regenerate.

As planned we arrived back home in mid-August and Vancouver welcomed us with almost two months of spectacular weather—the first of the summer we learned. After taking over the house, which was in fine shape, we went down to the Yacht Club. It was a perfect evening, the sea and sky bright blue then turning a brilliant orange at dusk. Across English Bay soared the mountains with just the odd speck of white glistening on the peaks. What a beautiful setting Vancouver has; as a city it is only rivalled for us by Sydney in Australia and Cape Town, South Africa. The racers with spinnakers full were an attractive sight and I suddenly had a pang of longing for *Bagheera*—we should have been sailing in on a night like this, returning our vessel to her home port after her grand voyage.

We had a royal welcome back. "You've been away awhile," said not a few. "Is it two or three years?"

"How about six?" we answered.

"Surely it can't be six," they replied aghast, "surely six years of our lives can't have gone by so quickly."

Epilogue

So ended our six years away from the mainstream of life. In all we completed just over 50,000 nautical miles or 93,000 kilometres and visited 82 countries, colonies and possessions. We experienced an incredible variety of diverse cultures, scenery and wildlife but we were saddened to see how western culture is pervading the world. Junk foods, scruffy attire and pop culture videos are fast replacing food, clothing and entertainment that for us were far more creative in the past, and displacing values that had much greater depth and meaning. There is no doubt that consumerism and tourism have hit the world; many old customs are visibly disappearing, often between one visit and the next.

Outstanding in our memories are the people we met, particularly other yachtsmen, with whom we enjoyed great camaraderie. An incredible bond develops from sharing new experiences, helping each other in crises and being 'out there' on the ocean together. We frequently hear from our offshore friends by letter, phone or in person. The Faures from Singapore are currently cruising on *Bagheera*; the Youngs from Pittwater in Australia, who used to take Jamie to soccer practice, have just 'dropped in' for a visit. Last week Jamie participated in CORK sailing regatta in Kingston, Ontario and we stayed in the beautiful lakeside home of Michael and Elaine Davies from *Archangel*. Michael generously took us for a ride in his new *Archangel*—a helicopter!

It is wonderful to reminisce, but we also discuss the difficulties of adjusting to a regular lifestyle with its lack of constant new stimuli and stultifying programming and routine. Without doubt Andy was the one who most felt the adversities of returning. Although fortunate to be offered the job of managing a yacht broking business, he initially had to battle with a recession, as well as adapting to the demands of a busy office and telephone. Now he has his own yacht broking business again, which he finds more gratifying, and gets great pleasure from our garden—but he still yearns for the blue-water life.

A few months after the family returned *Bagheera* was trucked from Florida to Vancouver. It was a comfort to have her at Royal Vancouver Yacht Club, just a short distance away from our home. However, even going cruising was an adjustment. Although British Columbia is a spectacular area, full of islands and safe, pleasant anchorages, we had to drastically change our perspective. Because the scenery and culture is familiar the joys of sailing are the relaxation, the escape from the demands of work, and being with friends in known places—rather than what we had become used to, the exhilaration of new horizons.

With house prices having soared in our absence we were fortunate in having kept ours, and refurbishing and planning for the boy's different needs initially consumed most of my time. But I also had to make a decision about my future career. Would I return to work as an educational psychologist or could I fulfil my desire to write a book. During our trip I had kept a daily diary, as well as most of our cruising guides and travel books. I had already experienced the difficulty of getting articles accepted in cruising magazines—those that pay well anyway! The problem was how to write and make money at the same time. Fortunately a friend told me about 'homestay' overseas language students. We had the room for extra dwellers in our large basement and the family seemed agreeable; it would after all keep the international contact.

Writing my first book *Just Cruising* has given me a whole new career. Not only have I travelled all over the States, Canada and Britain doing media book promotions, I have also been invited to give many slide presentations and seminars. My audiences vary widely from those at boat shows and yacht clubs, whose focus is boating, to business, professional and university organizations who enjoy the travel aspect. I've also been a guest teacher at both Elementary and High schools, and for a university travel writing course. My new life is most interesting and varied, and a bonus is that I'm travelling again.

The boys all enjoyed coming back to Vancouver, (but Jamie at eight would have also loved a few more years offshore). Although they lead a completely regular lifestyle, without doubt they have a different perspective of the world. They continue to be avid readers, and have a knowledge base that has daunted more than a few adults as well as some of their teachers! We realize from their comments, particularly when watching documentaries on television, the extraordinary depth of perception they gained from having experienced the 'real thing.'

Duncan is now in his second year of sciences at university. He had a wonderful first year, with a definite focus on rugby and parties! In fact he has been very successful in rugby, playing on both university and provincial teams, and has been awarded a university rugby scholarship. This summer he had a job in forestry and is now planning to enter this field as a career. Before starting a forestry programme, however, he is taking a few months out—to travel in South East Asia and play rugby in Australia, also to work he assures us! He definitely has the travel bug in his blood.

Colin has just entered his last year of High School. He has continued with his artistic pursuits, working in a variety of mediums and subject matters, and is hoping to go to art school. Recently his painting of gargoyles was chosen to be in the Vancouver Law courts. He also plays the base guitar in a band. He has just asked for a regular, electric guitar for his birthday and promises us some melodies!

As Tom mentioned in his poem, Jamie is our boat kid (although Duncan has now started taking *Bagheera* out with his friends). Since taking his first Optimist dinghy course on our return, Jamie has never looked back. This summer he spent his entire holiday on the water racing, participating in events across Canada as well as in the States, and cruising on *Bagheera*. Recently Duncan was looking at Jamie's trophies, "I think I chose the wrong sport!" he commented. Jamie is now in high school, having just entered Grade 8.

"Are you going to do another trip?" we're frequently asked. Of course we are! Our plan is to cruise the canals and rivers of Europe between Holland and Russia, after Colin has finished High School. It will be a very different experience, powering instead of sailing, in confined waters instead of the vast ocean, and coping with the disparities of locks rather than weather systems. From what we have read and previously experienced it is a fascinating way to travel and meet the local people. Will there be another book? Definitely! It will be entitled *Go Cruising – on the waterways of Europe*.

Offshore Cruising – Some Practical Tips

Preparations, route planning, the boat, equipment, provisioning, budgeting, travel, the differences

Cruising is a wonderful lifestyle and I thoroughly recommended it to you and your family, whatever your ages. For a cruise to be a success, however, every crew member must have realistic expectations.

Modern, comfortable designs, efficient gear and electronic equipment, and increased boat speed that gives time for travel in exotic lands, entice increasing numbers to go offshore. Many adapt like 'ducks to water' while others feel they have been deceived. It comes as a shock that life on board takes considerable adjustment. One needs to be extremely flexible. It is far harder work than expected. One even has to work at having fun.

In the dreaming stage it is easy to ignore the negative aspects—passages that can be uncomfortable, boat maintenance that is ongoing and cannot be neglected, the sometimes arduous organization that is required when visiting many different countries and planning new experiences, culture shock from different customs, foods and languages, coping without the support of old friends and relatives, to say nothing of the dynamics of living with your partner twenty-four hours a day, seven days a week in a tiny space—which you have probably never done before!

Often one of a couple is more enthusiastic than the other. Urged on by the dream of shedding a lifetime of responsibilities ashore and the lure of distant horizons, they cannot wait to sell up and head out, not recognizing their partner's reservations. In my experience most women want the stability of keeping their home, despite the management difficulties.

If you are planning to sell up and take to the high seas analyze your plans carefully and objectively. There are a huge number of decisions to be made, as I recount in the Appendix of *Just Cruising*, but knowing what to expect in advance so that one can be prepared both materially and psychologically will make a huge difference to your success at bluewater cruising.

As North America offers such scenic diversity we find that many Americans and Canadians have travelled little overseas before going offshore, and it comes as a surprise that several things are done differently at home compared to the rest of the world. Conversely those visiting North America have similar reactions. As a regular traveller these would be of little significance but, when having to maintain a complex yacht, the differences—such as in voltages and cycles, imperial versus metric measurements and fittings, propane versus butane for cooking, even finding that there are different television systems, to say nothing of a different buoyage system and meteorological terms—can produce considerable frustration. This can be compounded by the varying rules and regulations when entering countries, different cultural customs, the lack of familiar foods, problems with making phone calls, getting money and mail etc.

When walking marina docks or scanning a group of cruising boats at anchor, one soon realizes there is no such thing as the perfect cruising boat, although Andy, as a yacht broker, is frequently asked for it. Every yacht is an accommodation to personal needs. Many variables such as one's personal priorities for safety, comfort and seaworthiness, whether one plans to cruise coastal waters or offshore, in well frequented areas or off the beaten track, in tropical or temperate latitudes, the number and age of the crew and the budget available, have to be taken into consideration. It is no small task choosing a boat and its equipment, as it is a combination of practical analysis from one's own knowledge, experience and needs, of evaluating the advice of others, then finding a boat which technically and emotionally also feels and looks right. In the end every boat is a compromise and as with the cruising lifestyle one has to continuously weigh up the pros and cons and be flexible.

I hope the following list will help, not only with some of the decisions but also in preparing you for a very different lifestyle. For easy access I've listed the subjects in alphabetical order and rather than overlap with my earlier book *Just Cruising* I make reference to it with page numbers. The list is by no means exhaustive—that would take another book—and headings are certainly not equally weighted. Hopefully, however, it will be a starting point to get ideas, food for thought to help acclimatize to the realities of the cruising life. Again I would like to make it clear that these ideas and suggestions are completely from our own experience and observations.

You will find a list of *Bagheera's* equipment in Appendix B.

ANCHORS, ANCHOR WINDLASSES AND RODES The Bruce and c.q.r were overwhelmingly the most popular anchors with the experienced sailors, though with the latter one should avoid the many cheap imitations. The Danforth style and aluminum anchors were not good in coral and sea grass.

The kedge anchor was used in series with the Bruce at times, shackled to the crown with 20′ of chain. This combination gave tremendous holding power yet was easier to recover than two anchors streamed separately from the bow.

An all chain main anchor rode is safer, particularly around coral and was commonly used in the South Pacific and Indian Ocean. It can be marked with paint or dacron. 18″ lengths of ¼" dacron woven through the chain and heat sealed works well. For example white, blue and red at 30′ intervals. We used a nylon strop, that clipped into the chain and fastened to the bow cleat, to take up the load and minimize the noise. The availability of high tensile chain means one can go down one size with increased strength and much reduced weight. For a storm anchor heavy chain combined with a good quality nylon rode cushions the shock loads but one has to keep clear of coral and guard against chafe at the bow fairlead.

An electric anchor windlass is high on our list of priorities. Ours not only saved our backs and enabled anchoring in deep water without concern, it also took Andy aloft in the bosun's chair to do regular rig inspections and was used to hoist the dinghy onto the deck.

BATTERIES See *Just Cruising* p.298. You should never penny pinch on the ship's batteries as all your equipment depends on them. We charged the two banks of deep cycle batteries totalling 660 amp/hours from the wind generator, solar panels and running the main engine using a high output alternator with a 'Smart' three-stage regulator. In particular the solar panels were very affective. These are commonly put on a bracket at the stern above the helm, although are also found in other places such as on dodgers. Ours can be angled to the sun but obviously the angle has to be constantly monitored. They need to be accessible for regular cleaning. Downwind we often didn't have sufficient airflow for the wind generator. We monitored our batteries with ammeters for charging and load together with a voltmeter and low voltage alarm.

Stock up on special batteries for equipment. We found rechargeable batteries useful for small items, especially for the childrens' radios, keyboard, games etc.

BOAT CONSTRUCTION is the most important factor and yet often one of the hardest to analyze when purchasing a boat. Stresses offshore soon find out weaknesses.

Four areas to check are:

1. The hull to deck join, which is best if internal and permanently bonded either by being glassed over or with a structural adhesive. Through bolting using bedding compounds is not sufficient but is still commonly found.
2. Bulkheads should be bonded to the hull **and deck** throughout their perimeters and on both sides; screws or bolts are not enough.
3. The rig loads need to be properly distributed to the hull, not the deck.
4. Fiberglass is a very flexible material and the hull construction must be such that it cannot bend and twist at sea. The grid system of bonding an inner fiberglass backbone to the hull is effective when properly designed and combined with 1, 2, and 3 above. Modern cruising boats using a grid can be stronger and yet lighter than older boats, contributing to safety, ease of handling and performance.

BOATING EXPERIENCE See *Just Cruising* p.277- 279. Get to know your own boat, seek out bad weather, learn how your boat behaves when lying ahull, practice heaving-to and man overboard drills. Hoist the storm sails and make sure the sheet leads etc. work. You will have to reef in pitch dark and driving rain, so make sure you can do it blindfold. Go out into the ocean and experience the swells and the isolation when out of sight of land.

Understanding weather and being able to interpret weather charts is of paramount importance.

Take courses for all aspects of sailing and maintaining your boat. Several people have mentioned the merit of less experienced women taking a sailing course independently to gain skills and confidence. A further offshore course taken as a couple not only gives practice at working together but a place to work out differences of opinion with an instructor. The ideal situation is where a couple can independently handle the boat and its equipment and share the navigation and the cooking.

BILGES Need to be kept dry. In hot climes water soon fouls from the action of bacteria on any dust, fuel or other contaminants which find their way under the floor boards. Any unpleasant odour will considerably increase one's tendency to seasickness, so has to be treated immediately with bleach. (A permanent item on your provisioning list.) It is also recommended that a dripless stern gland be fitted to any boat going offshore. Adequate limber holes are necessary for water to drain to the lowest party of the bilge quickly.

A powerful bilge pumping system, both manual and electric, is usual and one should know how to use the engine's raw water pump in an emergency. It is a good idea to have effective strum boxes or filters at all pump intakes so that they do not get choked. Labels on cans and bottles stowed in the bilges might wash off or disintegrate when wet and disable your pumps.

BUDGETING/MONEY See *Just Cruising* 274. Although it seems currently popular to suggest $1000 US a month for a couple to cruise, this generally only includes the actual cruising budget; not insurance, major inland travel expenses and visits back home. As prices vary hugely around the world it is definitely worth selectively stocking up, both for provisions and for boat needs such as spares and bottom paint. Watch out for varying exchange rates, you might be spending considerably more than you thought. If using travellers cheques have both large and small denominations—low amounts for a quick shop in a remote area, where the exchange rate will probably be poor, and high denominations as there are often charges per cheque changed.

We used credit cards to access cash. VISA and MASTERCARD were common everywhere. Now direct debit credit cards overcome the interest taken with a cash withdrawal, but one has to have money in one's account!

BUGS ON BOARD
Cockroaches: some large tropical species fly aboard but are usually easy

to find because of their size. The real pests are the small cockroaches found throughout temperate and tropical climes. These get aboard along warps and gangplanks, in containers and produce. We always discard all boxes and packaging ashore, inspecting all containers that have to come aboard for eggs or young 'crawlers', (particularly the folded ends of cartons) and cleaning all produce immediately. Where you use a plank to get ashore as is common in the Mediterranean, suspend it a few inches above the ground. When you find a cockroach on board—and you will!—assume that there are others. There are many different commercial baits. Cockroach Hotels are popular, and borax mixed with icing sugar is a good home remedy.

Weevils and flour moths: can be a nuisance, laying eggs in anything that is made of grains. They can penetrate plastic bags and cardboard packs so all cookies, rice, cereals, pasta etc. have to be in robust sealed containers. Bay leaves seem to discourage them. The traditional sailor may prefer to ignore them, since the Royal Navy of Nelson's day appears to have flourished on weevilly ship's biscuits!

Rats: Large funnels on the mooring lines facing shoreward will prevent them boarding that way, but they also swim well.

Termites: Once established on board, wooden bulkheads etc. may be weakened. Professional fumigation is the best answer using a gas which disperses rather than one of the highly toxic chemical sprays which can affect health. (Also see mosquitoes)

CHAFE: Much damage can be prevented by careful preparation. Downwind sailing is hard on gear due to the constant rolling in the ocean swells. A preventer should be used (line must be light in case the boom goes in the water). Avoid rigs with severely swept back spreaders. Full batten mains are very vulnerable to chafe downwind where battens rest against the shrouds. Carpeting can be taped to the backs of spreaders and around shrouds where sails touch. Chafe patches should be applied where sails contact spreaders including when reefed. Adhesive chafe tape protects seams where they rub on shrouds.

All running rigging should be inspected for wear before each passage, particularly halyards where they turn on the masthead sheaves. To stop the jaws of a whisker or spinnaker pole eating through genoa or spinnaker sheets we protected them with plastic tubing. (Also see sails)

CHARTS: See *Just Cruising* p.292. Are a major expense, but you should never have too few as you can end up in unexpected places; a common compromise for extras is to photocopy. Chart plotters are becoming popular but may give limited information. As they rely on equipment and power, they can never be a substitute for regular charts.

Most cruisers found the British Admiralty charts the best. Compared with U.S. charts they are of more uniform size for stowing, are printed on better quality paper and when purchased are up to date with all the latest amendments. Canadian, Australian, South African and other ex. British countries produce their own charts to the same standards. Be prepared for metric or imperial measurements and varying symbols. (Also, beware older French charts which have the prime meridian going through Paris!)

The well written cruising guides have chartlets of harbours and anchorages that save the purchase of many detail charts.

NOTE: One cannot always rely on G.P.S. to give safe landfalls or to navigate through a confined passage at night. The G.P.S. is far more accurate than many charted positions and an island can be a mile or two out of position, often fixed by a survey dating back many years.

CHILDREN ON BOARD: See *Just Cruising* p.281
   Education: See *Just Cruising* p.283
   Safety: See *Just Cruising* p.285

CLUBS AND ASSOCIATIONS: Most yacht clubs around the world welcome cruisers who are members of a recognized yacht club at home. Take a letter of good standing. Cruising clubs and associations such as the Ocean Cruising Club, the Seven Seas Cruising Association and the Bluewater Cruising Association are invaluable sources of information for both fitting out and for route planning.

COMPASSES: If a boat is purchased in N.America or Europe it is likely that the magnetic compass will have been corrected for dip in northern latitudes. Sailing south this will cause the compass card to tilt until eventually it will cease to rotate freely. A compass corrected for mid latitude dip may be substituted or a second compass for southern latitudes carried.

We carried a small compass at the chart table and two hand bearing compasses in addition to the binnacle mounted unit. This was swung and corrected at the start of our cruise and again after *Bagheera* was struck by lightning.

KEEPING COMFORTABLE:

On deck: Most boats have spray dodgers on a stainless steel frame with an opening portion in the centre to allow a through breeze whilst at anchor (Essential in the tropics). Many also have removable side curtains. Being able to see over the dodger when standing at the helm is most advantageous.

As the sun is one of the greatest hazards, a bimini over the cockpit is desirable; it also protects from rain. Ideally it should be high enough to stand under but must clear the boom. Ours could be left up when sailing in all but the strongest winds. Side curtains on the lifelines from forward of the companionway to the stern pulpit help keep the cockpit dry and shielded us from reflected sun's rays off the water. Also psychologically they made the cockpit seem much bigger and safer at sea. An awning stretching from behind the mast to the backstay above the boom was rigged on *Bagheera* when at anchor. This shades much of the deck and funnels the breeze through, cooling both above and below deck. Ours was also rigged to catch rainwater. It rolled up tightly to stow permanently across the double backstay. Although fewer boats now have these large awnings, as they are considerably more work, they are highly desirable if anchored for a long period of time.

Cockpit cushions: The further you go the more you need for night watches! Must be waterproof, such as closed cell foam, easily manageable in size and comfortable. Flotation cushions can also double for safety.

Gates in the lifelines are useful to facilitate boarding but should be taped against accidental opening at sea.

Below deck: Hatches which open forward allow a through breeze to flow below when at anchor. The more the better. Cloth wind scoops which direct air down and into hatches are effective and inexpensive. Opening ports also help with ventilation. It is particularly good to have one beside the galley. Dorades are not effective to create a cooling draught but do ventilate in cool climates.

Light coloured decks reflect the heat and the core material makes a big difference to the protection given from the sun's heat or extreme cold, so check on this detail before buying. Thick balsa or closed cell foam is good insulation, plywood coring is not. Teak decks not only increase the insulation but give a positive cooling effect if wetted down.

Dark hulls are hot in the tropics; the lighter the colour the more it will reflect the heat of the sun. Uncored hulls need insulation material or liners with an air space between to protect against the transfer of heat from the sun or condensation when it is colder outside.

Fans made a huge difference to our comfort below. We have the German Hellas which draw a minimum of power, have two speeds and are quiet. There is one at every berth, in the galley, and two over the settees. They were frequently on 24 hours a day and made sleep possible when no natural wind found its way below.

For cabin heat we have a simple bulkhead mounted diesel heater which vents the combustion gases outside. The furnace type of heaters with forced draught circulation are wonderful for cool climates but do not take kindly to long periods of non-use in the tropics, where the high humidity, temperature and salinity combine to rot them out in short order.

If clothing and food etc. is to stay free from mould all storage lockers need to be well ventilated. Salty clothing should always be kept separate until the salt has been washed out. Mould has to be removed immediately otherwise it will 'run' rapidly through the boat. Spray-on bleach based cleaners work well.

Cushion covers can quickly deteriorate in a liveaboard situation, particularly in the tropics with salt, sand, sweat and sunscreens abundant, and the common 'tweed' style is scratchy in the heat. On *Bagheera* we used cotton slip covers fastened with velcro over the regular covers which could be easily removed and laundered.

We also used regular sheets and duvets, beds being permanently made up like home, and had plenty of pillows and cushions so we could be comfortable if heeled over.

Lee-cloths were on all the berths, double berths being split down the middle.

COMMUNICATIONS:

On Board: A vhf radio with its limited range is used for calling port authorities, to alert ships to your presence and for communicating with anyone else within range. We also used a portable v.h.f. when ashore to keep in touch with *Bagheera* and for safety when on dinghy expeditions, and it was an item to be taken in the liferaft.

An hf Ham or single side-band radio with receiving and transmitting capabilities is extremely useful on long trips for safety, weather, medical assistance etc; and great for one's social life. Phone patching, using E-Mail and the 'Packet' communication system is an advantage of having a Ham license, as well as meeting people who enjoy communicating with offshore cruisers. No business can be done on the Ham frequencies.

Using the marine operators through the s.s.b. radio for phone calls is very expensive. Regular and weather faxes can be received and sent through the HF radio via a computer and printed out with the appropriate hardware and software. Incidentally in weather forecasts wind strengths may be given in metric or imperial or in the Beaufort scale. Temperatures are generally in centigrade except the U.S.

On Shore Regular phone cards can increasingly be used, check for overseas usage before leaving, but don't be surprised if a phone call takes all day to make in the more remote areas. Many countries have local phone cards that are bought in advance, some use the p.o. for international calls others have a central office in town where calls can be made. Facilities for cellular phones are increasing, into the Caribbean for example.

COOKING FUELS: Almost everyone uses gas for cooking. In much of the world butane is used rather than the propane that is the norm in N. America. Butane can be put in propane bottles but not the other way round, as butane is stored at a lower pressure. Some countries will require high-pressure (hydro) testing of your bottles at yearly intervals.

We carried a three month supply using large (20 and 30lb) aluminum bottles. There was never any trouble finding gas, but different fittings are used and a series of adaptors is useful on board. In many places there is a system where they exchange bottles rather than filling privately owned ones. You hand in an empty bottle and take away a full one. Unfortunately one has to put up a large deposit to get your first bottle, but it is possible to transfer the liquid from their bottle to your bottle if you make an adaptor. It goes without saying that this is to be done with great care, but sometimes it is the only way of filling your own bottles.

In Europe the easy way is to use Camping Gaz bottles and regulators which are available everywhere.

Compressed natural gas is not commonly found and a three month's supply would leave no room for anything else on board due to the number of cylinders one would have to carry.

Stove alcohol and kerosine of a useable quality are not obtainable in most parts of the world.

Microwave ovens are popular on vessels with ample battery power and large inverter or a generator.

COURTESY FLAGS: It is traditional and good manners to fly the flag of the country you are visiting from your spreaders. It is ironic that buying a country's flag in advance is often very expensive compared to the cost in the country itself. Although you may offend people if you don't do this it is rare that officials will take action, although in Turkey they did make yachts without or flying a frayed or faded flag put up a new one that day. In Indonesia it was obligatory to fly a courtesy flag at least as large as the ensign and in the Dominican Republic officials tried to insist that new arrivals buy a flag from them at an exorbitant price.

Many cruisers make their own flags, but accurate reproduction is necessary to avoid offense.

CRUISING GUIDES, PILOTS AND SAILING DIRECTIONS:

All the commonly cruised areas have cruising guides. They vary greatly and can be expensive but they are useful for providing clearing procedures and details and chartlets of anchorages. Most also give accounts of facilities ashore and sometimes tips for sightseeing. (Also see Travel Books) Admiralty Pilot Books and American Sailing Directions are government publications providing weather, navigation, ocean and land information which is invaluable. Lists of lights, aids to navigation, radio stations and weather services should also be carried. Routing charts (U.K.) or Pilot charts (U.S.) are a must, combining for each month information on currents, winds, fog, ice, hurricanes, wave heights and much more.

DINGHIES AND OUTBOARDS

The pleasure of rowing a small wood or fibreglass dinghy is hard to beat, but unless one's boat is large enough to safely stow both a hard dinghy and an inflatable the latter is favoured by nearly all long distance cruisers. Remember your dinghy is your vehicle, your link with the shore, as you will mostly be at anchor.

Inflatable dinghies are stable, they carry huge loads, they don't damage your topsides, they deflate and can be stowed on the deck for ocean passages but at the same time tow well for short trips. They are easy and stable to climb into for divers and swimmers. Minor damage is easy to repair. We had a 10'6" inflatable which with the 8 HP outboard could plane quite easily with four on board and we used it extensively to explore up rivers, through shallows and for diving expeditions. It did take some time to dismantle the floorboards and for future cruising we will use one of the inflatables with roll-up floorboards which are now available. Those with inflatable floors are another option and light to carry. Swing-down wheels at the transom enabled us to pull it up the beach as our dinghy was heavy for two to lift.

An outboard powerful enough for long expeditions is quite heavy. We have a four-part tackle hanging from the wind generator mast on the starboard quarter which hoists the motor onto a mount on the stern pulpit. An outboard is the most attractive item on board to thieves almost everywhere in the world. Preventative measures are needed. This not only includes locks and chain, hoisting the dinghy out of the water at night but also making one's motor less attractive.

Fluorescent paint stripes were applied to our outboard to make it a chore for a thief to repaint before it could be used or sold. We found having a small engine in addition was useful. The 3 HP was economical, a good commuter engine, and not so desirable to thieves as the large one.

Hydrofoil fins on the engine work well, keeping the dinghy flat when only one person is on board.

ELECTRICITY: Whilst most of the world has standardized with 220 volt 50 cycle A.C. power, North Americans (and some of the Caribbean and South America) have 110 volts and 60 cycles.

Aboard *Bagheera* we carried a transformer which enabled us to use 110 volt power tools, charge batteries etc., whilst plugged into a 220v shore side facility.

We also had a small 110v A.C/12v D.C. portable generator. Invertors are useful for items with small power consumption like computers.

ELECTRONICS: The availability of inexpensive and reliable electronics has made navigation very easy and accurate. However, traditional methods can't be neglected; we carried a sextant and navigation calculator, plus sight reduction tables and almanac. Also a trailing log. Duplication of, say, a G.P.S. is no guarantee that you will always be able to calculate where you are; we lost all electronics through a lightning strike.

ENGINES and PROPELLERS: Many areas lack reliable wind, have strong currents or have tricky, narrow entrances and are inaccessible without a reliable engine.

Fixed propellers create drag, and can make a difference of days in a long ocean passage. Also, with a hydraulic gear box some sort of shaft lock will be needed.

On *Bagheera* we used a geared folding propeller which gave excellent performance both ahead and astern. The two blade fixed prop. which came with the boat was kept as a spare. The advantage of a folding prop. over a feathering prop. are lower cost, less vulnerability to damage and less likelihood of fouling on fish nets, floating lines or plastic bags.

FENDERS AND MOORING LINES: Have enough for both sides of the boat, particularly in areas where Med moor (anchored from the bow and stern-to) is common. Cloth covers protect the boat and are easily washed. In many remote areas our topsides were getting scarred by the local craft that so often swarmed around us so we made up fender mats made from canvas covered backpacker's foam sleeping mats.

Have at least six mooring lines for extra springs, etc. Rubber 'snubbers' considerably reduce jerking in turbulent areas. (Particularly with Med-moor). They are also good on the dinghy towline.

FISHING: We carried a gamefishing reel on our stern pulpit with 100lb test line and used very small lures on a steel trace to try to keep the size of the fish to manageable proportions but we still lost a lot of lures to big ones. Fish were put to sleep by squirting alcohol into their mouths and over their gills before they were hoisted on board.

Ciguatera poisoning is a common hazard and we avoided fishing near land unless we knew it was safe. This is a toxin which originates on dead coral and travels up the food chain, accumulating in fish without affecting them, but which can make people very ill. Symptoms are itching, tingling, pains in the joints and vomiting. Predators of reef fish such as barracuda are particularly affected. In French Polynesia we met a medical officer who told us 80% of his clinic was related to ciguatera.

FUEL MANAGEMENT: Don't take the quality of fuels for granted. Be prepared! Diesel in many places is of a poor quality, with high sulphur content and contaminants such as water, rust and other solids. Use a fine mesh filter when filling and always add **biocide** to avoid infestation of your tank with microbes. When getting fuel from drums, wait for several hours after the drums arrive before drawing the fuel to allow solids to settle and then leave the last few inches of fuel in the drum. If carrying aboard in jerry cans, again allow to settle.

Much trouble will be avoided by having a good fuel filtering system. Primary filters ideally should be duplicated so that you can switch from a dirty one to a clean one without having to bleed the system. *Bagheera's* primary is a water separator and particulate filter, the secondary and tertiary progressively finer particulate filters. We carried 140 litres in our tank and also used jerry cans on long trips.

GARBAGE DISPOSAL: Garbage is becoming an eyesore around the world; even in remote Chagos rubber thongs, light bulbs and plastic containers were all over the beaches.

Garbage amasses quickly on a boat; it needs careful management.

1. Before leaving on a passage we dispose of all unnecessary packaging. Dry goods go into reusable containers which also keep the goods fresh and free from weevils. We also try to buy liquids in glass rather than plastic, and schedule oil changes in ports.

2. During a trip we divide the garbage into 4 categories: a)biodegradables, b)metal and glass containers, c) plastics, and d) chemical materials. When we are many days or weeks from disposal facilities we put biodegradeables, glass (broken into small pieces) and metal cans (pierced and crushed) over the side when in at least 100 fathoms of water and many miles from land. Plastics can be burnt ashore, and all solids can be buried deeply where they will not be washed out or dug up by animals. Whether burning or burying, extreme care must be taken of the environment with all traces of the garbage removed. Chemical items such as batteries, medications, cleaners are stored until we reach civilization again.

The U.S. coastguard give guidelines for dumping at sea which conform to the international Marpol Treaty. Of significance is that dumping should not occur within 3 miles off shore, and outside this limit only if pieces are less than an inch, and that plastic must never be dumped.

We always checked out local disposal facilities before taking our garbage ashore. In some places it is thrown over a convenient cliff straight into the ocean! We were also aware that one man's garbage can be another man's treasure and would leave 'good' garbage in full view beside the disposal bins for the locals to sort out.

GIFTS: Trading or giving gifts is common in the more remote areas. The problem is that while the locals give gifts from the land and sea, you have to come up with them from what you have on board. Our typical gifts were fishing hooks and line, soap, t-shirts, (although in some of the more frequented areas they wanted designer shirts!), coloured pens and pencils for children, also outgrown childrens books and clothing, fuel to fishermen for their outboards, occasionally canned goods and local gifts such as kava root in Fiji. We also frequently entertained on board, serving large quantities of newly baked bread and cakes, with juice and coffee or tea. The boys usually quickly made friends and disappeared into the village to play, often returning with local shells and carvings.

GUNS: We did not carry firearms aboard *Bagheera*. There is a continuing argument about the pros and cons of guns on board, as discussed in Chap. 6, but we found that the more experienced cruisers were, the less likely they were to carry firearms. If guns are carried they have to be declared and deposited ashore with the authorities; a license issued at home for a weapon has no validity in another country. If hidden guns are found the consequences are usually very severe and can include seizure of your vessel and goal.

Research and safe route planning is the key to avoiding most problems. We kept a careful lookout and monitored other craft at sea by radar, using our powerful searchlight to warn off suspicious vessels. Travelling in company with another yacht is best in the areas with a poor reputation. At anchor, we had a contingency plan which involved lights and making considerable noise, and had the tape of dogs barking handy. An Australian friend put great faith in his electric sheep fence which was rigged to give an uninvited guest a nasty jolt.

INSURANCE: See *Just Cruising* p.273. We arranged for coverage through Lloyds of London. Rates varied depending on our proposed routes which we submitted annually. We were fortunate in that because of our past offshore experience they relaxed the rule after the second year that requires a minimum of 3 experienced watchkeepers on board, and our 10 year old became No. 3. Some cruising clubs now have arrangements with insurance companies for a boat to be insured with just two on board we understand.

Our only claim was a large one after being struck by lightning. This was handled quickly and courteously by our broker in London and Lloyds agents in S. Africa.

INTERIORS: See *Just Cruising* p.290. Some modern boats look very roomy but have little storage below. Always go through the mental exercise of trying to stow the basics when looking for a liveaboard boat. Imagine life under constant motion and at an angle. Look for robust handholds, sea berths, a head compartment and galley which can be used in a rough sea.

LIGHTNING: See Chap. 14 and Appendix D

MAIL: We used a variety of addresses of friends, friends of friends, yacht clubs and Poste Restante or had visitors bring it. As itineraries are flexible it is important to choose a place far enough on in your route, even though you have to wait longer to get your letters. You will need someone at home to sort and send the mail to you. In our case my eldest step-daughter Alison Kinsey kindly managed our affairs. Most people seemed to have willing friends or relatives, although some used agencies.

MAST STEPS: Are useful to have up to the spreaders for visibility when in shallow water. (The boys also loved escaping up there!). Our steps stow against the mast, individually clipping out for use. A pair of steps about four feet down from the top of the mast facilitates repairs at the masthead.

MEDICAL: See *Just Cruising* p.286. Besides having the required vaccinations diet and climate are two of the most important influences on health. One of the advantages of travelling by boat is that if one is worried about hygiene one can always go home. One generally doesn't have to eat the food or drink the local water and all fruit and vegetables can be carefully washed. Local remedies for stomach upset generally seem the most potent, we found Imodium a good general purpose 'stopper'.

Be prepared for the sun (see *Just Cruising* p.288 and 'comfort on deck') and for the effects of heat and cold. Also be careful of abrasions in the tropics as the tiniest will flair up if in salt water, contrary to the temperate maxim 'saltwater heals'.

Dental: A small cotton ball soaked in oil of cloves with help relieve tooth ache. When the pain has subsided a mixture of oil of cloves and zinc oxide, inserted with a flat-ended toothpick, will set-up and seal the cavity.

Insurance: Many had it but it is expensive.

MOSQUITOES: If they like you be prepared! As several tropical diseases can be transmitted by mosquitoes they must be kept out of the boat. We made mesh screens for all the ports and hatches which are fastened by velcro. Awareness about malaria, dengue and yellow fever etc. danger areas is important and suitable medications and immunizations arranged ahead of time.

I found I became allergic to the smell of pyrethrum coils which are commonly burned as deterrents as it pervaded all the upholstery, but a 12 volt unit that used pyrethrum tablets worked well without odour.

OFFICIALS: Procedures and officials vary greatly, some requiring you to stay on board for clearance, others that you go ashore, either just the captain or both captain and crew. For a smooth entry it is important to know the ports of entry, the correct procedure and have acquired any necessary documents and visas in advance. Jimmy Cornell's World Cruising Handbook is very useful in this respect, besides giving much other information.

Most countries require a clearance document from the last place visited. Have copies of crew lists, at least four, with names, rank, nationality, date of birth, passport number, place and date of issue, and boat documents at hand. A few countries will hold your passports until you leave which can be concerning and also is a problem if you have to show your passport to change money or collect a parcel. Be warned, in several countries you have to check with officials at every stop. After our visit to Fiji, for example, they had 32 pieces of paper on us! Just the initial check-in had taken more than one day. Being prepared, looking present-able, and being polite and patient definitely helps the process.

Having children on board was a big asset; it was a rare official that didn't have a smile for them. We never bribed.

We would always offer tea or coffee when the officials arrived. When the paperwork was over we would also offer beer. Frequently the officials liked to stay and we found them extremely informative both with practical and sightseeing suggestions and insight into the local political, cultural and economic situation.

English is the accepted language for international traffic.

PETS: Those who want to sail with a cat or dog need to plan their route to avoid countries where rabies has been eliminated and where the authorities require a quarantine period of several months before the pet can go ashore. This includes much of the former British Empire.

Penalties for infractions usually involve the pet being destroyed and huge fines for the owners. Rabies shots are not acceptable as the animal can still be a carrier.

In many places you may not even lock the pet below and take your boat to a marina or fuel dock but must carry everything out in your dinghy. Some countries like New Zealand have a quarantine official make regular unscheduled visits to the yacht to check on the pet and the boat is charged a hefty fee each time.

The boys all wanted pets which is why we settled on a budgerigar, a tiny and very endearing parakeet, which did not seem to worry any officials, although it was sealed in its cage in Australia to ensure that it could not fly off to join its wild cousins.

PHOTOGRAPHY: With so many new places it was difficult to stop taking pictures. We ended up with 16 albums on board! We took photos, slides and videos, although 3 cameras between 2 people can be hard to juggle. Since returning home we look at the photos the most, although slides have been useful for giving talks. Not knowing that we would be asked to give so many presentations we only had average camera equipment and have since much regretted it. Although the action in videos is fun for others be prepared to do a lot of editing!

Film varies in price and quality around the world as does the cost and quality of processing. Ideally film should be kept cool as it deteriorates in heat and humidity, and should be developed as soon as possible. A polarizing filter brings out the colours of the sky and water.

Some local people strongly object to being photographed, particularly being videoed. It generally helps to ask their permission; some will want payment.

Saltwater and sand devastate cameras. A good quality waterproof bag, or waterproof container if available for your model, helps greatly. We stored our cameras in sealed containers with moisture absorbing silica gel.

PROVISIONING: The more you do it the easier it becomes and the fewer lists you'll make! In fact provisioning in this day and age is easier than it used to be because of the variety of products and types of packaging, and the fact that we are becoming used to bulk buying in regular life.

Although at first people can find provisioning for long periods very threatening, with copious lists and shopping expeditions being completed, the task does becomes easier with practice. Now I only make lists for essentials, such as tea and toilet paper for Andy who has a phobia about running out of either at sea! It's important to be adaptable. We both have the philosophy that if an ingredient to a particular dish is missing we'll substitute and make a new recipe—who knows the new dish might be even better!

We found you can get most things everywhere, although you may have to search through several stores and brand names probably won't be the same. Accepting that products are going to be different from home is important, otherwise you will constantly be frustrated when shopping. Personally we found expeditions to the market and trying new foods part of the excitement of travel.

I mentally divide stocking up into three types: **general, emergency** and **luxury**. Luxury items are personal favourites, such as particular brand names, goods that are easy to prepare like muffin mix and goods you can't live without, such as peanut butter for North Americans and Vegemite for Australians. Not liking powdered milk we stocked up heavily with cartons of UHT (Longlife) milk. When we find a favourite product that we've not had for a while, it's a special treat.

Shopping for a passage is like any regular shop, only one fills several carts instead of one, and will be buying a greater quantity of canned and packaged goods. By going around the supermarket (and all main centres around the world have them) methodically one generally doesn't forget too many items that are critical, but just in case I shop, when possible, at least two days before we leave. Naturally along the way I top up with goods when I see them. We always eat out on the evening of a large provisioning expedition—I've earned it!

The 'emergency' shop is done at the same time but includes a variety of provisions that are kept separate in case a situation arises causing one to be much longer at sea than planned. These supplies are continuously rotated so they do not get too old. I like to have at least one month's extra provisions, and generally have considerably more, beyond our estimated day of arrival at known shopping facilities.

We generally cook and eat as we do at home, using regular pans that stack for storage, and a non-stick frying pan. Our oven takes 3 bread pans across but as they vary in size it is worth measuring the oven so you can fit in the maximum, likewise for roasting and muffin pans. We seldom used a pressure cooker, though some find them indispensable. For those who like pulses and stews etc: they do save gas. They are also good for conch and octopus, however we either beat these to tenderize them, or cut them up finely. A pressure cooker is needed if you plan to do canning/bottling (the water bath method generally not being safe on a boat). When buying the pressure cooker ensure it is big enough to take preserving jars and that there is a reliable control to maintain a steady 15lb. pressure. For us, a large pan to cook crab and lobster was indispensable; incidentally always cook these in salt water.

Have tables for recipe conversions, measuring cups, etc: A general purpose cookery book is always useful, also local cookery books can help with cooking and shopping. For example meat cuts are different even between N. America and Europe.

Produce should not only be as fresh as possible, ideally it should not be washed and particularly the machine scrubbed supermarket veggies rot very quickly. Baskets and nets work well for storage as produce needs to be exposed to circulating air. If one item goes mouldy it will spread quickly through the rest so must be checked daily. Apples and citrus wrapped in paper towel, placed where they can't bruise, keep well. Fresh, never refrigerated eggs can be covered with vaseline and will last over a month.(However, always crack them separately!). Cheese and margarine only need to be kept cool; for long term storage cheese can be vacuum packed or immersed in salad oil in a jar. Home vacuum packers are inexpensive and can be used on a regular basis to keep food fresh. Many of the items that we commonly refrigerate such as mustards, sauces, jams etc: usually don't need it. Bay leaves in flour help keep out the weevils. If you are keen on fishing, stock up on ingredients to marinade fish. Also get plenty of nibbles for night watches.

REFRIGERATION: If you haven't got a generator the choices are between a 12 volt system and an engine driven system with holdover plates. Some lucky people have both. *Bagheera* had a 12 volt system for the first two years which provided some cooling in the tropics but which could not keep frozen food. In Australia we replaced it with a compressor, belt driven by the engine and a custom made holding plate. It keeps frozen foods well, though when very hot we had to run the engine for 45 minutes both morning and evening. Water cooled systems seem to be more effective than air cooling in a 12 volt unit; although considerable battery power is needed, particularly in the tropics. It greatly helps to beef up the insulation of the ice box, eliminate drains at the bottom and to have a lid that is insulated and seals well. With an engine driven system carry spares and gauges, learn how to change a filter-dryer and to recharge the system. Make sure that there are valves either side of the filter dryer so that the whole system doesn't evacuate when you do this.

Whilst Freon 12 is disappearing in the first world it is probably the only refrigerant available in most of the third world, so carry spare gas if your system uses one of the new kinds.

For those without a freezer but who have an efficient refrigerator, vacuum packing has become very popular. Dry ice can also help you keep food cold for a long time. Sometimes available through welding shops even in third world countries frozen meats etc. well wrapped in newspaper can be kept for many days in a solid state. As this is solid carbon dioxide the boat needs to be kept well ventilated as although there is no odour and it is not poisonous it is heavier than air and will displace it in an enclosed space, reducing the available oxygen.

RIGGING: Our standing rigging was 1x19 stainless wire. This is easier to repair than rod rigging. We carried spare wire, Norseman terminals, toggles etc: as spares and inspected the rig before each long passage.

Running rigging was all rope which we favour over wire or a combination because it is quieter; if overlength can be shortened when necessary to cut out chafe from the masthead sheave, and can be used for less demanding jobs when it has been replaced.

ROUTE PLANNING: The initial route you choose can contribute hugely to the success or failure of your trip. For those who have little experience or with young children on board, easing into the lifestyle with short trips in an area where goods and services are available, will greatly facilitate the adjustment to living on board. This is why with our young family we started our trip in Europe, spending a year mostly day sailing around the Mediterranean rather than leaving on a 2,300 n.mile passage Vancouver to Hawaii. The Caribbean is another ideal area to cruise where one can mostly daysail. After you have experienced several overnight runs, and varying weather and sea conditions, you will take an offshore passage in your stride.

Several people have commented that as we were out for six years we must have had no deadlines, that we could stay as long as we wanted wherever we wanted. In fact this was not the case. When cruising offshore one is constantly co-ordinating one's route with the seasonal weather patterns (See Safety – at Sea). Crossing the South Pacific, for example, should to be done between March and November, then yachts head down to either Australia or New Zealand or north of the equator, to avoid the cyclone season. Caribbean cruising is best between November and June with the north coast of South America being a place to go for the rest of the year as it is out of the hurricane belt.

SAILS FOR CRUISING: Dacron is still the most popular material for cruising sails. Not only is it cheaper than laminated and exotic materials but it lasts much longer, is more resistant to chafe, is easier to handle and fold, can be repaired at sea. We found it pays to get the best quality cruising cloth with a very dense weave and a minimum of fill.

When furling gear is used for the genoas, and almost no-one was without it, then one needs some system for hanking on a storm jib so this sail doesn't rely on a luff tape to stay in place. On *Bagheera* we have an inner forestay which can be attached to a padeye on the foredeck for this purpose.

We found that at sea if you need to reef then you want to reduce sail drastically, not the few inches found on most sails at home, so when we had a new mainsail made in Australia we had the reefing points made at 25%, 50%, and 75% of luff height. We had all seams triple stitched, and reinforcement tape applied wherever the sail touched the shrouds and spreaders downwind.

Bagheera's main was cut with the clew higher than the tack so that rain would run forward along the boom to be caught and led to the water tanks. Regular leech battens rather than full battens were chosen to avoid chafe problems when sailing downwind in ocean swells.

Roller furling mains are becoming popular for offshore and all we met who had them were happy and trouble free. It would seem sensible to carry a trysail as well if using a furling mainsail.

Our 150% genoa was used 99% of the time and has over 50,000 n.miles on it. It worked well when partially furled, and we only resorted to smaller jibs for upwind trips in heavy winds.

Cruising spinnakers are excellent. We used our old racing spinnaker on passages when the wind was light though we learned that it was best taken down before nightfall. Coping with a sudden line squall short handed in the rain, wind and darkness does not need the 'chute to add to the excitement.

SAFETY – AT SEA: Although cruising life is for the most part comfortable and enjoyable inevitably there will be some excitement. Many of the worst situations can be avoided by preparing the vessel and by careful planning of routes and timetables. Hurricanes, cyclones and typhoons are for the most part seasonal, as is most of the extreme weather in the high latitudes. We, like most cruisers, always planned to be in the right place at the right time, and zig-zagged north and south of the Equator accordingly. We used our weatherfax to monitor developments around us and were prepared always to divert to avoid unpleasantness.

Having sailed many types of yacht offshore, our first safety requirement in a boat after quality of construction is sailing efficiency, the ability to sail away from trouble and to cover many miles in a short time both upwind and down.

Preparation: Before going offshore much can be done to minimize the devastation which can result from very severe conditions. Hopefully you will never experience a knock-down or worse but you should think out the consequences of such an event and prepare.

Above decks look at the security of all gear: Will the anchors stay in place if you are rolled? What about the dinghy and liferaft? Cockpit lockers should have positive catches and the lids should be gasketed to seal out water. Warps, chafe gear and bolt cutters easily found? Strong points for attaching life harnesses, secure companionway boards?

Bagheera was new when we started our circumnavigation, but one of the changes we made was to go up one size on all the standing rigging. If preparing to cruise in an older boat replace all the rigging, and consider going up in size; old wire and swages will have lost some of their strength. Make sure that the rigging loads are properly transferred through the chainplates to the hull; even today some of the manufacturers have inadequate chain plates with the loads taken by the decks or by poorly secured bulkheads. Carry a supply of the correct sizes of Norseman or Staylock terminals, also heavy duty wire clamps for temporary rigging repairs.

Below, batteries need to be effectively bolted down, not simply held in place by straps, and the stove secured robustly in its gimbals. Injuries and damage from these heavy items if they fly free can be severe. Stoves also need rails that are high and strong enough to stop pans from flying off.

All drawers need catches. The ones which drop into a slot when closed don't always remain closed in violent conditions. Lockers should have strong latches, not spring or friction ones. Floorboards can be screwed down and locker bins under berths and seats secured with turnbuttons or barrel bolts.

The security of fuel, holding and water tanks should also be checked; 100 gallons of water, for example, weighs nearly half a ton.

Fires are most likely to occur in the engine compartment, the electrics or most common of all, in the galley. Good extinguishers which can cope with different fire sources are essential. A fire blanket, common on European boats and available from most of the mail order firms found in British yachting magazines is great for those flare-ups on the stove which can so easily get out of hand; anyone who prefers to cook with kerosine or alcohol should certainly have one. Using a powder extinguisher leaves a mess which can take weeks to clear up.

SAFETY – ON DECK: Attachment points in the cockpit and safety wires leading from the bow to the stern along the decks are necessary to clip harnesses onto. They need to be robust enough to stop heavy people should they get airborne. Although flat dacron tapes have the advantage over wire of lying flat on the deck, this material may be weakened by the sun even when looking good can fail when stressed if not replaced at frequent intervals.

We have seen boats where stanchions are poorly secured, lifelines very light and deck handholds flimsy. This is an important area to upgrade. Nylon netting prevents pets, people and gear from sliding overboard when rigged from a robust top lifeline to the toerail. It was most comforting to know that the children couldn't slip overboard.

Cockpit drains should be large. A bridge deck or barrier to prevent water going below is necessary, as is an engine exhaust system which does not allow water to flood the engine in extreme conditions. If a shut-off valve is used be sure to have a system for remembering, such as hanging the engine key on the valve!

Make sure you can be seen in poor visibility and at night. Always conserve enough battery power to display adequate navigation lights. A masthead trilight is best offshore, being visible from many miles. For coastal cruising the conventional nav. lights make it easier for other vessels to judge your distance.

A good radar reflector, or better still, two reflectors are some of the most important and least expensive pieces of safety equipment. Fiberglass hulls and rounded spars give a very poor radar echo (for example we have a blind spot astern with our reflector mounted on the front of the mast. Ships do not expect small craft in the middle of the oceans and often the first indication of your presence will be a radar alarm; your echo must be large enough to make it go off! The efficiency of a reflector is a function of the area of reflective surface, and tiny gizmos should be avoided.

Inexpensive radar detectors are now available that draw a minimum of power. These detect any vessel with radar on.

Safety equipment: A good liferaft, inspected at the required intervals should contain survival equipment and sustenance to last several days. Ours included a second e.p.i.r.b., space blankets, a solar still for water making, fishing gear, heliograph as well as flares, food and water. It was stowed in a fiberglass container in a cradle at the transom. Research where the next facility will be for liferaft service; they are not common.

A man overboard situation in the ocean is highly dangerous even in fine weather and should be avoided at all costs. Our rules were that no one could leave the cockpit and go forward on the deck unless someone else could watch; lifeharnesses were worn on night watches always and during the day in bad weather, or if deck work, such as rigging the spinnaker pole onto the genoa, involved leaving the cockpit; males use the head or a bucket in the cockpit and **never** pee over the side. (This is the commonest cause of people falling overboard).

Our 'overboard' strategy is to come to a stop immediately. In ocean swells one can loose sight of a person after only a few lengths even in fine weather. Life rings, cockpit cushions and other floatable items should also be thrown over the side immediately to help mark the position. Life slings are good for securing someone in the water and getting them on board. Practise the procedure.

SEASICKNESS: See *Just Cruising* p.125 and 279. Also some people find ginger works well.

SELF STEERING GEAR: Hand steering on long passages is exhausting and to be avoided if possible as it doesn't allow the flexibility to do other important tasks. With a young family it was a necessity to have a reliable system. *Bagheera* was fitted with an Autohelm 6000 with a powerful series 2 linear drive coupled directly to the rudder quadrant. 'Otto Van Hellum' proved able to cope with almost any condition and was certainly our preferred steering system downwind in ocean swells.

An Aries wind vane also worked well as long as we took down the bimini which created turbulence so became our second choice. We also had a small tiller pilot, the Autohelm 800 which when coupled directly in place of the sail on the Aries steered powerfully and accurately with very little current draw.

To minimize the loads on both electronic and mechanical steering systems a yacht must be well balanced and directionally stable.

SPARES: Fewer problems will be encountered should you need service if you equip your vessel with gear which is popular internationally. Lewmar, Autohelm, Brookes and Gatehouse, Furuno, Icom, Perkins, Yanmar, Jabsco are typical brand names found world wide and there will be service and spares available in major cities.

Within the confines of storage space available carry spares for all equipment giving priority to items which need regular servicing, which are indispensable such as the steering gear, wind vane and furling system or which are necessity and have limited availability. Get advice from the local dealers; ensure you have on board workshop manuals and wiring diagrams. Fuel and oil filters may be hard to find, also good bottom paints, varnishes and quality lube oils. Carry complete spare raw water cooling and fuel pumps, also bilge, water and head pumps as well as parts.

Zincs, cutlass bearings, propeller shaft diameters, tapers and threads on N. American boats are different. Carry plenty of spares including a propeller.

Stock up on any other parts with imperial rather than metric measurements, including hoses, fasteners and plumbing fittings, 110 volt light bulbs etc., the other way round if you are a yacht visiting N. America.

Also circuit breakers for DC panel, spare bulbs for 12 volt fixtures, special batteries for EPIRBS, GPS, laptops, camcorders.

Open an account with a good mail order marine supplier. Customs duties are usually avoided if your packages were clearly marked 'to Yacht Bagheera, Canadian yacht in transit'.

TOOLS: For power tools when in places where the voltage is different *Bagheera* had a 1000 watt transformer built in to the A.C. system. We also carried a small gasoline powered portable generator. Boats with inverters can also run tools from the D.C. supply.

Tools and gauges specific to the yacht's machinery should be obtained from the manufacturers before leaving. Doing one's own maintenance before leaving helps develop an adequate tool kit. It is advisable to carry full sets of wrenches, allen keys and drills in both metric and imperial sizes.

TRAVEL AND REFERENCE BOOKS: We found the best information for sightseeing in the backpackers travel books. I particularly liked the Moon Publications Guide for the South Pacific, otherwise we have the Lonely Planet series. Every time they are published these books get fatter, bulging with tips and exciting destinations. They also provide pertinent details on topics such as visa requirements, money, health hazards and travel, and give excellent historical, political, cultural, geographical, fauna and flora information, although we would also get local books on nature as this was a particular focus for us. Travel and reference books generally need to be purchased in advance, firstly because it is unlikely you will find them at your first port of call, if at all, and secondly because they provide excellent reading on passages when there is plenty of time to sort information and make tentative plans.

It made a huge difference to our enjoyment of a place if we were already familiar with the layout of the town, where to change money, the market etc: and the sights we wanted to see. We also felt more comfortable knowing the local customs, how to dress appropriately and what not to do. Probably the single most important issue, in this regard, is for women to dress conservatively. It is fascinating how customs vary; while we think terrible that moslem women have to wear purdah, the long robes and head covers that are so hot, and hide their identity, others think wrapping the contents of our noses in a handkerchief and keeping it in our pockets quite extraordinary!

TEAK, CARE OF: The tropical sun is hard on teak and many boats are now produced with no wood on the outside to minimize the need for maintenance. For those of us who like a bit of traditional teak trim any varnish like finish requires work to keep it in top condition. The varnish aboard *Bagheera* was re-coated every 3 months with a one part non synthetic product with ultra violet inhibitors. We tried several 'wonder' finishes which seemed to last no longer but which were far harder to re-finish. Some sailors allow their teak to weather and bleach out, but we neither like the look of this nor care for the erosion that the surface of the wood suffers.

Teak decks of course should not be coated with any finish. Salt water rather than fresh keeps them healthy and handsome in the sun, and only a soft bristle brush should be used for cleaning to minimize wear.

WATCHKEEPING and LOGS: Almost every boat we met had different strategies, what worked best for them. On passage in *Bagheera* we always kept watch 24 hours daily, a routine which is hard for the first day or two but then becomes acceptable when one's body has adapted. Andy and I did three hour watches, with the boys sharing one three hour period during the day. This meant we alternated watch times daily. Whoever was on 4:30-7:30 watch cooked dinner. If we had a guest on a long passage then they would also stand watches which gave us more sleep, but the downside is losing one's privacy.

At sea a log was kept at hourly intervals with time, course steered, log reading, n.miles covered in last hour, wind speed and direction, barometric pressure, position (electronic, celestial or D.R.). Also noted was any significant information such as ship sightings, gear problems, weather changes or radio contacts. Reminders for the next watchkeeper of weatherfax broadcasts to be printed out or light characteristics for an expected landfall were also entered.

WATER: We carried about 550 litres in four tanks and for longer passages also carried 60 litres in cans which could be put in a liferaft. We always strictly rationed water at sea, pumping it manually, cooking such things as potatoes in sea water (part mix with pasta), washing up in sea water and washing ourselves down with a cloth using no more than a cupful. We easily managed with under a gallon per person per day and were never short.

No opportunity was lost to top up the water tanks with rain whether at sea or at anchor. We went many months without being able to put a hose to a tap ashore. When sailing we caught rain in the mainsail and it flowed to the tanks through a permanent catchment system at the gooseneck. We also dammed the foredeck with wet towels and let the water flood into the tanks. At anchor the big sun awning had two drains with hoses attached.

Quality of the water from taps, wells and other sources must be monitored to prevent contamination of the tanks. Filtration and sterilization are sometimes required.

We did not have the luxury of a watermaker. Next time, perhaps, but we will still maintain an ample reserve in case of problems.

Although all of this may seem daunting, along with decisions about work, the house and finances etc: don't be put off. Start planning, take courses, and read everything in sight. Go sailing on the days you would have previously stayed home to get practise in inclement conditions and take some charters to get a taste for offshore conditions. Then set a date to go, one not too far down the road.

One never knows what life will bring. Of just the people I mention in this book Salvio Tanderella and Reg McNicol from Australia, Don Windsor from Sri Lanka, Colin from *Moonshine* in South Africa, Tony Garton from St. Thomas and Mary off *Counterpoint* from the States have since passed away. We met people of all ages and all walks of life as we cruised, you don't have to wait until you retire, everyone has assimilated successfully back into the 'real world'. The only problem is, they can't wait to get back offshore!

As we were cruising in *Bagheera* this summer and I was discussing this section with Andy, we realized that an expanded form of this material could be very useful, both for new cruisers as well as those who are planning to venture further afield. If you would be interested in such a book please fill in the form at the back. If we get a good response, we'll write it!

Appendix B

Equipment List

SAILS
- mainsail with 3 reefs—321 sq.ft.
- medium air 150% Hood furling genoa—533 sq.ft.
- No. 2 130% genoa—320 sq.ft.
- No. 3 100% short hoist Genoa 210 sq. ft.
- No. 1 storm jib—83 sq.ft.
- No. 2 storm jib—36 sq. ft.
- spinnakers—asymmetric cruising and tri-radial racing

RIGGING
- anodized aluminium 55′ keel-stepped mast with double spreaders and internal halyards
- anodized aluminium boom with 3 internal reefing lines and topping lift
- 1 x 19 stainless steel shrouds and stays: lowers, uppers, intermediates, baby stay, forestay, split adjustable backstay and running backstays
- aluminum and stainless steel blocks, chromed bronze turnbuckles

DECK FITTINGS
- genoa tracks and cars
- cabin top main traveller and car
- boomvang (5-1 purchase)
- preventers (rope with light weight shackles (see chapter 10)
- 2 genoa halyards and 2 spinnaker halyards—all lines (except genoa halyard and reefing) come back to the cockpit
- teak handrails
- teak covered cockpit seats
- teak grating in self-bailing cockpit
- wheel steering and binnacle compass
- emergency tiller
- 2 lazarette lockers and one cockpit locker
- opening transom for propane and spare fuel
- 2 Goiot (500MM x 500MM) opening hatches with vents (main and forward cabins)
- 1 Goiot (185 MM x 320 MM) opening hatch with vent in main head
- 5 Goiot portholes for aft cabins and aft head ventilation
- 2 opening hatches added aft in stern cabins for through ventilation
- 2 life rings and man overboard pole
- Beaufort 6-man liferaft in offshore pack—with food, water, fishing gear, anchor, EPIRB, solar blankets and solar still
- 2xSolarex 50 watt solar panels
- Rutland wind generator

- Rope and block tackle to hoist the outboard engine from wind generator support
- Manual bilge pump
- salt water deck wash/emergency pump
- Beaufort 6 man liferaft
- 10 Lewmar 2 speed winches (various sizes)

ANCHORS AND EQUIPMENT

- 2 anchor rollers
- 33lb (15 kilo) Bruce anchor
  —with 120' CHAIN AND 200' octoplait rope in the Mediterranean
  —with 300' high tensile chain for the remainder of the voyage
- 24 kilo (53lb) FOB anchor
- 18lb (8 kilo) Danforth Kedge anchor
- anchor windlass—first a Simpson Lawrence manual 555 replaced by an electric Nillsen Maxwell V700
- self-bailing anchor locker

SELF-STEERING

- Autohelm 6000, Series 2 linear drive
- Autohelm 800
- Aries windvane

ENGINE and BATTERIES

- PERKINS 4-108M diesel engine in sound insulated engine compartment
- s/s fuel tank 35 Imp. gals
- 2 x 120 amp hr batteries at the beginning, 6 x 110 amp hr deep cycle at finish
- Charging system—90 amp hr alternator with high output, multistage regulator
- 40 litre hot water tank

ELECTRICS AND ELECTRONICS

(Changes due to a lightning strike off South Africa)
- Navigation—Navstar Transit Satnav A 300s then GPS Navstar XR4
- Log: Brooks and Gatehouse then Autohelm
- Wind instruments: Plastimo then Autohelm
- Depth Sounder: initially Seafarer with alarms then Autohelm
- Weather fax: FAX MATE, then SEA with a Kodak Dikonix Printer linked to HF radio
- Radios:
  —VHF Demek RS 1000   —VHF SMR Handheld
  —HF Icom 735   —Panasonic shortwave receiver
- Radar: Apelco LDR 9910, 8 mile range
- Radio Direction Finder (RDF): Brooks and Gatehouse
- Refrigeration: initially a 12 volt electric refrigerator, in Australia changed to deepfreeze/ refrigerator engine driven with hold-over plates
- EPIRB x 2 (Emergency Position Indicating Radio Beacons)

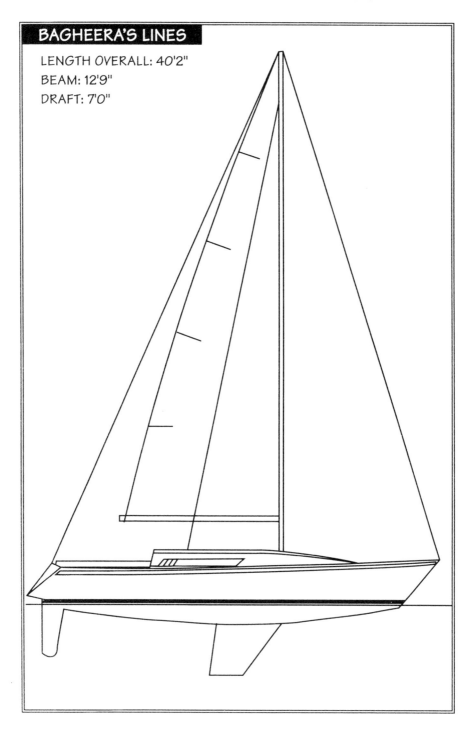

BAGHEERA'S LINES

LENGTH OVERALL: 40'2"
BEAM: 12'9"
DRAFT: 7'0"

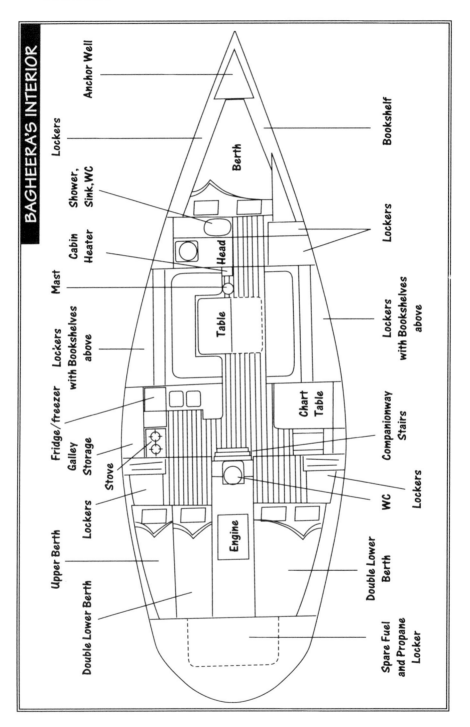

BAGHEERA'S INTERIOR

Lightening Strike–
Effects and Strategies

It has been estimated that there are roughly 2000 thunderstorms in progress over the earth's surface at any given time. Together they may produce 6,000 cloud to ground charges each minute, over 8 million per day. Sheltering golfers are the group most frequently struck by lightning, those on the open water run second.

Immediate effects of *Bagheera's* strike

Radios, radar, wind instruments, depth sounder, log, weather fax, Satnav, were all dead; several of the electronics were emitting the stifling smell of fried circuitboard. The v.h.f. radio was still smoking.

Two interior fans were affected but the other five still worked. The bulbs on about half the lights had been blown. Some spare batteries were dead. Engine electrics were blown as were some fuses on the elctrical panel.

The alternator was molten.

The compass reading was out by several degrees.

The autohelm 800, that we attached to the windvane, survived. It was connected to electrical power and turned on at 'standby'. Our large autohelm 6000 was in England for repair.

The electric anchor windlass, connected but not turned on, was also not affected.

The navigation calculator never worked again. Some functions of the electronic typewriter didn't work. The colour T.V. worked fitfully and had a purple side to the screen.

Anodising disappeared from the top of the mast. A large hole was blown in the top radio insulator on the backstay.

What did we learn?

We escaped structural damage and personal injury because Beneteau had provided lightning protection by connecting the rigging and the keel. They had also installed a 'positive gap' connector in the ground wire which was designed to keep an 'open' circuit until the electrical discharge, caused by the difference between the negative charge at the base of the cloud and the positive charge on the ground below, jumped the gap and dissipated into the sea. As there was no sign of burning at the bottom of the mast, from heat build-up due to resistance to the path of the electrical discharge, the system appeared to have worked satisfactorily. It would also have served to bleed off any static charge from a nearby strike and stopped electrolysis between the different metals of the rig and hull.

We have since installed a copper strap directly from the mast to the keel bolts but have to watch carefully for electrolysis. The strap provides alternate conductor capacity, particularly in case of a double strike, or the possibility that the 'positive gap' could vaporise, or 'blow-up', with a flash of extreme voltage. It joins the mast and keel in a straight line as the electrical discharge will not follow sharp angles. The engine, V.H.F. and H.F. radios are grounded to the same place.

We have also installed 'positive gap' connectors on both radio antennae with a direct ground to the keel. By diverting the electrical charge to ground this should protect the H.F and V.H.F radios from direct damage should the antennae be the source of the strike. We were reminded that a lightning protection system gives no protection when the boat is out of the water or if it comes in contact with power lines, whether in or out of the water.

As mentioned a side effect of a lightning strike, and the resultant equalisation of the positive and negative charges, is an simultaneous electromagnetic pulse. This radiates out across the spectrum of wavelengths, through very low to very high frequencies. Effects caused by this phenomenon are varied and controversial. Due to the fact that a lightning strike never happens twice in exactly the same way, there can be no comparative analysis. In our case it was suggested that it was the electromagnetic pulse that caused much of the damage to our equipment. An example was our molten alternator. It was theorized that the EMP destroyed the diodes in the alternator creating a massive short circuit. This is turn caused the battery bank in use (330 amp hour), to discharge rapidly to ground through the alternator, parts of which melted from the heat of this reaction.

It seemed to make no difference whether electrics and electronics were in use or turned off regarding damage. Also some pieces of equipment had functions affected even though they were not connected to the ships electrical system in any way. This included our portable electronic typewriter, colour T.V. and navigation calculator.

The compass had to be re-swung. Apparently as the change in the magnetic field of the engine had altered the deviation of the compass above.

Although the V.H.F. radio was affected directly through its antenna, that was struck with the top of the mast, most units were damaged by a massive current flowing back up through the ground system. This was ascertained when electronics were assessed for possible repair. Although it has been suggested that this could have been caused by a build-up of the electrical discharge, most suspect damage was due to the electromagnetic pulse.

The current pulse last tens of microseconds, with an average of about 20 millionths of a second. Local experts have suggested that since the current produces a magnetic field which varies with the same time scale, this time varying magnetic field will induce high voltages in any closed electric circuit nearby. Also, that the induced voltages, which can do damage to closed loops, may effect electrical equipment even if it is not turned on, and in many different ways.

Some equipment such as the H.F radio and V.H.F. radio could be repaired. Other electronics could not be fixed, or turned out not to be worth while financially. In the case of the radar, for example, replacing one circuit board wasn't successful. If we had replaced all three circuit boards it would have been more expensive than an entire new unit, including the scanner.

There was considerable controversy over the effect on our stainless steel rigging. Some riggers insisted it would have been considerably weakened by the heat and should be changed, whilst others thought no damage would have occurred. Of concern was a large hole in our top radio insulator. It was presumed that the electrical current had flowed down the backstay but on reaching this obstruction had sideflashed back to the mast, for an alternate route. We also found that all the anodizing at the top of the mast had disappeared, not so surprising when temperatures at the source of the strike can be up to 55,000°F. The aluminum mast did not appear to be affected structurally but we could not risk having suspect rigging, as we had 7000 nautical miles of ocean passages planned during the next six months. Because of the signs of heat damage we decided to replace the main rigging forestay, backstay, lower and upper shrouds. Recently we read that the American Boat and Yacht Council, Inc. recommend that all shrouds, backstays, preventers, sail tracks and continuous metallic tracks on the mast and boom should be grounded.

In this day and age most offshore yachts have extensive, sophisticated, electronic equipment. Several boats have back-up systems. Losing all our navigational aids simultaneously shocked the cruising community, most of whom like ourselves were soon to complete a circumnavigation. It particularly showed us the vulnerability of electronics and that we should never abandon our navigation skills with a sextant.

APPENDIX D

Glossary of Terms

(Definitions Specific to **Still Cruising**)

ABEAM Off one side of the boat

AFT At the back of the boat; behind

ANTIFOULING Bottom paint, to deter growth of weed, barnacles etc.

ASTERN To go backwards; behind the boat

AUTOPILOT Electro/mechanical steering device for automatic course keeping

BACKS, BACKING When the wind changes in an anti-clockwise direction

BACKSTAY Wire supporting the mast which attaches to back of boat

BAGGYWRINKLE Material on the shrouds, to stop chafe damage to sails, traditionally made out of old rope

BEAM Width of a boat at its widest point; 'On the beam'—at right angles to the length of the boat

BEAM REACH Sailing at about 90° to the wind direction

BEAR AWAY To alter course away from the wind

BEATING To sail into wind by zig-zagging (TACKING) towards it

BEAUFORT SCALE International scale of wind strength, Forces 0-12

BELOW Inside the boat

BERTH A bed; To berth—to come into the dock; A berth—the place in which a boat lies at the dock

BILGE Space under the floor boards

BINNACLE A stand in the cockpit on which the compass in supported. On Bagheera it also supports the steering and engine controls

BLOCK A pulley

BOOM Horizontal spar supporting the bottom of the mainsail

BOOM VANG Tackle from the boom to the deck to keep the boom from lifting (also called a kicking strap)

BOSUN'S CHAIR A chair for going up the mast generally made from wood and canvas and hooked onto a halyard

BOW   The front of the boat

BROACH   Heading up into wind uncontrollably

BULKHEAD   An interior divider like a wall in a house

BUOY   A floating device anchored to the sea's bottom. Used as markers for navigation, automatic weather reporting, to enable vessels to tie up, as fishing net markers etc.

CAST OFF   Undo a mooring or towing line

CATAMARAN   Boat with two hulls

CHAIN PLATE   Place on the hull where rigging supporting the mast is secured

CHART   Nautical map showing navigational aids, depths, hazards and land forms

'CHUTE   Spinnaker

CLEAT   Fitting on which to secure a line

CLEW   Aft bottom corner of a sail

CLOSE-HAULED (on the wind)   Sailing the boat as close to the wind as possible, sails are hauled in and boat may heel

COCKPIT   A recessed part of the deck in which to sit and steer (in the stern in *Bagheera*)

COMPANIONWAY   Entry and stairway to get below

DEAD RECKONING (DR)   Estimate of the boat's position based on course and speed

DECKHEAD   Underside of the deck (ceiling in a house)

DEPTH SOUNDER   An electronic instrument that measures the depth of the water below the boat

DEATH ROLL   Side-to-side uncontrollable motion when going downwind

DINGHY   A small boat or tender

DRAFT   Depth of the boat below the waterline

DRAGGING   When an anchor slips along the bottom

DROGUE   A device trailed behind a boat to create drag

EPIRB   Emergency Position Indicating Radio Beacon

FATHOM   A measurement of depth still used but being superseded by metres. 1 fathom = 6 feet

FENDERS (bumpers)   Inflated cylinders used to protect the sides of the boat when berthed

FEND OFF   To push the boat away from an object so no damage occurs

FIDDLES   Strips of metal or wood to stop objects from sliding off e.g. the stove or table

FLOOD TIDE   A rising tide

FOOT   Bottom edge of a sail

FOREDECK   Deck at the front of a boat

FOREGUY (downhaul)   Line to pull down the spinnaker pole

FORESTAY   Wire supporting the mast which is attached to the front of the boat

FORWARD   Towards the front or bow

FREEBOARD   The height of the hull between the water and the deck

FRONT   Leading edge of a moving mass of cold or warm air. Cold fronts are usually associated with rain, lightning and squalls. Warm fronts are associated with heavy clouds and rain.

FURL   Mainsail—To drop and lash to the boom. Genoa—To roll round a vertical aluminum extrusion which rotates around the forestay

FURLING GEAR   Equipment used to enable furling of the genoa

GALLEY   Boat kitchen

GENOA   Large foresail (overlaps the mainsail)

GIMBALS   A device to enable an object, such as a compass or galley stove, to remain horizontal regardless of the boat's motion

GOOSENECK   Hinged fitting which attach the boom to the mast

GPS (GLOBAL POSITIONING SYSTEM)   Position indicating electronic navigational aid

GO ABOUT (to tack)   To turn the bow through the wind when sailing

GUST   Sudden increase in wind

GYBE (jibe)   To change course downwind so that the sails change sides (can be dangerous when unplanned)

HALYARD   Line for hoisting sails

HANKS   Clips for attaching foresail to the forestay

HATCH   An opening through the deck

HEAD(S)   Boat toilet

HEAD OF SAIL   Top corner of the sail

HEADSAILS   Sails that attach forward of the mast

HEAD-TO-WIND   When the front of the boat, or bow, points into wind

HEAVING-TO   A method of stopping the vessel and allowing it to maintain a comfortable attitude, usually with a reefed mainsail, backed jib and lashed helm.

HEEL   When boat leans over at an angle (most severe when beating in a strong wind)

HELM   To steer; steering device (*Bagheera* has a wheel)

HOIST   Pull up

HULL   Main body of the boat

JIB   Small foresail (in front of the mast)

KEEL   Appendage under the hull running fore and aft, needed for vertical stability and to prevent leeway. (*Bagheera* has a cast iron keel encased in epoxy and bolted onto the hull

KNOT   One nautical mile per hour; method of fastening a line

LAZARETTE   Storage lockers on deck aft of the steering wheel

LEE CLOTH   Length of Canvas secured at the side of a berth to keep occupant in when boat heels or rolls

LEECH   The trailing edge of a sail (back edge)

LEE SHORE   Coast onto which the wind is blowing

LEE SIDE, (LEEWARD)   Side of the boat away from the direction of the wind

LEEWAY   Sideways drift

LIFELINE   Lines around the boat to stop people falling overboard (*Bagheera* has double lines)

LIFERAFT   Specially designed inflatable raft with food, water and an EPIRB for use when the yacht has to be abandoned

LIFERING   Floating ring to throw to a person who has fallen overboard

LOG   Measures distance through the water (ours also gives boat speed and water temperature)

LOGBOOK, OR THE LOG   Regular record of boats progress with position, speed, weather etc.

LUFF   Front edge of a sail

LYING AHULL   A technique useful in heavy weather, with bare poles and helm lashed such that the vessel lies beam on to the seas.

MAINSAIL   Sail attached to the main mast (*Bagheera*'s is smaller than #1 genoa)

MAKE FAST   Tie securely

MAST   Vertical spar which supports the sails

MASTHEAD   Top of the mast

MOORED   Boat is tied to a permanent object e.g. a mooring buoy

NAVIGATION LIGHTS   Lights used at night. Red faces port (left side) and green faces starboard (right), white faces aft. (*Bagheera* had 2 sets, one at deck level and the other at the top of the mast)

NEAP TIDES   Smaller changes in the height of the tide, occur twice monthly at the half moon (alternate with spring tides)

OARLOCK, OR ROWLOCK   Fitting which acts as a pivot point for an oar

OFF THE WIND   Sailing on a reach or run

ON THE WIND   See close-hauled

OUTBOARD   Outside the perimeter of the deck; portable engine for a dinghy

PADEYE   A fitting on deck used for attaching lines or blocks

PAINTER   Dinghy tie-up or towing line

PORT SIDE   Left side of the boat when looking forward

PORT TACK   When the wind comes on the port side,(sails will be to starboard)

PREVENTER   Line leading forward which holds the boom at right angles to the boat when going downwind, to prevent a gybe

PULPIT   Metal railing at bow and stern to which the lifelines are attached

QUARTER   Between astern and abeam (back and middle) of the boat

RADAR Electronic instrument for detecting other vessels, land and storms

RADIO, HF High frequency for long distance
VHF Very high frequency for short range

RAFT UP Tie alongside another vessel

REACHING Sailing when the wind is on the beam, the sail is approximately halfway out.

REEF A ridge of rocks which is at or near the surface; a portion of sail furled and tied down to reduce the area exposed to the wind

RIG To prepare a boat for sailing; the mast and its supports

RIGGING The equipment required to use sails, i.e. spars, sheets, shrouds, stays and halyards

RODE Rope or chain joining the anchor to the boat

RUNNING To sail with the wind from behind the boat

RUNNING BACKSTAYS Adjustable lines supporting the back of the mast

SAILS Shaped dacron, or other strong material, used to catch the wind and propel the boat through the water

SAIL TIES Webbing strips used to tie the sails when furled

SATELLITE NAVIGATION, OR SAT NAV Electronic device that aids navigation

SET Trimming a sail for the wind direction; course error due to current

SEXTANT An instrument used to aid navigation by measuring altitudes of celestial bodies and hence determining position of the boat

SHEET A line attached to the sail used to adjust its position

SHROUDS Wire supports on either side of the mast

SOLE Floor of the interior of the boat

SPAR A mast or boom

SPINNAKER Lightweight, parachute-like sail (usually colourful) used when the wind is aft of the beam

SPINNAKER POLE A boom attached to the mast at one end and the spinnaker at the other, used to support and control the spinnaker

SPREADERS Short struts between mast and shrouds to add support to the rig

SPRING TIDES Greatest change in the height of the tide, occurs twice monthly at the new and full moons (alternates with neap tides)

STANCHIONS Metal supports for lifelines around the boat

STARBOARD Right side of the vessel when looking forward

STARBOARD TACK Sailing with wind on the starboard (right) side of the boat, (sails will be to port)

STAY Wire supporting the mast fore and aft

STERN The back of the boat

STOWING Securing or putting away

TACK   Act of passing the bow through the wind when sailing; the front corner of the sail

TIDE   The rise and fall of the sea level due to gravitational pull of the moon and sun

TOPPING LIFT (uphaul)   Lines supporting main boom and spinnaker pole

TOPSIDES   Area of hull above the water line

TRANSOM   Flat part across the back of boat

TRIM   Fine tune a sail

TRIMARAN   Boat with three hulls

VEER   When the wind changes in a clockwise direction

WATERLINE   Demarkation between portion of hull above water and below

WEATHER FAX   Instrument for receiving graphic weather charts

WINCH   Round metal drum with detachable handle for winding in lines

WIND GENERATOR   Wind driven electricity-producing device

WIND INSTRUMENTS   Devices that measure wind speed and determine its direction

WINDLASS   Mechanical or electrical device to lift anchor and chain

WINDSHIFT   Change in wind direction

WINDVANE steering   A device which automatically steers a boat at a pre-set angle to the wind

WINDWARD   Direction from which the wind is blowing

WING ON WING   Sailing downwind with the genoa and mainsails on opposite sides to catch more wind

Send A Copy To A Friend!

If not available at your local bookstore please order through

Romany Enterprises,
3943 West Broadway,
Vancouver, BC, V6R 2C2,
CANADA
Tel:(604) 228-8712
Fax:(604) 228-8779

Please send the BOOK

☐ **JUST CRUISING** – Europe to Australia

☐ **STILL CRUISING**–– Australia to Asia, Africa and America

TO:

Name:_____   Name: _____

Address:_____   Address: _____

_____   _____

City:_____   City: _____

Province/State: _____   Province/State:_____

Postal Code: _____   Postal Code _____

Country: _____   Country: _____

$19.95 + $4.00 shipping and handling ($8.00 outside N.America)

                                                        . . . over

Please send the VIDEO - JUST CRUISING

Based on **'On board 5 for Six'**, a finalist in the CANPRO TV Documentary Awards, this video shows the lure of life afloat around the world, besides giving much practical boating and travel information. 55 mins.

Name:_____   Name: _____

Address:_____   Address: _____

_____   _____

City:_____   City: _____

Province/State: _____   Province/State:_____

Postal Code: _____   Postal Code _____

Country: _____   Country: _____

$29.95 + $4.00 shipping and handling ($8.00 outside N.America)

☐ Payment enclosed (Sorry, no CODS)

☐ By cheque (made payable to **Romany Enterprises**)

I am interested in **GO CRUISING – Practical Tips for Offshore Cruising.** Please inform me when published.

Name:_____

Address:_____

City:_____   Prob/State: _____

Postal Code: _____   Country_____

Send to: Romany Enterprises,
                      3943 West Broadway,
                      Vancouver, BC, V6R 2C2, CANADA
                      Tel:(604) 228-8712 Fax:(604) 228-8779